G. EDWARD ORCHARD is associate professor of history at the University of Lethbridge.

The opening decade of the seventeenth century was, for Russia, one of great turmoil. Political unrest was compounded by natural calamity. On the death of Boris Godunov, the Russian throne was seized by a pretender claiming to be the long-dead son of Ivan the Terrible, allegedly murdered at Boris's instigation in 1591. The False Dmitry made a triumphal entry into Moscow in June 1605, only to be assassinated less than a year later by the supporters of Vasily Shnisky, who then seized the throne for himself. Rumours soon spread that Dmitry had in fact escaped, and soon another pretender was advancing on Moscow with his Polish supporters.

Eyewitness to many of these events was Isaac Massa who came to Moscow from the Netherlands in 1600 as a merchant apprentice and remained for eight years. His history, written after his return home for the benefit of Maurice, Prince of Orange, lay undiscovered until 1859. This is its first English translation.

Massa was an astute and observant youth and his account provides a unique description of the famine in Moscow (1601-3), the appearance of the rulers (whom he had apparently known intimately), the entry of the Pretender, and the subsequent exhibition of his mangled corpse on Red Square after his downfall.

Massa's dramatic accounts are complemented by a unique topographical sketch of the city of Moscow provided to Massa by an elderly soldier, one of his many Muscovite friends. Three portraits of Massa by Frans Hals, an intimate in his homeland, are also reproduced in this fascinating volume.

A Short History of the Beginnings and Origins of These Present Wars in Moscow under the Reign of Various Sovereigns down to the Year 1610

BY
ISAAC MASSA

TRANSLATED AND WITH AN INTRODUCTION BY
G. EDWARD ORCHARD

UNIVERSITY OF TORONTO PRESS
Toronto Buffalo London

© University of Toronto Press 1982
Toronto Buffalo London
Printed in Canada
Reprinted in 2018
ISBN 0-8020-2404-1
ISBN 978-1-4875-7919-7 (paper)

Canadian Cataloguing in Publication Data

Massa, Isaac Abrahamszoon, 1586-1643.
A short history of the beginnings and origins of these present wars in Moscow under the reign of various sovereigns down to the year 1610

Bibliography: p.
Includes index.
ISBN 0-8020-2404-1

1. Soviet Union – History – 1533-1613. I. Title.

DKI11.M37   947'.045   C82-094211-1

Acknowledgments

This book has been published with the help of a grant from the Social Science Federation of Canada, using funds provided by the Social Sciences and Humanities Research Council of Canada, and a grant from the Publications Fund of the University of Toronto Press. I am also indebted to the Canada Council for a grant which enabled me to visit the Netherlands during the spring and early summer of 1978. In connection with this visit, I am deeply indebted to Mrs H. Peeters of the manuscript division of the Koninklijke Bibliotheek, The Hague, together with the staff of the Gemeynte Archief, Haarlem and the library of the Rijksuniversiteit, Utrecht.

For invaluable assistance in obtaining the illustrations for this volume, I have to thank the Koninklijke Bibliotheek for permission to reproduce the illustrations from the Massa manuscripts; for the Frans Hals portraits of Isaac Massa the Art Gallery of Ontario, the Rijksmuseum of Amsterdam, and the Fine Arts Gallery of San Diego; for the portrait of the false Dmitry by an unknown artist, the Hessische Landes- und Hochschulbibliothek, Darmstadt.

Finally I would like to thank my colleague, Professor I.D.C. Newbould, for his assistance in overcoming some of the difficulties posed by translation from the Dutch, and express my gratitude to Professor Hugh F. Graham and Mr Richard Howard for their helpful reading of my manuscript and suggestions for its improvement.

When it has seemed desirable to do so, I have included proper names from Massa's original Dutch, in square brackets, after my English renderings of them.

G.E. ORCHARD
November 1981

Contents

INTRODUCTION ix

Isaac Massa: A Short History of the Muscovite Wars 1

APPENDIX A
Letter of Isaac Massa to the States-General (1614) 183

APPENDIX B
1 / Letter of Isaac Massa to the States-General, 4 September 1618 186
2 / Report of Isaac Massa to the States-General, 2 March 1620 189

ABBREVIATIONS 199

NOTES 201

BIBLIOGRAPHY 217

INDEX 221

Introduction

Isaac Massa remains a rather shadowy figure, even though his outstanding gifts as an annalist, geographer, merchant, and diplomatic agent are well documented. Not the least of our difficulties is the fact that his writings contain very little autobiographical detail, and the only extensive biography, Antonius van der Linde's, is in many respects erroneous.[1] Unfortunately, these errors have been incorporated into many standard works of reference, so a brief biographical essay may not be out of place here. In fairness, it should be pointed out that the information in Johannes Keuning's essay, published in 1953, is basically correct, but he was concerned principally with Massa's achievements as a cartographer.[2]

It must also have hampered van der Linde that in his day the demographic records for Massa's lifetime had not been fully collated. For instance, he is able to trace the baptismal records of Isaac's brothers, Christiaan and Lambert, but not Isaac's own. Similarly, the biography tells us nothing about his marriages or family life; indeed, the biographer concludes Massa's life prematurely in 1635, whereas the records clearly indicate that he lived until 1643, marrying a second time and begetting two children in the interval.

Even the Massa family's origin is a matter for speculation. In the records preserved in Haarlem, the family name is spelt variously as Massa, Massaert, Mastaert, and Masse, a variant used by a cousin, Pierre, whose marriage was entered in the registers of the Haarlem Walloon church. It appears that the Massa family, like that of the painter Frans Hals – with which there are several intimate links – had migrated to Haarlem from Antwerp. Abraham Massa (Massaert, Mastaert) appears in the baptismal records of his two children, Abraham (1590) and Susanna (1592), with the suffix 'van Antwerpen.' His wife, Sara, is given the surname Texor in Isaac's baptismal record. The Massa family may be further traced back to the province of

Liège, if we are to believe the patent of nobility granted to Isaac in 1625 by King Gustavus Adolphus of Sweden, where he is described as being descended from the Velroës family of that province.³ It was not unknown, however, for members of the aspiring bourgeoisie to fabricate antecedents which, then as now, would be impossible to verify.

With regard to the earlier provenance of the Massa family, the name has something of a northern Italian ring. In the dedicatory epistle to his *History*, Massa said that his family had migrated and lost everything for the sake of religion,⁴ but this may simply refer to the two migrations within the Netherlands already mentioned. Another possibility, given its evident preference for Old Testament names, is that the family may have been of Jewish origin. Yet even a cursory knowledge of the social history of the Reformation will tell us that the early Protestants had a similar predilection. Moreover, all the Massas who left any trace were baptized, married, or buried in the Calvinist rite, and Isaac's writings bristle with impeccable Calvinist sentiments.

Isaac, the eldest child of Abraham and Sara Massa, was baptized in the Great or St Bavo Church of Haarlem on 7 October 1586.⁵ He was followed by five other children: Jakob (1588), Abraham (1590), Susanna (1592), Christiaan (1595), and Lambert (1596). It appears that the father had been forced to abandon all his property in Antwerp when the city was captured by the Spaniards in 1585, and he found it very difficult to get back on his feet in his new home. Certainly, he did not have the wherewithal to provide a formal education for his children, beyond the elements of literacy and numeracy, and yet Isaac somehow acquired a taste for Latin verse, which he sprinkled through his *History*, and later published his geographical treatises in Latin as well as Dutch. He was a boy of quick intelligence, and so, even though financial stringencies meant that the road to grammar school and university was closed to him, his parents did the next best thing, and apprenticed him to a firm of Amsterdam merchants engaged in the Russia trade.

So it was that in the year 1600 the 13-year-old Isaac Massa travelled to Russia as a merchant apprentice, to live in his employer's household for the next eight years. He became fluent in the Russian language, and struck up acquaintance with a number of Muscovite junior functionaries who were to rise through the ranks of the bureaucracy and be invaluable to him on his later visits to Russia as a diplomatic agent. Massa was also an indefatigable compiler of notes, which later formed the basis of his *History*. He was well received at the court of Tsar Boris Godunov, who listened eagerly to his accounts of the history of the Netherlands and the fortunes of the Spanish wars. He also shared the passion for cartography of the tsarevich, Fyodor Borisovich, three years his junior. Massa was also privy to 'inside information' on Siberia, both from Russian sources, whom he did not feel at liberty to reveal, and from the brother of his employer, who had been invited to participate in one of the Siberian expeditions mounted by the tsar.[6]

During the eight years he was to remain in Moscow, Massa was witness to many spectacular events. He gives a harrowing account of the famine of 1601-3. He recounts in detail the usurpation, reign, and violent end of the false Dmitry, and can vouch for his death after personally seeing the Pretender's naked corpse on ignominious public view in Red Square. He was also able to obtain a unique map of the city of Moscow from a Muscovite friend. His is one of the most remarkable accounts of Russia during the Time of Troubles, even though the struggle was far from concluded when Massa made his perilous exit from Muscovy at the opening of the 1609 shipping season.

While at Archangel, he was invited by a group of Dutch navigators to join an expedition in search of the North-east Passage, but he declined. He might have done better to accept; in the unsettled conditions of the time, trade between Russia and the Netherlands was at a standstill. In his dedicatory epistle, Massa alludes to his current lack of employment. His father's death in 1602 had made Isaac the mainstay of his mother and her younger children. Initially, he approached the stadholder, Prince Maurice, using his book as an introduction with a view to obtaining employment. He also stressed that he had much to relate orally concerning the state of Muscovy. He does not appear to have been given the opportunity to do so, and so in 1609 and 1610, he translated from the Russian two narratives on Siberian topography, since lost, under the title *Beschryvinghe vander Samoyeden Landt*.[7] The significance of these accounts was quickly realized by the renowned cartographer and publisher Hessel Gerritz, who wrote an introduction to the work, which was first published in Dutch in 1612 and came out in a Latin version shortly afterwards. The author's name does not appear in these editions, but the second Latin edition, published in 1613, is signed 'Isaac Massa Haarlem.'[8] Massa's maps of Siberia, the first to appear in western Europe, were used in successive atlases throughout the seventeenth century, and numerous prints were sold separately.

As the Muscovite wars ground to a halt with Moscow's recapture from the Polish occupying force and the election of a new tsar, prospects for renewing commercial relations began to brighten. Yet settled conditions and a definitive peace between Muscovy and the Polish and Swedish interventionists still seemed remote, and in fact were not realized for a number of years. Nevertheless, the hastily improvised government of Michael Romanov felt confident enough to reopen negotiations with foreign powers, and in 1614 sent

S.M. Ushakov and his secretary Semeon Zaborsky to tour the European courts. Massa had been befriended in the meantime by the influential merchant and politician Gerrit Witsen, who brought him to the attention of the States-General as an acknowledged expert on Russian affairs.

Ushakov and Zaborsky had been conveyed from Archangel to Hamburg on a Dutch man-of-war, and on disembarking had sent letters to Prince Maurice, informing the stadholder of the election of the new tsar, the machinations of the Renegade Monk, and the attempts of King Sigismund to undermine Russia's independence. The ambassadors were empowered to ask for assistance and offer Dutch merchants freedom to trade throughout the Muscovite tsardom, with greater protection than had been afforded by any previous tsar.[9] The matter was taken up at a session of the States-General on 23 January 1614. Finally, on 12 March, it was resolved to send an emissary to congratulate Tsar Michael and request the same trading privileges in Russia that the English then enjoyed. The Dutch also wished to sound out the possibility of transit facilities for the Persian trade, a constant element in briefs to Dutch emissaries until the matter of the grain trade assumed greater urgency with the onset of the Thirty Years' War. Two letters were to be sent to Moscow by the hand of 'an astute merchant,' and Caron, the Dutch ambassador in London, was instructed to be helpful to the Russian ambassador when he arrived to present his credentials to King James.[10] On their return from Vienna, Ushakov and Zaborsky were intercepted at Hamburg by the Dutch residents, Voght and Bass, and in May appeared in person before the States-General. On 23 May they were given a solemn farewell, and then escorted from Texel to Archangel by a Dutch naval vessel.

In the meantime, Massa had been sent to Russia, probably with the opening of navigation in March. By the homeward dispatch of the Russian embassy, he received a letter from the States-General charging him with presenting their letters to the tsar and promoting Dutch interests at the Russian court.[11]

Massa received these instructions on 16 July at Archangel, where he had gone from Moscow on commercial business, evidently bypassing the returning ambassadors on his way. His letter of 2 August is a particularly succinct summary of recent events in Russia, and in many respects rounds out his *History* (see Appendix A). In a subsequent letter, he pointed out that in view of the unsettled state of affairs and the lateness of the season, it would be as well to delay his departure for Moscow.[12] While he was writing these lines, the English agent John Merrick, whose career so curiously parallels Massa's own, arrived in Archangel. Massa was highly suspicious of English motives, and wrote the States-General that Merrick was doing his utmost to discredit the Dutch and further English interests by his offer to mediate in the peace talks with Sweden. The States-General were urged not to allow peace to be concluded between Russia and Sweden without Dutch, as well as English, mediation.[13] In yet another letter, dated 30 August, Massa urged that the Dutch should have a permanent diplomatic representative in Russia, and hinted broadly that he himself would be suitable for the post.[14]

Early in December, Massa set out by the 'winter road' from Archangel to Moscow, where he obtained an audience with the tsar on 3 January 1615. He presented the letters from the States-General and Prince Maurice, together with a petition from a group of Dutch merchants concerning trade with Russia. He was then referred to Peter Tretiakov, with whom he spent most of January in negotiation. Massa certainly exceeded his instructions, since he gave the Russians to understand that the States-General were sending an ambassador to Sweden to ensure a fair peace, knowing that Merrick had come on just such a mission for his own government. He also requested clarification of the peace terms conveyed to the Swedish envoy by the tsar so that he, Massa, might send a brief to the Dutch ambassadors. He further assured the tsar that the Dutch were likely to have greater influence than the English on the Swedes, and that they were also prepared to give double the amounts of money and military supplies the English were ready to offer.

Eventually, Massa was summoned to the Ambassadorial Chancellery and told that he was being sent home with answers from the tsar. Massa insisted on a personal farewell audience with the tsar, which took place on 31 May, the tsar handing him letters identical with those given him in the earlier interview at the chancellery.

Massa's mission, then, was not a total failure. While he had admittedly failed to achieve the specific aims contained in his brief, the willingness to assist Russia expressed by the States-General had awakened a desire there for closer relations with the Netherlands. Michael was offended that the Dutch had not yet sent an embassy, but merely an unofficial emissary who had come 'for trade,' but he had received this emissary graciously none the less, and was dispatching him home with letters for the prince and the States-General.

Massa was accompanied on the return journey by the Muscovite embassy of I.G. Kondyrev and Mikhail Neverov, who were to visit the Netherlands and France. They set sail from Archangel and cast anchor at Texel early in October 1615. Arriving in The Hague, the ambassadors were greeted personally by the stadholder, and on 22 October formally addressed the States-General.[15]

In their formal reply, the States-General pointed out that they had already sent ambassadors to Sweden to assist with the peace talks, and that these Dutch emissaries would do their utmost to achieve the desired results. The question of financial or military aid to Russia, however, was studiously avoided. The Russian emissaries proceeded by ship to Bordeaux, where they attended the wedding celebrations of Louis XIII and Anne of Austria, and by January 1616 had returned safely to the Netherlands to renew their request for financial and military assistance. Despite this even more pointed demand, the emissaries were obliged to go away empty-handed.

Massa's proposal for a permanent consulate in Russia was also aired. There was a suggestion that Massa should be sent back to Moscow to safeguard the interests of Dutch merchants at an annual salary of two or three thousand guilders. This did not meet with general approval, and was shelved indefinitely. It was decided, however, to send Massa with letters for the tsar and await his reply. For his services in 1614-15, Massa received a grant of eight thousand guilders. The accounts he had submitted for his last visit to Russia struck the States-General as exorbitant, and so this time he was set a limit of three thousand guilders and sent specifically not as an ambassador, but as a simple emissary.[16]

Prior to his departure, on 17 May 1616, the States-General awarded Massa a gold medal in recognition of his services. He left in the company of the Russian ambassadors. He had been ordered to return without delay, but neither he nor the States-General could possibly have anticipated that his task in Moscow would be complicated by the patent bias of the Dutch envoys at the Swedish peace talks, who visited Stockholm and were decorated by King Gustavus Adolphus, but declined to visit Moscow or take part in the final negotiations leading to the Peace of Stolbovo.

Massa arrived at Archangel on 2 July after a 37-day voyage, and reached Moscow on 19 September. The reception was cool, and he was treated to a series of stern lectures by Tretiakov, who was not only notoriously anglophile, but had evidently conceived a strong dislike for the brash young Dutchman. Massa was kept waiting nearly half a year before being granted an audience with the tsar, and in this time he had constantly been kept short of provisions. In his letter to the States-General, he blamed his privations on the conduct of the ambassadors: 'The reason for my close confinement was the ambassadors' conduct in Sweden, and if peace had not been concluded, I should have had to sit and wait indefinitely for the arrival of ambassadors from the Netherlands to secure my release. As each day passed, my situation deteriorated, and we were often denied half the rations allocated to us.'[17]

His reading of the situation was correct, and the decision not to break off relations with the Netherlands was reached on the basis of the favourable treatment accorded to the ambassadors to the Netherlands in 1616, the conclusion of peace with Sweden – though the final sessions of the peace talks had taken place without the Dutch, but with the assistance of the ubiquitous Merrick – and the continuing war with the Poles, with whom the Dutch were at odds too. All the same, Dutch blunders had left Massa with a lot of explaining to do, and it was largely because of his diplomatic finesse that relations did not founder at this time.

When he was finally received by Michael on 6 April 1617, Massa congratulated the tsar on the peace with Sweden, but warned him about the league of Catholic rulers that was bent on world domination. He also pointed out that the Dutch, even though they had shaken off the Spanish yoke, still had to maintain a war footing to protect their merchants and fishermen. The Dutch ambassadors' apparent discourtesy was explained away in terms of their advanced age, which made them unequal to the strain of an arduous winter journey from the Swedish border to Moscow.

From that day, Massa never again had reason to complain of his treatment at the hands of Russian officials. The tsar, it is true, was not persuaded by Massa's arguments, but all the same he expressed willingness to continue negotiations. To this end, he reiterated his request that the States-General send ambassadors with plenipotentiary powers. On 20 June Massa took his leave of the tsar, receiving his passports, together with letters of conduct for the proposed Dutch embassy, as he left Moscow a week later.[18]

Despite its fortunate outcome, this last journey had been most unpleasant as far as Massa was concerned, and had also, by his own account, put him out of pocket to the tune of 4,654 guilders. Yet he still strove with all his might to point out the advantages to be gained from closer relations with Russia. He also argued that the States-General should send military supplies. The tsar would probably agree to pay in cash, but even if such a transaction did show a loss, it would be offset by the benefits of friendlier contact.[19]

The States-General took up Massa's report, and appointed commissioners to examine its recommendations and audit Massa's claim for reimbursement. There was some abortive discussion about a scheme to levy an excise tax to defray the costs of maintaining a permanent Moscow consulate. The commissioners approved Massa's expense claim, but a plenary session of the States-General pared the award down to two thousand guilders, adding a further five hundred when Massa protested that this was not enough. Despite this rebuff, he offered to take the States-General's letter to the tsar. The assembly voted him three hundred guilders with the rider that he waive any further claim against the state treasury over this mission. Massa asked instead for a gold chain to replace the one he had been given in 1616 and parted with as a gift to his Muscovite friend, the secretary Savva Romanchukov. He was told that if he wished, he could use the three hundred guilders to order a chain for himself. Angered by this ungracious response, Massa declined to undertake the mission.

He was still at The Hague in June 1618 when the Russian ambassador Baklanovsky – erroneously called 'Bornalofsky' by van der Linde – arrived unannounced with a fresh request for aid against the Polish king. The States-General asked Massa to assist the ambassador, who had heard of him through his predecessor, Kondyrev. Massa moved into the Russian's quarters. On 11 June the States-General studied Baklanovsky's request for a loan of 70,000 rubles plus military supplies to the tsar. They redrafted the letter they had written the tsar earlier, but the terms remained unchanged. They resolved to send the ambassador back to Archangel on 15 June aboard a Dutch ship, and awarded him a chain to the value of 1,500 guilders, together with chains worth a hundred guilders each for his secretary and translator. Courteously persistent, Baklanovsky reiterated his demands. It would be a mistake, he said, to judge Russia by her present condition and the currently limited resources of the tsar, since Russia would soon recover, God willing, and be in a position to afford assistance to her friends.

The Russian proposal was declined once again, but the deputies from Holland and Zeeland then suggested that if the States-General as a whole were unwilling to supply this aid, the two provinces would undertake to oblige the tsar themselves. Finally, on 22 June, after much hesitation, this project was accepted for debate in the assembly. After another impassioned plea by Baklanovsky, the States-General agreed to send military supplies to a maximum value of 20,000 guilders. Massa was assigned to accompany the shipment. He was to supervise its unloading at Archangel and then see to it that the cargo was shipped to Moscow at the Russian government's expense. As soon as he got there, he was to present the bill of lading to the tsar, convey the Dutch request for transit facilities for the Persian trade, and ask for plenipotentiaries. If such talks seemed feasible, Massa was to report on how best to achieve the desired results. If he met with refusal, he was to report on the reasons for this, so the Netherlands government could avoid wasting money in future. If the tsar rejected the war materials, or if the military situation made it impossible to get them past Archangel, Massa was to dispose of the shipment and remit the proceeds to the States-General.[20]

Massa and the Dutch ambassador weighed anchor at Rotterdam on 16 July. Shortly after they had left The Hague, the States-General were alarmed by news of the latest English initiative. Sir Dudley Digges was on his way to Moscow with a gift of 200,000 crowns and a petition that the Dutch be excluded from the Russia trade. The English plan misfired badly, however. Digges reached Archangel and had gone as far inland as Kholmogory when he heard that the roads to Moscow were infested by Poles. He took fright and fled with a treasure valued at 100,000 rubles.[21] The next year, the English sent Digges's uncle, Sir Thomas Finch, with a mere 16,000 rubles. So offended were the Russians by the stinginess of this present, plus the fact that Finch was not a properly accredited ambassador, that they almost rejected the money, especially as by then the war with Poland was at an end.

The English had made the mistake of promising much and delivering little, while the Dutch, despite the meagreness of their promises, had been as good as their word. Yet Massa's overland journey to Moscow was such that it appears Digges's fears were not wholly unjustified. Just as Massa and Baklanovsky arrived at Archangel, they witnessed the Englishman's precipitate departure. The report Massa now sent back on the activities of the English (see Appendix B.1) was far from truthful, but he rightly and exultantly pointed out that these rivals were embarrassed, and the Dutch would soon be back in favour.

Massa set off from Archangel on 15 September on what proved to be a harrowing journey, including shipwreck, foul weather conditions, and attacks by marauding Poles. He did not get to Moscow until 1 February 1619, and even then he had been compelled to leave most of his cargo at Yaroslavl for later shipment (see Appendix B.2). When he reached Moscow, he found that his old adversary Tretiakov was dead, and his position filled temporarily by Massa's old friend Savva Romanchukov. On the other hand, there was a great deal of uncertainty, since the end of hostilities with Poland meant the imminent return of the tsar's father. On 14 June, Patriarch Filaret made his triumphal entry into Moscow, and shortly afterwards there was a large turnover of Muscovite officials. Massa had made a point of ingratiating himself with Ivan Nikitich Romanov, the tsar's uncle, and gained a sympathetic hearing from Filaret's trusted adviser, the new conciliar secretary Ivan Kurbatov. Massa left Moscow on 7 August and reached Archangel on the 26th. There he saw the evidence of a fire that cost the Dutch merchants some one and a half million guilders, even though they had managed to retrieve about half of their possessions. Massa blamed the fire on the English, whom he evidently viewed as compulsive incendiaries; he also held them responsible for a fire in Yaroslavl on his outward journey, though in this instance citing 'tobacco smoking and drunkenness' rather than cold-blooded arson. In the Archangel blaze, which occurred in his absence, he claimed to have suffered heavy losses. Sailing from Archangel at the end of August, he reached the Netherlands on 20 November after a stormy and generally unpleasant passage, and presented the tsar's messages to the States-General.

After this voyage, Massa seems to have settled down. His mother died in April 1621, and on 25 April 1622 he married Beatrix van der Laen, the daughter of a former burgomaster of Haarlem, who at that time lived in Lisse.[22] We are indebted to Frans Hals for an exquisite portrait of the bridal pair, replete with symbols of conjugal bliss.[23] Two children, Abraham and Magdalena, were born of this union. By 1624, however, Massa was ready for another voyage to Russia.

Russia's gradual recovery from the economic dislocations of the Time of Troubles, coupled with the disruption of European trade patterns by the Thirty Years' War, meant that the pressing area of Russo-Dutch relations became the grain export trade. Certain Dutch merchants came with letters of credence from their government, requesting permission to purchase from the state granaries for export to the Netherlands. On this occasion Massa travelled by the Baltic route, by way of Novgorod, armed with a letter from the stadholder accrediting him as an official representative of the republic. On 26 September he conferred with Savva Romanchukov and his colleague Ivan Gramotin, who expressed concern that the tsar had now been on the throne for 12 years, but the States-General had yet to send a formal embassy. Prince Maurice had also written independently on behalf of a number of Dutch merchants, and Massa sent a supplementary memorandum to Gramotin, vouching for the fact that the merchants named by the prince were men of substance who, as deputies to the States-General for the city of Amsterdam, had voted for Baklanovsky's petition in 1618. Massa also petitioned the tsar on behalf of his two brothers, Christiaan and Lambert, asking that they be permitted to trade toll-free in Russia, and that Christiaan be placed directly under the jurisdiction of Filipp Oblezov, head of the Customs Chancellery. The request for toll-free trade by Massa's brothers was rejected on the grounds that this would arouse the envy of other foreigners, but Christiaan was placed under Oblezov's protection.[24] Massa was dismissed on 30 November 1624, and left by way of Novgorod, Vyborg, and Abo. While visiting Stockholm, he was received by King Gustavus Adolphus, from whom he received a patent of nobility on 7 March 1625. In addition, the king recommended Massa to his agent at The Hague, urging close consultation with the Dutchman on matters touching Swedish interests.[25]

Massa returned to the Netherlands this time with several proposals. He outlined a scheme for building a canal to link the waterways between Moscow and Novgorod, thus developing a continuous route from Persia, by way of the Caspian Sea and the Volga, to the Baltic. Massa also stressed his potential usefulness in negotiations over the grain trade, pointing out very adroitly that affairs of state were now in the hands of the tsar's father, who was a deadly enemy of the Poles, and therefore of the entire Hapsburg coalition. He urged further that he be given a 30-year monopoly in the Russian grain trade.[26]

Massa's proposal was taken up by the States-General in January 1626, but it was apparently buried there, since Massa states in his petition to Tsar Michael, dated 21 March 1629, that in 1626 his ideas had aroused great enmity among the Amsterdam merchants, a number of whom had sent the States-General a memorandum full of slanders against him.[27] Massa did not deign to reply to these accusations, but retired to a country estate he had acquired near Almelo, in the province of Overijssel.

From there, he wrote the tsar a series of informative letters, two of which survive in the original Dutch (20 April and 20 June 1626) and three in contemporary Russian translation (16 May 1627, June 1627, and June 1628). It was quite common practice at this time for the Ambassadorial Chancellery to keep abreast of political events in foreign countries through selected correspondents, of whom there were several at this time in the Netherlands, but Massa was very frank in his remarks, and his correspondence was intercepted by some of his bitter rivals, notably Georg Clenck and Karl de Molin. Copies of the two 1626 letters were in fact handed over to the Dutch authorities, who placed them in the secret archives with the notation, 'Two letters written to the detriment of the Republic.' In 1628, Massa attempted once again to get letters of credence from the States-General, which had already granted such letters to his rival Clenck. This time some members of that assembly asserted that Massa was a traitor, since he had written to the tsar volunteering information about the prince and the States-General. Prince Maurice summoned Massa to his presence, demanding to know whether these allegations were true. Massa admitted that he had written to the tsar, but denied that the letters had contained anything disrespectful, let alone treasonable. The stadholder let it go at that, and while Massa was refused letters of credence, he was empowered to negotiate on behalf of a consortium of merchants to whom such letters had been granted.

Though still useful for his uniquely intimate knowledge of Russia, Massa had apparently lost standing with the Dutch government. In December 1628 he travelled to Stockholm, and arrived in Moscow on 17 March 1629 in the company of Anton Monier, the Swedish ambassador. Massa and Monier were received in formal audience on 21 March, and it was at this audience that Massa presented the petition referred to above. The nature of the relationship between Massa and the Swedish ambassador is unclear, though it is known that he had been in correspondence with Swedish ruling circles since 1625 through the resident at The Hague.

Very little is known about Massa's last visit to Moscow in 1633-4, except that he went afterwards to Sweden, where he addressed the Riksdag on 18 April 1634, describing his Moscow journey and giving an account of relations between the States-General and the Muscovite government. After he had made his report, the Riksdag debated whether the Swedish government should employ him. Jakob Delagardie told the assembly that Massa was a skilful man who could fathom the secrets of men's hearts and be useful in dealings of some note, but that he should not be entrusted with matters of prime importance. It was decided to give Massa four thousand pounds of bronze, two hundred reichsthalers for the expenses of his journey back to the Netherlands, and an annual pension of a thousand guilders. Massa expressed his gratitude, and stated that he would always be ready to carry out the Swedish government's commissions so far as his conscience would allow.

We know nothing more about Massa's diplomatic activity, except that in the early months of 1635 the tsar's translator, Ivan Angelaer, arrived in The Hague during a tour of England, France, and the Netherlands, with documents concerning the Eternal Peace with Poland and the death of Patriarch Filaret. Massa was asked to translate the tsar's letters and accompany Angelaer to Amsterdam.

Thereafter, Massa seems to have lived in retirement. The Frans Hals portrait painted in 1626 shows him at age 39 in the prime of life, while the later portrait, painted in 1635, shows us a more portly, prematurely aged man. Adriaen Matham made an engraving from the latter portrait, though it came out as a mirror image of the original, with a profusion of drapery in place of Hals' stark background. Below the engraving is a fragment of verse, perhaps written by Massa himself: 'Pursued by hatred and envy, he obtained honour from the tsar and the Swedish king, and sought their favour, while fulfilling the commissions entrusted to him by the States. When envy brought accusations upon him, he continued on his way, relying on God, and obtained greater honours from the commander of the Goths, while laughing at envy. Promoted now to the nobility, and having become rich, he now calmly awaits his eternal bliss.'[28] Indeed, the superscription *In coelis Massa* led earlier biographers to conclude that Massa actually died in 1635. It is true that he seems to have taken no active part in public affairs. In 1639 his first wife, Beatrix, died, and about a year later he was married a second time, to Maria van Wassenburgh, by whom he had two children, Jakob and Willem.[29] Relations with the Hals family had been very close. Not only did Hals paint at least three portraits of Massa, but Massa also stood as godfather to one of the painter's children in 1623. In the year before Massa's death, however, the relationship between the two families was clouded by an unseemly incident. On 31 March 1642, the painter's eldest daughter, Sara, was brought to the workhouse in Haarlem 'for hope of improvement.' Later witnesses declared 'that they were present in the house of mother Lysbeth, in the Achterstraat, Haarlem, and that they have seen that Sara, the daughter of the said Mr Frans Hals, was delivered of a girl. And that they have heard her say in deepest distress, being questioned by the same midwife, that Abraham Potterloo, the son of Susanna Massa, was the father of the child, and no one else ... Upon further questioning by the said midwife, if she had not been with some other men, she replied: "Yes, I have been with more."'[30] The putative father was, of course, Isaac Massa's nephew.

Isaac died in 1643, and was buried in the Bavokerk between 14 and 21 June.[31] His son Abraham later accompanied the embassy of Conrad de Burgh as a translator. Of his two sons by his second marriage, Jakob studied at the University of Utrecht in the 1660s, and Willem served as a public notary at Haarlem from 1667 to 1684. The last trace of the family is the burial of Pieter Massaert, recorded on 24 April 1772.

MASSA'S TEXT

Until the later nineteenth century, Isaac Massa's chief claim to fame was as a cartographer and author of one of the earliest western geographical treatises on Siberia; his achievements as a historian were all but unknown. Yet while living in Moscow between 1600 and 1609 he had kept copious notes on contemporary events, on the basis of which he wrote down his impressions on his return, and filled some 84 folio pages excluding the dedicatory epistle to Prince Maurice.[32] The completed manuscript was presented to the stadholder, but it is not known whether the stadholder ever read it or, if he did, how he received it. In fact it remained on the shelves, apparently unread, for nearly two and a half centuries. There is a vague entry in the eighteenth-century catalogue of Prince Frederick Henry's library that may be taken as pertaining to Massa's manuscript.[33] Massa himself made two subsequent allusions to his *History*. One is contained in a letter sent in 1614 from Archangel to the States-General, describing the current Russian situation and referring to Maryna as 'the daughter of the palatine of Sandomierz, as Their High Mightinesses the States-General may read in my work on the troubles in Muscovy, which I have dedicated to His Excellency the prince.'[34] Massa's other reference occurs in his treatise on Siberia. Friedrich von Adelung, who published his biographical survey of foreign travellers' accounts of Russia in 1846, did not fail to notice this reference; yet, despite his five-page entry on Massa, this is the only trace he could find of the *History*, which he evidently presumed lost.[35]

The manuscript came to light in 1859, when the Amsterdam antiquarian and bookseller Frederik Muller published his list of volumes dealing with early Russo-Dutch relations. Muller expressed an interest in having Massa's *History* published along with a French translation of it, and even went so far as to copy out the text, but was daunted by its 263 foolscap sheets, 35 lines to a page.[36] The task fell therefore to Antonius van der Linde, a Dutch scholar of very diverse interests. In 1864, by way of a preliminary report, he published a short biography of Massa in Dutch.[37] Translated into French with some important additions, it was essentially incorporated into the apparatus of the first printed edition of Massa's *History*, which was published at Brussels in 1866.

In preparing the Brussels edition, van der Linde secured the co-operation of Prince Mikhail Obolensky, who had previously, in 1839, reprinted the pamphlet *La légende de la vie et de la mort de Démétrius, dernier Grand-Duc de Moscovie*, issued originally at Amsterdam in 1606,[38] to which certain parts of Massa's narrative bear a close relation.

The Brussels edition comprises two volumes, the first containing the Dutch text, six of Massa's missives to the States-General, two of Massa's treatises on Siberia, and the text of *La légende*. The second volume includes an introduction in French, which is a slightly updated version of the Dutch biography of 1864, the French translation of the text, and 75 pages of scholarly annotations.

A pirated edition of the French translation was put out in 1868 by the St Petersburg bookseller and publisher Yakov Isaakov, under the title *Démétrius l'Imposteur, par Isaac Masse* [sic]. The Dutch text was reprinted in 1868 by the Archeographic Commission in the second volume of *Rerum Rossicarum Scriptores Exteri*, and in 1874 the same body published the first Russian translation in a volume entitled *Skazaniia Massy i Gerkmana o Smutnom Vremeni v Rossii*. The definitive Russian translation, by Alexander Morozov, was published at Moscow in 1937 under the title *Kratkoe izvestie o Moskovii v nachale XVII veka*. Morozov was able to point out most of the discrepancies between the two printed versions, but was apparently unable to check them against the original manuscript to verify the correct readings. This I have been able to do.

The work's importance was immediately seized on by scholars. S.M. Soloviev, the eighth volume of whose monumental *History of Russia* had been published in 1858 and 1866, had to make substantial revisions before publication of his third edition in 1873. Later historians dealing with the Time of Troubles have cited Massa extensively.

In relating events prior to his arrival in 1600, Massa is generally repeating gossip, and much of his reporting on that period is inaccurate. This is the least valuable part of his *History*. But when he deals with the first decade of the seventeenth century, his testimony is particularly valuable, and has the immediacy of an eyewitness report that I shall leave to speak for itself.

The main textological problem is posed by the middle section, from Basmanov's defection through the death of the false Dmitry to the bill of accusations brought against the Pretender by the government of Vasily Shuisky. This section would appear to be largely derivative, though Massa has undoubtedly added touches of his own. His source appears to have been the same as that of the *Légende*, which bears the subtitle '*traduicte nouvellement l'an 1606*,' probably from the German or Dutch. An English version of the same account, published at London in 1607 by order of William Russell, the local agent for a consortium of Dutch merchants, appeared under the title *The Reporte of a Bloudie and Terrible Massacre in the Citty of Mosco*.[39]

In 1606 a similar pamphlet appeared in Dutch, entitled *Warachtige ende eygentlijcke Beschryvinghe vande wonderbare ende seer gedenckweerdighe geschiednissen die in Moscovia zyn voorgevallen*, 'all faithfully recorded by a trustworthy merchant who was present at the time.' I would hazard a guess that this pamphlet, of which the only extant copy known to me is in the University Library at Utrecht,[40] is the common source of the *Légende* and the *Reporte*, and also, ultimately, of the corresponding section of Massa's history. Could Massa have written it himself? The autobiographical information in the pamphlet does not fit this hypothesis. Yet it is more than likely that Massa knew the author of the protograph, and certainly by the time that Massa wrote his own account, printed versions of the earlier narrative were readily accessible in three languages.[41]

Unlike other foreign observers and participants whose accounts survive, Massa was able to compile notes during the reign of Vasily Shuisky from the perspective of the Muscovite camp, and his story is one against which contemporary Russian sources can be verified. During the reign of the Romanovs, Muscovite annalistic reporting was subjected to an extensive 'operation rewrite,' culminating in the many variants of the *Novyi Letopisets* from 1630 onwards. Massa had no partisan motives in compiling his history, except perhaps to expose the machinations of the Poles, whom he saw as instruments of a world-wide Jesuit conspiracy.

The Jesuit historian Paul Pierling has noted Massa's marked anti-Catholic bias; and indeed Massa was something of a seventeenth-century cold warrior, inclined to view every untoward event as the consequence of a cosmic popish plot. Pierling is quite correct when he asserts that this preoccupation tends at times to warp Massa's judgment, but he overstates his case when he implies that this weakness tends to impugn the reliability of the narrative as a whole.[42]

Massa's style is also sometimes erratic, his sentences disjointed, and it has been quite a challenge to render his text into what I hope is readable English prose, to say nothing of the problems posed by his snatches of doggerel.[43] My rather elementary Dutch was aided considerably by triangulation with the French and Russian versions. The former is marred by a number of errors and omissions, whereas the Morozov translation is generally accurate, and the notes invaluable, though some of the biblical citations are misleading. I am confident, however, that the reader will consider my labour to have been worth while. Massa's promise, made in his dedicatory epistle, to report the events he had seen faithfully and to the best of his ability was, on the whole, ably fulfilled.

A page from Massa's manuscript with his sketch of the palace built by the false Dmitry (see p. 115). *By kind permission of the Koninklijke Bibliotheek, The Hague*

The map drawn by Massa's Muscovite friend, from the manuscript (see p. 130).
By kind permission of the Koninklijke Bibliotheek, The Hague

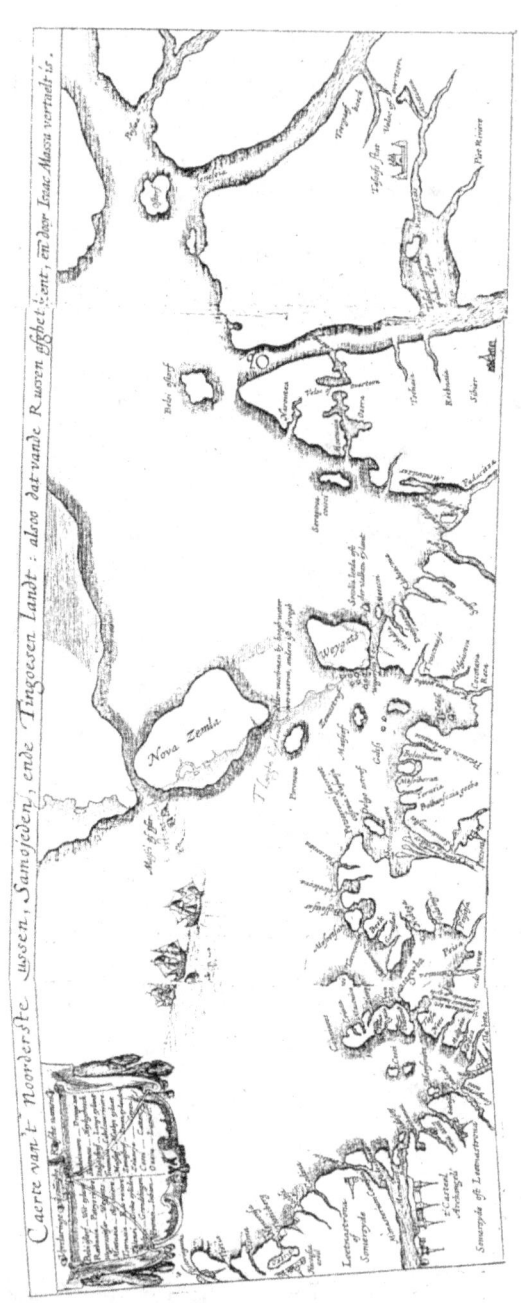

Anonymous portrait of the false Dmitry.
By kind permission of the Hessische Landes- und Hochschulbibliothek, Darmstadt

LEFT: Map of Arctic Siberia from Massa's *Beshryvinghe vande Samoyeden Landt* (1612). *By kind permission of the Koninklijke Bibliotheek, The Hague*

Frans Hals, *Portrait of a Married Couple* (Isaac Massa and Beatrix van der Laen), ca. 1622.
Amsterdam: Rijksmuseum. 1852; by kind permission of the Curators of the Rijksmuseum

Frans Hals, *Portrait of Isaac Massa*, 1626.
By kind permission of the Art Gallery of Ontario, Toronto; bequest of Frank P. Wood, 1955

Frans Hals, *Portrait of Isaac Massa*, 1635.
By kind permission of the Fine Arts Gallery of San Diego; gift of the Misses Anne R. and Amy Putnam, 1946

A Short History of the Beginnings and
Origins of These Present Wars in Moscow
under the Reign of Various Sovereigns,
down to the Year 1610

by
Isaac Massa

A Short History of the Muscovite Wars

Letter to Maurice, Prince of Orange[1]

Gracious and most illustrious Prince! All nations that are endowed with the true faith and conscious of their duty to love and honour the Almighty and sing his praises, are bound to sing yours equally and in hymns, dramatic spectacles, and sublime verses, celebrate the noble and prodigious feats you have accomplished for the country's good, and the great victories you have procured with the aid of the Most High.

Yes, even the infidels and heathen cannot admire these deeds enough, as I have persuaded myself after discoursing from beginning to end of your own high glorious feats and the love the illustrious Prince of Orange, your father,[2] bore his country. I also recounted to them the Spaniard's implacable tyranny, partly from my own experience and partly from what was told me by my parents, who have suffered it so much, and do still. Persians, Muscovites, and Tartars were in ecstasy over my speeches. Enraptured, they fell at the feet of their gods and made supplications and offerings that heaven might grant such a hero as yourself long-lasting health for the good of the state. For the considerable time I was employed at Moscow, and frequented the court and served there, I used to send for engravings representing the sieges of towns taken and battles won under Your Excellency's leadership, and I translated their inscriptions into the Muscovite tongue for the children of the tsar of Muscovy. I have also helped to propagate the glory of Your Princely Grace in this part of the world, a glory which inspires admiration and has become the subject of increasing praise by the Muscovite princes. The Persians also, when I gave them my accounts for the shah of Persia, their sovereign, did not cease, with the arrival of their annual caravans of merchants on the opposite shore of the Caspian Sea, to ask me for the continuation of the story, as so agreeable was it to their sovereign that he took pleasure in hearing of your fine deeds. Nor did he ever fail to present his wishes for Your Excellency's prosperity.

For this reason, I have often wondered to what purpose I was born, if not to use my existence in the service of my prince, and I have always wished for the time when I could repay a debt of gratitude to my country in accomplishing a work that would obtain it some advantage.

The first wish I could have would be to be received by Your Princely Grace and speak with you, and I would bless that happy moment should the favour of the Most High grant me my desire. I would present Your Princely Grace with this little work dealing with the origins of the disastrous wars in Muscovy. I must point out that I know the history in depth, seeing that I have lived in Moscow, the capital of that country, for the past eight years; and being very curious, I was in a position to find out everything in consequence of my relations with a number of nobles and secretaries of the court, whose friendship I continually sought. All I have been able to learn in this manner I have noted down as accurately as possible, though not with the care and knowledge with which a historian might have done so, for I am unschooled in letters, nor have I pursued any studies except the little learning I have acquired on my own account.

I hope that my book, despite its want of merit, will be received kindly by Your Princely Grace, who I trust will appreciate the affection the humblest of his subjects bears to him. At the least, it may be as acceptable to him as the pomegranate given by Rizom[3] to the king of Persia, or the cup of water offered the same king by a peasant. There is no one as worthy as Your Princely Grace, so greatly inclined to all that is good, to receive in homage what is but newly composed and written down. As meagre as my work may be, it is to Your Princely Grace that I purpose to present it first.

I beg Your Princely Grace to excuse my great presumption, and consider a young man's zeal and affection towards his prince rather than the boldness he displays.

Meanwhile, may I express the desire to enter the service of my country, whether on sea or land, declaring without fear that with the grace of God I would conduct myself as bravely as any in the world? From my earliest years, even though my parents had sent me to Moscow to learn of commerce, I have been seized by the desire to be useful to my country in the same way Heemskerk[4] and many others have been, and in whatever employment might be entrusted to me. And it seems to me it is these ardent spirits that should be helped, and not merely those wanting for nothing, who are rich and live in luxury. I mean young men who have nothing, but who feel in them the passion to work for the glory of their country; they are the ones who should be advanced. If I dare write these words, it is my zeal that moves me, and the good inspiration that watches over me day and night. Being descended from an honourable family, I would wish to make my way in the world honourably, in accordance with my condition. At this moment, commerce with Moscow is non-existent, and I have no means of making a living.[5] Would it not be deplorable if one were unable to give employment to men full of zeal who are exiled far from their friends, who have lost everything for the cause of religion, and who show also that they are faithful to their country unto death?

Once again, I pray that Your Princely Grace will deign to accept this meagre present from one of his humblest subjects. For henceforth, I will feel bound to make my prayers to heaven unceasingly, that Your Princely Grace may be always in good health and assured the continuation of your triumphs. The kindness of Your Princely Grace to me, your most humble subject, will be complete if you will permit me to come and read my little book to Your Highness and Princely Excellency, so that Your Princely Excellency may become well acquainted with its contents, since my poor handwriting will not permit it to be read easily. If I may obtain this audience which I so much desire, I would then be able to tell Your Highness in person a number of pieces of information about these lands, and the voyages undertaken by order of the Muscovite princes to the lands of Cathay and Mongolia, as well as the wars that have taken place in Muscovy. And once again I beg Your Highness to pardon my boldness and accept the wishes I express for his prosperity, his health, and victory over all his enemies. Amen.

Your Excellency's most humble servant,
Isaac Massa

IVAN VASILIEVICH

> Kazan, Astrakhan, and other powerful kingdoms
> By force you vanquished, not your valour.
> They fell under the yoke which all abhor.
> You were nothing but a scourge;
> To your great dishonour
> History accords you the name of Basilisk,[6]
> And no other tyrant has ever inspired such dread.

1530. Birth of Ivan Vasilievich; his father Vasily dies; the death of his mother

Ivan Vasilievich, Grand Prince of Muscovy, called 'the Tyrant' for his acts of tyranny, was born in Moscow, capital of the country, in the month of August in the year 1530. His father, called Vasily Ivanovich, a virtuous prince according to the chroniclers, was seized shortly after the tyrant's birth by a serious illness that grew worse from day to day and carried him off at last in 1534, leaving behind the young prince, who at that time was only three years and three months old, and the Grand Princess, named Elena, a virtuous woman who, with a number of noblemen whom she thought to be among the wisest and ablest to serve the public good, took the reins of government into her own hands. But this regency, which was an age of peace and concord, lasted only four years. Elena went to rest with the Lord and died in 1538, when Ivan was about seven years old.[7]

Government of the Muscovite princes; dissension among the Muscovite lords

For some time, the government remained in the hands of the leading lords, those who had sworn to the people to govern the country well and defend it against all enemies until the prince had attained his majority. But it was soon obvious that several of the magnates were men given over to injustice, oppressing the innocent at every occasion, pillaging and stealing all they could get their hands on, and little concerned for the public good. Furthermore, they were continually arguing and quarrelling among themselves, and these differences could not always be reconciled. Some deadly event was to be feared, perhaps even the ruin of the state. Seeing these afflictions, the clergy and some of the most notable and distinguished members of the community came together to discuss the means of saving the country and the sanctuary of Christ's saints, as they call it. They were of the opinion that what most needed to be done was to restore the authority to the prince, regardless of his extreme youth, crowning the Grand Prince as his father's successor, and thus check the growing power of the magnates. Therefore, together with the clergy, they entrusted him with the reins of the state, but did not crown him until they had chosen him a wife. This happened when he attained age seventeen and a half.

1548. Coronation and marriage of Ivan Vasilievich

He ascended the throne of his ancestors in 1548 and was betrothed to Anastasia, daughter to Roman Zakharievich, the most powerful lord in Muscovy after the Grand Prince himself. The betrothal ceremony and coronation were celebrated according to national custom and with extraordinary grandeur.[8]

The troubles came to an end. Several guilty men were judged and sent into exile, where they died in hunger and poverty.

In the first years of his reign, Ivan Vasilievich governed as a good prince, but when he had learned the spirit of his subjects, he began to curb them with severity and tyrannize them cruelly.

Ivan's sons

The Grand Princess gave him three sons, of which the oldest, Dmitry, drowned while still a child. This was at a time when the Crimean Tatars had just invaded the country in a manner both violent and sudden, causing such immense damage that Moscow's inhabitants were obliged to flee. The Grand Prince himself withdrew with all his treasure and his court to Beloozero, a town fortified with good ramparts and surrounded by a great lake, which serves as a very strong defence.

1548. His son Dmitry drowns

One day Ivan was crossing the lake to inspect the Muscovite camp, which was all around the shore. The Grand Princess with the small Dmitry went with him in another boat. At a certain moment, husband and wife were to embark at the same time. In an access of fatherly joy, the Grand Prince asked for the child. The mother made haste to pass the child over to him, but, unhappily, he slipped from her arms, fell into the water between the two boats, sank like a stone, and was never found again. So died their first son, and the whole country was moved with grief at the news of this loss.[9]

The second son born to them was named Ivan after his father, to whom he bore a resemblance in both appearance and character. It was feared that he would even surpass him in tyranny, for he took great pleasure in seeing blood spilled. At the age of 23[10] he died by his father's own hand. The Grand Prince used to pass the summer in one of his country residences called the Alexandrovskaia Sloboda, 12 miles from Moscow. Several military leaders, as they were preparing to march against the approaching Crimean Tatars, begged the tsar to permit his son, who was already a grown man, to go with them on this campaign, saying that in their opinion such news would sow fear among the enemy. They added that this was the prince's most earnest desire.

The tragic end of Ivan's son

On hearing this proposal, the Grand Prince flew into a violent rage, and raising the stick he held in his hand against his son, struck him such a violent blow on the head that the young man died three days afterwards. This tragic event took place in 1581.

It is said that the Grand Prince suspected treason in his son, a noble young man, fearing that he wished to depose his father. Ivan also looked with misgivings on his love of foreigners, especially of German origin. The young Ivan was continually saying that when he became tsar, he would order all the wives of the nobility to dress in the German fashion. These and other such schemes sometimes reached the father's ears, and he became fearful of his son.

The third son of Ivan and Anastasia was called Fyodor. He was a virtuous, good, pious, and mild-mannered prince, and it was he who succeeded his father.

Apart from these three sons, of whom only one survived, the Grand Prince had from his first marriage three daughters who died unmarried.

After his wife died, he married several other ladies, but he had few children by them, none in fact except by his seventh lawful wife, who belonged to the Nagoi family. She gave him a son who was called Dmitry, of whom I will have frequent occasion to speak.

The second Dmitry, prince of Moscow

I could tell you much about Ivan's great tyranny, but that would be to digress from my subject. All the histories, however, tell of it in detail. I would add that there are so many versions of the story that no writer could begin to guarantee the veracity of his account. I will restrict myself to writing briefly of the wars he undertook and the conquests he made, from which he derived the name of tsar or emperor, although the word in the Slavic language signifies simply 'king.' I repeat, I will be brief, in order to get to the cause of the present wars in this country.

Treason in Moscow; a great conflagration

He began building a new earthwork around the city of Moscow, which he later reinforced with a ring of walls, so that he made this city much greater than it had been in his father's lifetime.[11] During his reign, he fought many wars with the kings[12] of Kazan, and the inroads of the Crimean Tatars caused him great hardship. His reign was also notable for frequent treason in Moscow, as many times there were cases of incendiarism. After one of these disasters, only about fifty churches remained. One can judge from this how few houses were left.

Rebellion in Kazan

Kazan, a kingdom in Tatary which in his father's time had been paying tribute to the Muscovites in acknowledgment of Muscovite suzerainty, fell away from Muscovy, and raised a great rebellion. To subjugate them, therefore, Ivan had to employ all his forces, and sent his army against them six times in six successive years. In the seventh year, he marched in person against this rebel country at the head of a formidable army of four hundred thousand able-bodied men.

The Poles attack the Muscovites and then conclude peace

The Poles, as eternal enemies of the Muscovites, took advantage of the occasion to attempt to regain several strongholds that had been recently taken from them by one of their great lords, Mikhail Glinsky by name. This lord, having been subjected to great outrage in his homeland, had taken flight and placed himself and his vassals under the protection of the Muscovites, who held him in great honour during his lifetime. He had often made war for the Muscovites, and wrought great harm on the Poles, from whom he took several towns, such as Smolensk, Polotsk, Starodub, and others of like importance. The Poles, finding this a sufficient reason for war, made vigorous preparation to recapture the towns. Preoccupied with the revolt of Kazan, Ivan concluded a peace of several years with Poland, giving back Polotsk, Starodub, and some other towns, so as not to be hampered from that side in his undertaking.[13]

Siege of Kazan

He left Moscow, therefore, in 1551, entrusting the affairs of state to Metropolitan Makarius on behalf of the Grand Princess and the young Prince Fyodor, or Theodore,[14] his son, and came with his army before Kazan. After several vigorous assaults combined with stratagems, he finally succeeded in capturing the town by storm. This success was greatly aided by a mine that passed under the Volga and emerged within the city. The sapping operation was conducted by an able engineer of German origin, called Erasmus.

Conquest of Kazan

Having conquered Kazan by the sword, the victors captured the king of Kazan, Safa Girei, who died of grief standing upright.[15] Of his two sons who were captured with him, one died in the same manner. The other was brought to Moscow, where he received baptism and the name Alexander. He was formerly called Utemish Girei [Neefcirej]. He was married to a highborn Muscovite lady who had three patrimonies, the towns of Torzhok, Tver, and Toropets, which let him live in a manner befitting his rank.

Captivity of the tsar of Kazan

Among the captives from Kazan was yet another prince of royal blood, who was baptized and named Simeon.[16] He also was married to a Muscovite lady, the daughter of a great lord, Duke Ivan Mstislavsky. This young prince was so greatly favoured by the Grand Prince that he even put him on his throne, the crown on his head, and gave him territories to govern for two whole years. Simeon carried this task out faithfully. Until the two years were up, the Grand Prince withdrew to a stronghold outside the town, where he lived as an ordinary lord. Thereafter, Ivan rewarded young Simeon generously, showering him with honours and riches.

After the conquest of the empire or kingdom of Kazan, Ivan Vasilievich abolished its privileges and settled a great number of Muscovites there. He then added to his title that of tsar, for until then he had simply borne the name Veliky Kniaz, or Grand Prince.

1553. Description of Astrakhan

Thus, for a short time the country enjoyed peace and tranquillity. Astrakhan, which had previously borne the name Motrogan,[17] was formerly a Tatar province that elected its own ruler and had under its permanent dominion vast territories close to the Volga and on the shores of the Caspian Sea. A populous commercial town, Astrakhan was a meeting-place for numerous merchants from Persia, Arabia, Media, Armenia, Shemakha, and Turkey. Those from Armenia brought pearls, turquoises, and precious leathers. Those from Shemakha, Persia, and Turkey arrived with cloth of gold, sumptuous tapestries, silk, and other valuable merchandise. Those from Arabia brought their spices. The Muscovites, for their part, came to sell other sorts of leather, cloth, serge, paper, and other inferior goods, and finally caviar, which the Turks buy in great quantities to export to Constantinople. This caviar is the roe of the sturgeon, which is caught in incredible quantities in the Volga, and makes a dish the Turks sought as keenly as the Italians do today. In short, it was an important city, which had been obliged to pay tribute to the tsar; apart from this, the inhabitants were free of obligations, and could do as they wished.

Dues paid by the inhabitants of Astrakhan

The boyars and Muscovite lords who governed the land along the Volga were avaricious and also great dissipators of wealth. They laid heavy impositions on the city and loaded it with taxes, of which the Grand Prince was well aware. Their conduct became intolerable, and the inhabitants, their patience with the Muscovites exhausted, sought all possible means of shaking off the yoke, and finally did so. When the collectors arrived to gather the tax, they replied by doing them injury, and refused several times to pay them anything. 'And if the Muscovites are bold enough to attack us,' they said, 'we will summon the Turks to our aid, and place ourselves under their domination.' This state of affairs dragged on for some time. Sometimes they submitted and sometimes they rose in revolt, until such time as Ivan Vasilievich made himself master of Kazan, as I have just related.

1553. The inhabitants of Astrakhan sue for terms

Learning of the siege and conquest of this town, and observing the daily growth of Muscovite power, the inhabitants of Astrakhan feared that the terrible Grand Prince would punish cruelly their many revolts. They wished to regain his good favour. Thus, they sent a costly embassy to Moscow, bearing rich gifts and empowered to implore the tsar's pardon, begging him to forget all resentment at their foolish conduct and promising to behave as befitted loyal subjects.

For his part, their king, named Abdul Rahman [Abdilrogman], had also sent ambassadors to the Grand Prince. Having accomplished their mission, both by sending petitions and by verbal promises, these envoys obtained the pardon they had come to ask and received numerous gifts. In addition, they were splendidly feted, and brought back letters full of friendship for king and people.

Nogai kings come to Moscow

At this time, two young kings of the Nogai, moved by the desire to become Christians, left their country and came to Moscow, where they were received with enthusiasm, overwhelmed with friendship, and generally entertained like the Grand Prince himself. They were given fine territories. One was called Ediger, the other Kaibula. The latter was the son of Akubek, the powerful Tatar prince of the Nogai. The Grand Prince offered Kaibula a town called Yuriev Polsky and married him to the daughter of Enalei,[18] the Tatar king. She was also the niece of Shigalei, who had been taken prisoner at Kazan. All these persons were of the blood royal.[19]

Death of the tsar of Astrakhan

Meanwhile, at Astrakhan, King Abdul Rahman died, and one Yamgurchai [Jemgoeretz], ruler of a land situated close to the Caspian Sea, was chosen in his place.

Hearing this news, Ivan Vasilievich sent the new king an embassy led by a learned man, a Wallachian called Sebastian, to offer him presents and invest him with the kingdom.

But when he arrived at Astrakhan, the ambassador was received in a manner even more outrageous than that in which David's envoys were received by Hanun, king of the Ammonites.[20] He was driven from the town with derision.

Ivan's anger against Astrakhan

Learning of this incident, Ivan Vasilievich was greatly angered, and swore that before winter he would raze Astrakhan to the ground and show no mercy, but put all its inhabitants to the sword. He summoned a man of war as cruel as he was brave, one Derbysh, who had for a long time been hetman over many Cossacks on the great steppes, and ordered him to be ready to march on Astrakhan. Derbysh received this command joyfully, and at once assembled a large army, with which he descended the Volga followed by most of the Piatagorian Cossacks, an untold host of men from all the towns along the Volga.

The Muscovites conquer Astrakhan

When he came near Astrakhan, he was joined by a large number of Nogai Tatars and their rulers, implacable enemies of the people of Astrakhan, from whom these had always suffered greatly. This formidable army besieged the town immediately, without any parleys or summons to surrender. Even though it was naturally very strong, and defended by a well-armed garrison, the unfortunate city was taken by assault after a siege of several days on 3 July 1554, old style. Men, women, and children all passed under the sword, and the town was razed to its foundations.

During the assault, King Yamgurchai succeeded in making his escape with several chariots and proceeded towards Tiumen. The victors set off in pursuit, but they got hold of only part of the baggage, along with his wives and concubines. He himself escaped.

Building in Astrakhan

Thus, three years apart, two illustrious kingdoms, Astrakhan and Kazan, met the same fate. But the town of Astrakhan, owing to its fortunate location, was soon rebuilt in a splendid manner with fine Muscovite churches and towers, more resplendent than before. Many Muscovites were compelled to live there, but a great number also went voluntarily, and in a short time prospered and multiplied. The town is now more flourishing than ever before.

The Crimean Tatars are defeated by the Muscovites

In the following year, the Crimean Tatars, on the orders of the Turkish sultan their overlord, launched a violent invasion of Muscovy with four hundred thousand men, destroying all the towns they could capture. Against them the Grand Prince sent a powerful army commanded by Ivan Sheremetev, Lev Saltykov, and Alexei Basmanov.[21] The two last attacked the Crimeans with great courage, while Sheremetev's contingent placed itself in ambush. The Crimeans were routed. More than eighty thousand were killed, either in battle or in flight. The Muscovites took ten thousand horses and five hundred camels. This was all the booty they could seize from these hordes, who owned nothing save their livestock. The victorious generals returned to Moscow in triumph, and were showered with favours by the tsar.

Ivan's tyranny

Victory continued to attend Ivan Vasilievich in all his undertakings. Every day he extended his sceptre over new lands and peoples, who feared his great might. On the one hand, he believed himself to be without equal in the world, and thus free from fear of anyone; on the other hand, he perpetually distrusted his lords and nobles. Them he held in cruellest tyranny. On the most frivolous charges, he would condemn them to shameful deaths. Some he impaled; others he subjected to the most inhuman tortures. He even set fire to his own cities, and had thousands of his subjects drowned. At their cries of despair, he laughed out loud and cried, 'How pleasantly you sing!'

His licentiousness

He was more given to luxury than Sardanapalus or Heliogabalus, and his strange quirks were almost always mingled with cruelty. I will give only one example, even though it is not relevant to the history I have undertaken to write, so that otherwise his actions would be sufficiently described. They have probably been described too much already, for they are so horrible that they have won him the surname 'Basilisk'[22] from the historians.

His cruel amusements

On a summer day, from the height of the palace, he looked at one of his country residences on the other side of the Moskva, immediately opposite the imperial palace. Abruptly, he called one of his pages and ordered him to summon to the palace at once all the chancellors and secretaries,[23] of whom there were many in Moscow. The message was conveyed instantly. When all these unfortunate folk had gathered, Ivan commanded them to take off their robes, and then had them whipped by ten or twelve stable-boys. Having reduced them to a piteous state, he permitted them to go after they had beaten their foreheads on the ground in gratitude for his clemency. One who had been delayed came in as the others were leaving. At that time the tsar was busy eating apples. He gave one to the latecomer and told him to go home. In view of this gracious greeting, he burst out in thanks to the tsar, and instead of going, started chattering. 'Oh, great tsar!' he said: 'I certainly did not deserve the treatment you have given the others, for my ancestors have always served faithfully at court, and as for myself, I have never felt the touch of the whip. It would have been too cruel to be punished unjustly!' 'Ho! Ho!' said the tyrant: 'You have never tasted the whip? You have never received a mark of favour, because nobody can call himself a man of the court if he has not undergone this trial.' And right on the spot, he had him whipped three times more than the others. That is what this unfortunate man suffered for not being able to control his tongue and content himself with an apple.

This characteristic, and others like it, are sufficient indication of his tyranny. If I had to write down all his actions, I would never have time enough, and it would be fruitless to describe his abuses and tyrannies, which were inhuman in their cruelty and scandalousness.

Devastation of Livonia

Neither will I describe the wars against the Swedes, or his devastation and ruin of Livonia, which have been told in sufficient detail in other histories. I should say a few words, however, about the victory he won over the Turkish army sent by Sultan Selim to conquer the town of Astrakhan.

He divorces his barren wives

At that time, or some time previously, he married several women whom he threw into a convent when, after three years, they had given him no children.[24] This is a custom among the Muscovite princes, to repudiate their wives after three years of barrenness and marry again.

At this time, Sultan Selim sent Ivan a letter in which he greeted the Grand Prince and conferred on him by special favour the title 'constable,' or 'head of the stables.' He further informed him that since the tsar's father, who was long dead, had left behind a son of tender years, namely himself, the sultan had wished out of pure affection not to disturb this young prince, and had waited for the moment when his domination over the Muscovites, his subjects, had been completely established. Finally, he demanded the tribute with all arrears since the death of Vasily Ivanovich of blessed memory. He also expressly recommended that this tribute be sent straight off without delay, for his father had always been faithful and obedient.

Answer given by the tsar to the sultan

This letter was brought to Moscow by an ambassador. When it had been read, Ivan sent at once for a rat skin and the hide of a black fox, which he shaved bald. 'For I wish to send to the great sultan,' he said, 'a few kindnesses in return for his favours.' Usually, the presents of Muscovite princes to kings or foreign princes consisted of precious furs, which they always had in abundance in their treasuries. The rat skin was to serve for the finishing of a robe, and the fox skin to make a cap for the sultan. Together with these presents, he sent a letter couched in these terms: 'If you dare write to me as you have done, you can expect your chief stableman to come and render you as bald as this fox fur, and give your country to be devoured by the Muscovite rats. Have you not learned what happened to the kings of Kazan and Astrakhan, your allies, who every year, stirred up by you, rose in revolt against my rule? I will subject your country to the same fate, and begin with Taman, Azov, and the land of Georgia. This time, however, I will overlook it.'

The sultan's anger towards the tsar

This insulting letter so deeply irritated the sultan that he resolved to destroy the Muscovite empire. He sent messengers to the kings and Tatar princes, commanding them to await his call. He even summoned the peoples who live in the neighbourhood of the Black Sea, those of the Crimea and the shores of the Caspian Sea, the Circassians, and their neighbouring tribes, and commanded them to assemble in the month of March on the shores of the Don, close to the town of Azov. This was in the year 1569.

Astrakhan remains loyal to the tsar

On 20 March of the aforesaid year, he dispatched from Constantinople a corps of thirty thousand men that included most of his army commanders and the greater part of the lords, noblemen, and grandees of the empire. To this he added five thousand janissaries armed with long muskets. These troops crossed the Black Sea on galleys and arrived without incident at Azov, where they joined with the formidable contingent of the aforesaid peoples, who were already encamped close to this town and along the banks of the Don. In Azov there was a great supply of provisions, ammunition, and other war materials, as there always had been, since Azov is a frontier garrison of the Turkish empire, on the banks of the Don.

The Turkish campaign plan, which had been known for quite some time, was to leave a garrison in Azov and march directly across country on Astrakhan, for they had no doubt that they would take Astrakhan easily, and then, afterwards, the Nogai and the Cheremissians, who hated Moscow for the cruel oppression they had suffered from time to time at its hands, or else simply wanting a change, would hasten to rally to their side. But these peoples went more in fear of the tsar than of the Turks, for Astrakhan was fortified with a strong garrison and well stocked with provisions and ammunition. Besides, the Muscovite government, which had a great predilection for this city, had granted it broad privileges, and the city was well satisfied with its prosperity. The inhabitants were also not unaware how fortune had favoured the Grand Prince. They swore once again to defend the country as true subjects, and prepared their forces for the defence.

The Muscovites prepare their defence against the Turks

In Moscow, where the people had had ample warning, everything was prepared to repel the enemy. A great number of commanders were sent to Astrakhan. From all around, they called in countless people proven in battle; they had orders to await the enemy outside Astrakhan and along the Caspian Sea, and spread out in the wildernesses of this country, which are very great. They expected to see the Turks encumbered and tired beyond measure from uneven paths, and it was proposed to surprise them piecemeal on terrain where they could not deploy en masse. Everything went according to plan. Having with them numerous Nogai and Cheremissians who knew the country perfectly, the Muscovites attacked and destroyed the Turkish army from all sides.

Distress of the Turkish army

So this army, having left Azov laden with victuals and water, had been obliged to divide into several columns during the night because of the uneven and rough roads, the mountains, and the forests through which it had to pass, and the soldiers were in great distress on more than one occasion. Among the Turks, thousands of men perished from shortages and fatigue, and the commanders were so greatly discouraged that they longed for death. More inured to fatigue, the Tatars did not fear the lack of provisions as long as they had at their side the two or three horses every man usually brought with him. The Tatars did not suffer from these privations, and nearly all survived; they were not, however, warriors like the peoples the Muscovites had as auxiliaries. The farther the Turkish army advanced, the greater its hardships, until at last it came to a fair country all covered with ruins, which appeared to be those of numerous and beautiful ancient cities. By the tradition of the Cheremissians, Alexander the Great had once prepared for war here, and established his camp. Ceremonies are still performed in his honour. They say also that a certain Timur-Askak [Tomiracsach] made great expeditions in which he ravaged the country completely, overthrowing all these fair cities whose ruins attest to their ancient splendour. They say that this Timur-Askak is none other than Tamerlane. There are also fine stone blocks in great numbers, several of which have inscriptions in Greek or Hebrew, very artistically engraved.

The courage of the Muscovites, and their victory over the Turks

It is in this place that the Turkish army rested for about two weeks, except for the ten thousand who had come to grief or perished on the march. There it divided into several columns and resumed the march on Astrakhan but, duped by poor guides, frequently went astray.

Fully informed of all these circumstances by the Tatars, either in the Turkish camp or living in the nearby mountains, the Muscovites were on their guard, and did not sleep. A corps of ten thousand men proven against fatigue was sent directly by the shortest road to surprise the town of Azov and put everything there to fire and the sword. They also set up numerous ambushes around Terek, Taman [Terek-Tumen], and other places, where they presumed the enemy would pass. Hidden in the forests and mountains, knowing the roads perfectly, and aware of all the enemy's manoeuvres from the reports of Tatar spies favourable to the Muscovites, these detachments immediately fell upon the Turkish army on the march, destroying piecemeal this host decimated already by four months' hardship and disaster.

Utter defeat of the Turkish army

During this time a corps of Muscovite troops, less than half in numbers of the one sent against Azov, arrived before the town, which they attacked briskly, falling upon the Turkish galleys, most of which were burnt or sunk to the bottom, and finally penetrating the city itself, which was consumed by fire. There was plenty of powder, the explosion of which demolished a large number of houses and killed many men, and those yet alive were slaughtered. In addition, an incredible number of inhabitants from both the town and the surrounding countryside were drowned in the waters of the Don. Others, mostly women and children, were rounded up as booty, along with camels, horses, and livestock. Hearing that a large body of Turks had followed the main force, the victors, with those waiting in ambush, began pursuing and harassing them from every side and destroyed them all. Of three hundred thousand Tatars, most of them horsemen, not one remained. The Turks suffered almost the same fate. About five thousand men, mostly grandees and commanders, managed to flee, but when they came before Azov they were massacred by the surviving inhabitants, so that not more than two thousand managed to get back to Constantinople. The destruction and pillage of Azov and the surrounding countryside, the loss of two hundred galleys and all the army – such was the outcome of the campaign. Since that time, the Turks have given up the idea of surprising Astrakhan in this manner. They are content to press the Crimean Tatars to invade Russia and take all the prisoners they can catch, but the Muscovites are used to this kind of attack and are not much concerned. From all sides, therefore, fortune smiled on the tsar. In his excess of prosperity he made himself redoubtable by his violence, and by his acts of tyranny.

It would be pointless to tell of all his wars with Stefan Batory, king of Poland, who inspired in him the most lively terror – they have been described in detail by Reinhold Heidenstein, secretary of the crown of Poland – as also of the cession of Livonia by the treaty concluded in Batory's camp before the town of Pskov on 15 January 1582.[25]

The birth of Dmitry; the beginning of my history

We come now to the history I have proposed to write, namely the cause of the current wars. Ivan Vasilievich, Grand Prince and tsar of the Muscovites, had contracted a seventh marriage to a lady of the Nagoi family called Marfa, or Martha in our language.[26] She gave him a son, called Dmitry. She was his last wife, and he had no children after that. He had, it is true, a great number of concubines, but we do not know if there are any bastards from these unions. It is improbable, for having known young girls, and there were constant expeditions to search them out for him, he handed them immediately to his officers and companions in debauch, who abused them in such a fashion that they could never afterwards bear children.

Fearful tyranny of the Muscovite tsar

In speaking of the birth of children, we have related how he lost or killed his son Ivan. This was about the year 1581. From that moment he gave himself over more than ever before to excesses of tyranny, and outdid all that had ever been heard about him. It is said that he fell into such despair at his son's death that he seemed driven by the Furies themselves. When he dressed himself in red, he let rivers of blood. When he was dressed in black, then disaster and grief dogged everyone as he ordered people drowned, murdered, and plundered. When he was seen dressed in white, however, everybody rejoiced, but not in a manner befitting Christian people.

Death of the tyrant

It is even said that he had the notion of destroying his country and exterminating all his people. Knowing that he had not long to live, he imagined everybody would be happy at his death, though no one gave any indication to that effect. But he died earlier than he had counted on. He grew weaker day by day, and was suffering from an illness in the head. His state was not desperate, however, nor was it hopeless. Yet one of his principal lords, named Bogdan Belsky,[27] who enjoyed his favour and was responsible for bringing him a daily potion ordered by the doctor, Johan Eyloff,[28] is said to have put poison in the cup while he was carrying it. God knows what the truth may be. But the tyrant succumbed immediately afterwards on 4 March 1584, old style.[29]

Fyodor is proclaimed tsar

After his death, there was great unrest in the populace of Moscow. Armed with bows, pikes, clubs, and swords, they hurried towards the castle, where the gates were shut in the face of the invading crowd. They turned to attack and plunder the shops and then the arsenal, where they took arms and powder, running to break down the doors of the castle and crying: 'Give us

Nikita Romanovich!' That was the name of the brother of Anastasia, the tyrant's first wife. This prince was well loved by the people for his own personal qualities as well as the affection they bore his sister. The crowd demanded to see him alive, afraid that in the interregnum someone would try to do away with him, his virtues having aroused enmity at court. From the Kremlin walls, the assailants were told to return to their homes and offer prayer and sacrifice for the repose of the soul of the departed; all would end well. For it was well known, since Ivan had left sons, which it was who should occupy the throne. At the same time, they proclaimed Fyodor Ivanovich tsar and Grand Prince in his father's place. Fyodor was already married, and so there was nothing to fear for the dynasty. Yet this still did not calm the crowd, who continued to shout: 'Give us Nikita Romanovich!' The lords, fearing some harm might befall Nikita, hastened to reply: 'He is safe and sound. Why should anyone do him harm?' This reply did not calm the assailants, who called even more loudly, naming the lords as traitors and scoundrels. Fearing that the people might break down the doors, they ordered the musketeers to fire two or three hundred rounds into the middle of the crowd, who fled from the doors. In an instant, the great square which stretches before the castle was entirely empty, and not a man dared show himself.

Unrest in the Muscovite populace

Nikita Romanov, fearing some move against his palace, or for some other reason, wished to return home. The lords implored him to stay in the castle, but since he insisted, they let him leave. No sooner had he come out with a score of his mounted retainers than the people rushed in front of him like a living tide, letting out shouts and cries of joy at seeing him again, and escorted him to his palace, where they guarded him carefully until after the coronation of the young prince, for they were convinced that traps had been set and someone would try to kill him by treachery. And so it continued until the Grand Prince was crowned.

Burial of Ivan

The funeral of Ivan Vasilievich was held according to the rites of the Greek church, to which the deceased belonged, in the presence of a large number of sobbing and weeping women.

Coronation of Fyodor

Although Tsar Fyodor had been proclaimed tsar and Grand Prince of Muscovy, his coronation was delayed until the following 1 September, which is the New Year's Day of the Muscovites. They crown their sovereigns on that day, and never any sooner.

The ceremony was brilliant and solemn but, since I did not see it, I cannot speak of it in detail. In everything that follows, however, I will relate facts of which I have been an eyewitness. We have seen that Ivan, after the capture of Kazan and Astrakhan, was the first to add the title 'tsar' to that of 'Grand Prince.'

At Fyodor's coronation on 1 September 1584, the new sovereign was given the following titles, which all his successors have borne after him: 'Fyodor Ivanovich by the Grace of God Tsar and Grand Prince of All the Russias, Autocrat of Vladimir, Moscow, Novgorod, Tsar of Kazan, Tsar of Astrakhan, Lord of Pskov, Grand Duke of Smolensk, of the lands of Tver, Yugoria, Perm, Viatka and Bulgaria, Lord and Grand Prince of the lowlands of Chernigov, Riazan, Polotsk, Rostov, Yaroslavl, Beloozero, Udorsk, Obdorsk, Kondinsk, and all the lands of Siberia, and of the Samoyeds, Lord of the Nogai, Supreme Overlord of the northern lands of Severia, Lord of Livonia.' These are the titles the Muscovite sovereigns place at the head of their documents.

Having briefly related the life of Ivan Vasilievich, we come to the reign of Fyodor Ivanovich. As I have said, his coronation took place on 1 September 1584. So now we come to the history which I have proposed to write.

1584. The Godunov family

There was in Muscovy during the tyrant's time the family of the Godunovs, a family of Tatar origin. They had lived for some time in Muscovy, as their ancestors had entered the service of the prince of Moscow, or Vladimir, which was formerly the seat of the Muscovite empire.[31] This was during the reign of Timur-Askak, who devastated all the country adjacent to the Caspian Sea and, among other regions, the cradle of this family, the land still called Zolotaia Orda – or the Land of Gold – because of its beautiful countryside.[32] There we can still see ruins of great and magnificent buildings, and discover curious inscriptions in Greek and Hebrew, artistically carved in stone and sometimes gilded.

During the lifetime of his father the tyrant, Fyodor Ivanovich had married a wife from this family. After three years of marriage, they had one little girl, who soon died. Tsar Ivan had wished that, following custom, his son would shut his wife up in a convent and take another.

But Fyodor, who was of a sweet and gentle character and had a tender affection for his wife, did not comply with his father's wishes. 'Let her stay with me,' he replied, 'or take my life, for I will never abandon her.' Tsar Ivan was greatly annoyed at having a son with so little respect for him, and greatly repented having so cruelly put his son Ivan, who much more resembled him, to death.

Boris Godunov

The empress, Fyodor's wife, was called Alexandra,[33] and she had a brother named Boris Godunov, who had married Maria, the daughter of a great lord called Maliuta Skuratov,[34] whose real name was Grigory. This lady Maria was a true Semiramis at heart, always nursing ambitious plans; she had nothing less in mind than to become empress, and she was all the more hopeful as the tsarina Alexandra had no children.[35] She always urged her husband to act so that none but he should wear the crown after Fyodor, though there were heirs presumptive, including Dmitry, son of Ivan the Terrible and Martha, his seventh wife.

The closest heirs to the Muscovite throne

Failing Dmitry, there were also the children of Roman Zakharievich, father of the tyrant's first wife. These were related in the second degree and quite numerous. It was therefore fairly difficult for the Godunovs to rid themselves of all these claimants as well as Prince Dmitry, who was very young. All went according to plan, however, owing to the extraordinary ability of Boris, brother of the Grand Princess.

The tsar's brother, young Dmitry, had been sent to Uglich, an estate on the banks of the great river Volga. There he was raised up and kept in the same high state as the tsar himself.

Boris seeks to do away with Dmitry

Boris immediately strove to get rid of this Dmitry, thinking that this would aid him in his design. Thanks to his sister, who had recommended him cordially, Boris had acquired great power from the tsar, who made him chief marshal and principal field commander of the armies of the empire, as well as giving him the most beautiful palace in Moscow, close to his own, and always showing great esteem for him. A pious and peace-loving man, the tsar took little part in the affairs of state, and was content to bear his title of sovereign. He gave the reins of government into Boris's hands and approved all he did. Boris then began to work his treasonous design.

His first step was to send Tsarina Martha as well as her son Dmitry and the Nagoi family, relatives of this princess, to various remote regions such as Tatary or elsewhere, by appointing them governors of provinces. But gradually, a number of them perished by Boris's orders, while several escaped, long wandering in destitution.

To avoid suspicion, he frequently sent rich presents to the young prince and the grandees of his court. He thought of a number of ways to rid himself of the young Dmitry. The principal one was to incite some enemy to attack the land, hoping that, having sown fear and dismay in the tsar's spirit, he would become master of the situation; for the emperor, who for the most part resembled an ignorant monk rather than a grand prince and was moreover credulous and over-trusting, had no ears but for Boris's insinuations and whatever else his favourite desired.

One day he persuaded the tsar to place himself at the head of an army and march towards Narva to retake Livonia, which had fallen almost completely into the hands of the Poles. It must be remembered that Russia had been obliged against her will to cede them this country temporarily. The truce had run out, and it would have been a pity for the Muscovite crown not to regain by force what the Poles would not restore out of good grace. Boris did all he could by his insistence to get the tsar to agree to this and leave in person with an army of three hundred thousand men, among them fifty thousand Cheremissians and Tatars, who at the first encounter were placed in the forefront, and not one survived. After wreaking much havoc and losing many men, this army retreated and seized Ivangorod and Koporie on the way. It is said that Boris wanted to attempt one more attack on Narva in hope of taking the town, and it is probable that he would have succeeded, for the inhabitants later asserted that there had not been more than eighty able-bodied men to defend it, and they had resolved to surrender at the first assault. But the Grand Prince, dismayed by all this blood-letting, had given them the order to return. Boris spread the rumour throughout the army by the mouths of some of his companions that it was he himself who, in his affection for the people, had persuaded the tsar to follow this counsel. In this manner he won the hearts of a great part of the masses. The commanders and magnates, however, conceived great scorn for him in their hearts, but dared say nothing.[36]

If he had captured Narva in the course of this expedition, Boris would then have ordered Dmitry's assassination, but since his campaign had been unsuccessful, he had to await another opportunity.

Moscow flourishes

Amid all these events, the country prospered in an astounding manner, and its population grew considerably. The fearful tyranny of the late sovereign had almost ruined the country, and by their pillage Ivan's officers, emulators of their master, had contrived to reduce it to poverty. Yet it recovered betimes and waxed rich through the paternal and just administration of Fyodor, and Boris's great abilities.[37]

1590. Rebellion on the Volga

The year 1590 was marked by the mutiny of a great number of Cheremissians on the banks of the Volga. This undisciplined horde, urged on by some disreputable hetmen, made depredations in the surrounding countryside. Troops of Germans, Poles, and Russians in the Grand Prince's service were sent against them, but when they came there they could find nothing. All the bands of pillagers had dispersed and gone away.

1591. The Crimean Tatars make an armed invasion of Muscovy, and approach Moscow itself

In the spring of the year 1591, news came to Moscow that the Crimean Tatars, by order of their tsar, had begun a campaign, and in rapid advance had overrun the neighbouring lands in a most alarming manner. The leader of these peoples, desiring to uphold his fame as a great warrior, had proposed to come and visit Moscow, and if he could not capture it, terrify the Muscovites and make off with captives. In fact the terror in Moscow was great, but Boris, who always maintained his cheerfulness and equanimity, had the confidence of the tsar and the people. He prepared busily for defence, and caused a formidable enclosure of wagons to be placed outside the city on the side where the Tatars would have to cross the Moskva, furnishing this at all points with artillery. Besides this, he enrolled all the city's inhabitants over twenty years of age, encouraging them to be perpetually ready and armed and take turns at guarding the ramparts. Knowing that the Tatar army was four hundred thousand strong, all horsemen, he chose not to march out to meet it, but resolved instead to await it on prepared ground, counting on attacking from several sides at once as soon as it halted for a time. But this plan did not succeed.

Couriers were constantly coming to Moscow with news of the enemy's rapid march. The enemy came within sight of the town even before the arrival of messengers sent out the previous night to reconnoitre. On 2 July, old style, early in the morning, an immense multitude was seen, like a cloud covering the land and making the earth tremble under its feet. This mass of men pitched camp at Kolomenskoe, a mile and a half from Moscow, and surrounded it with their entire army.

The two great armies came face to face. On the first day they did not move. On the second day, two Tatar horsemen advanced to the foot of the Muscovite entrenchment. The Muscovites began firing their heavy artillery on them, though to no good purpose. Then hundreds followed by thousands of Tatars moved up, falling like hail upon the entrenchment and firing arrows in such numbers that the sky was dark with them. After a long skirmish, they returned to their camp.

Simplicity of Fyodor, who loved his subjects

The Grand Prince Fyodor Ivanovich saw all this from his palace, which stood on a high hill near the Moskva in the middle of the town. He dissolved in tears, crying: 'See my people spilling their blood for me. If only I could die for them!' He was touched most of all by the conduct of a number of foreigners he had in his service, who showed themselves to be more courageous than the Muscovites. And such was his religious zeal that he would have willingly, if this were possible, exchanged his empire for a cloister.

The next day, despite heavy rain, the Tatars began again as on the previous one, and the Muscovites again received them with ill-directed fire. Though their artillery was formidable, it seems that they did not know how to use cannon, for they shot into their own ranks as much as into the enemy. After a second skirmish, the Tatars retired once more to their camp.

The following night, the Muscovites fired their artillery and musketry continuously from both the height of their ramparts and their entrenchment. Through all that night it seemed that heaven and earth were about to crumble. Nobody knew why these shots were being fired. The reason soon became apparent.

Boris, who in his capacity as chief commander represented the tsar, had, at a price, found a nobleman to take part in a stratagem. This nobleman allowed himself to be captured by the Tatars, who, unaware that this was a ruse, and seeing his rich raiment of cloth of gold sewn with pearls, believed they had a lord of high rank in their power, and brought him, bound hand and foot, into the camp before their tsar, who asked him why they had fired all night without doing harm to the enemy. The prisoner replied boldly that thirty thousand Poles and Germans were coming to Moscow's aid, and had entered the town from the opposite side. On hearing this, they put him to torture, but he suffered steadfastly, not changing a word of his story. Then the Tatar chief was convinced of the truth of the matter, and became so frightened that he fled the following night with all his army. This flight took place in unutterable disorder, and with such precipitateness that between Moscow and Serpukhov, a town situated about twelve miles away, they passed straight through a number of groves, uprooting trees and leaving thousands of men and horses entangled, their bodies heaped up and blocking the way in incredible numbers.[38]

It was exceedingly hot at this time, for there the summer heat is always very great, and the stench of the corpses was intolerable; and at the same time, hosts of worms and flies appeared, for the corpses had been crushed and slashed open by horses' hooves.

Only in the morning did reliable information reach the Muscovites that the entire Tatar camp had fled. Because of the cannonade of the previous night, their sentinels had heard nothing. They had also not suspected anything, seeing the large number of fires burning in the Tatar camp, which were not put out at daybreak. As soon as the Muscovites became aware of the enemy's flight, they sped large detachments of cavalry in hot pursuit to prevent him from burning everything in his path. Arriving in Serpukhov, they learned that the Tatars had already crossed the Oka that day. This seemed incredible to them. They could scarcely believe that such a vast army could, in one night and half a day, and in summer, make a march of 28 miles[39] and cross a great river. Yet so it was, for the enemy were endowed with inconceivable speed in flight, as in war they encumber themselves with neither munitions nor victuals. The Tatars, who feed on horseflesh, usually take two mounts for every man on their expeditions. When one of the two is tired, the rider jumps on the other, and the first follows his master like a dog, as these horses have been trained to do while very young. When a man happens to die, his companions kill his horses. Each of them cuts a slice, which he places under his saddle, the lower part of which is dry. There this flesh softens and is warmed; when it is tender enough, they savour it as a delicious morsel. Furthermore, pillage furnishes them with enough livestock for their subsistence. When they arrive at the bank of a river, each man attaches his horses to one another by their tails and bridles, throws his bow of wood and sinew on a horse's back so it will not swell through contact with the water, and, holding himself between the two mounts, crosses the river swimming with incredible speed. Clothed from head to foot in bearskins or sheepskins, these Tatars have the appearance of true demons.

Crossing the Oka, they took the inhabitants of all the hamlets and villages prisoner, and their cries of despair were piteous to hear. All these unfortunates were carried off to slavery in the Crimea, whence a great number, mainly women and children, were sent to Turkey; but many of the men managed to escape and return home. It was thus that the Tatars left the country having, without striking a blow, wrought great devastation, for those pursuing them came there much too late.

After these events, all the Muscovite army was paid and dismissed. The Germans, the Poles, and some other auxiliaries and commanders were given presents apart from their wages, and each man received a gold piece. About seventy individuals were arrested, mostly serfs who had tried to put the city of Moscow to the torch during the siege. Had they succeeded in their design, it would have meant the ruin of the empire. Also, through fear of conflagration, it had been necessary to prohibit the baking of bread, with the result that a number of poor people died of hunger in this short space of time, even though the enemy had stayed only three days before the town. The traitors were punished as they deserved.

Boris takes counsel with his confederates as to how he should succeed to the throne and dispose of Dmitry

As soon as peace had been restored, Boris turned again to manoeuvring for the accomplishment of his design. He conspired with his relatives the Godunovs – of whom he was the head, even though not the oldest – the Veliaminovs, Saburovs, and others, to a number of about seventy families. He plotted with them daily to secure the throne. But first he had to dispose of the young Dmitry, and he had no time to lose, for the prince was almost ten years old and very nimble-witted for his age. He was sometimes heard to say: 'What a pitiful sovereign my brother is! He pays no attention to the government of this great empire.' Often too, he asked: 'Who is this Boris Godunov who alone holds the reins of state?' Then he added: 'I would like to go to Moscow and see how things are there for myself. For with this blind trust in the magnates who are unworthy of it, I foresee that all will end badly, and it is time to attend to this.'

These sentiments and others like them were faithfully reported to Boris and his supporters, who grew very afraid that if they did not make haste, they would fall themselves into the trap they had prepared for others. And therefore they resolved to consummate their treason.

Prince Dmitry had a chancellor who never left his side, and whom he regarded as his most devoted friend. He was called Mikhail Mikhailovich Bitiagovsky [Petoegoffsci]. But this man had been bribed to assassinate the prince, and had agreed to do this thing. He entrusted the task to his son, Daniel Bitiagovsky, who had taken as his accomplice a man called Nikita Kachalov. These two went first to Moscow to see Boris, who made them great promises of honours and dignities. Receiving the sacrament and blessing from Boris's almoner, and also full and complete absolution for their sins, these two accomplices returned to Uglich with a letter from Boris to the elder Bitiagovsky.

The treacherous murder of Dmitry

One day, knowing full well what to do, he ordered his son Daniel and Nikita to hide themselves in the palace. For two or three young lords, he had arranged a game with walnuts that was to be played after dinner, and Dmitry had expressed a wish to take part. At a moment when the game was liveliest he sent the servants of the castle hither and thither on various pretexts, and to allay all popular suspicions, left the assembly himself and returned to the chancellery, ostensibly to look after his business in the presence of a crowd of people pleading and litigating against each other. At this time, when the game was liveliest the two assassins threw themselves on the prince and cut his throat. In their confusion, they left the other young men alive, and took flight on horses that had been made ready for them.

As soon as this occurred, the young nobles filled the palace with their clamouring. The news reached the chancellery forthwith, and spread through the town, and everywhere the cry resounded: 'Murder! The tsar has been murdered!' The townspeople leapt on their horses and assembled without knowing what to do. The people ran to the palace, seized all those who happened to be there, nobles as well as common folk, and led them off to prison until news of the murder reached Moscow. During the great tumult, a large number of people were killed.[40]

When the news came to Moscow, the town and court were stupefied. The tsar was filled with fear and prayed for death, though efforts were made to console him. As for the tsarina, she felt a mortal grief, and would have liked to retire to a convent, for she was afraid that the crime had been the work of her brother, whose desire for the throne she had remarked; but she was silent, and kept all she had heard to herself, not saying a word to anyone.

A revolt or a great tumult was to be feared at Moscow, but the tsar's presence prevented an outburst. However, it was murmured everywhere that the authors of the assassination were the Godunovs, whom everyone feared, for they had a great number of supporters; and the Godunovs were afraid all would be revealed, and that the inquest would be all too penetrating. But Boris knew how to speak to the tsar with such persuasiveness that Fyodor entrusted the conduct of the inquest to him, and Boris accepted.

Thus, one could say with justification that the lamb was placed in the wolf's care, for Boris led the investigation in such a manner that all the prince's court was arrested and charged with treason. They fell into the tsar's disfavour and were sent away in chains. Several noblemen were sent to prison at Ustiug, a town on the Dvina 200 miles from Moscow, where they suffered long privation. Some who had come under suspicion were put to death. So perished many good people who were completely innocent, along with their wives and children.

Dmitry is buried

One great lord named Vasily Shuisky, and another boyar or lord, Andrei Kleshnin,[41] were sent from Moscow to assist at Dmitry's funeral. After taking a good look, and identifying the young prince who had been assassinated, they set him in his coffin themselves in the presence of his mother, the tsarina and widow of the late tyrant. Then he was buried at Uglich, with great lamentations and cries, according to custom.

The former tsarina, Martha, was cast into a convent. All her remaining relatives of the Nagoi family were sent into exile, as has been previously related. There was great murmuring among the powerful lords throughout the country. But they could do nothing against the Godunovs so long as the tsar and his wife, Boris's sister, were living. As for the merchants and the populace, they spoke of this family privily, saying that it was a family of traitors, and aspired to the throne. These rumours caused Boris great unrest, and he sought means to dispel them at any cost.

Many crimes committed in Moscow at the instigation of the Godunovs

Thus, since fear still reigned in the people's hearts from the Tatar invasion, Boris several times ordered that the city of Moscow be set on fire.[42] Each time, in three or four of these incidents, more than two hundred houses were destroyed by the flames. The authors of the conflagrations were men hired by Boris. Several were arrested and brought before him. They were cast into various prisons and threatened with ignominious death. In this way, Boris sowed fear in all the land. He had established several of his adherents as governors in the frontier towns. They informed him in false reports that the Crimean Tatars were gathering once again in great numbers to invade the country. These letters, which were circulated in Moscow, caused such fear among the people that they forgot all else, and ceased to speak of Dmitry's death or murder. They were persuaded that the assassination attempts and incendiarism were Tatar deeds, and by these whisperings the Godunovs turned the people's suspicions completely away from themselves. Everybody was so taken up with personal grief or misfortune that they no longer thought of weeping for the misfortunes of others.

Fyodor's feeble-mindedness, and the munificence of Boris

Seeing that everything was going according to plan, Boris had substantial aid distributed to all those in Moscow whose houses and effects had been burned, allotting the money according to the position of each. He put his friends and servitors into the field, and told them to convey to the victims expressions of condolence and the most affectionate words of consolation in his name, as also offers of service for all that depended on him and support for the petitions they were addressing to the sovereign. And he kept his promises. He himself received all the requests and petitions laid before the tsar each day as he proceeded to church, and carefully followed them up. Thus did he keep abreast of all that was going on in the empire, and made himself the source of all replies and favours. In this manner, he won all hearts so completely to himself that no one spoke of any but him, and his praises were on all lips. People said that after the tsar's death he should inherit the crown. These sentiments fell in exactly with his own wishes. In a word, Boris was more honoured than the tsar himself, because the tsar was concerned exclusively with the church and religion. Administering everything as he desired, Boris was tsar or emperor in fact, and Fyodor Ivanovich, as I have already said, bore only the title.

The power of the Godunovs and Boris, their head

At the height of his power, having in his favour the attachment of the masses, who regarded and venerated him as a god, Boris was not satisfied. One more barrier stood against him. This was the existence of the children of Nikita Romanovich, brother of the tsarina, Ivan's wife. Failing direct heirs, the crown was to revert to one of these children, who belonged furthermore to the most noble, ancient, and exalted family in the land. To complete the fulfilment of his desires, Boris had to rid himself of these claimants, and this was no easy matter. He had the court to fear, the nobles, and the tsar himself, who was very fond of his Romanov uncles. There were no charges he could level at them. They lived in retirement, were generally popular, and each was seen as a potential tsar. The eldest, Fyodor Nikitich, was adored by everybody and so personable that by Moscow's tailors anyone who was well dressed would be told: 'You are a second Fyodor Nikitich.' His horsemanship provoked universal admiration. The other brothers, quite numerous, were worthy of their elder.

1594. Boris is reproached by the tsar; Boris's revenge on the children of Fyodor Nikitich

Boris had to devise a favourable occasion for hatching his designs against them. For despite all his machinations, their conduct gave rise to no reproach. Indeed it was because of them that one day he earned himself a reproach from Tsar Fyodor in words he never forgot. It was during one of the tsar's pilgrimages to the monastery of the Trinity, 12 miles from Moscow. The route was broken into three or four stages, and when they had arrived at the third, a place called Vozdvizhensk where the tsar owns a palace, the boyars' servants went ahead of their masters to prepare lodgings for them in the peasants' cottages and bath-houses. Only those of Boris and Alexander Nikitich arrived, and they met in a certain place where each tried to claim the quarters for their own lord. Boris's people, being more numerous and better armed, fell upon their adversaries and drove them out violently. Alexander's servants complained to their master, but he made no response, except to keep ordering them to give way; however, he did lodge his complaint with the tsar. The latter, moved with indignation, told Boris: 'You are truly working too hard for your place in the empire, but God, who sees all, will know how to find you.' To Boris these words, which rose spontaneously from the tsar's heart, seemed so bitter that he swore inwardly not to let this go unavenged, and he held to this oath when he later came to the throne. For having procured the deaths of all Nikitich's children by false accusations, he caused Alexander, who had been imprisoned at Beloozero, to be taken out and lose his life in a bath-house, as we shall see later on.[43]

While awaiting his chance, Boris continued to govern according to his will, but always in such a way as to favour the popular element. Thus he won the devotion of all the people, so that they loved him more than anyone else. In fact, it might be said that he was adored. He allowed the lands granted to army captains and commanders in recognition of their services to pass to their children, even if these lands had not been given in hereditary right. Anyone who presented a petition at his court obtained his wish immediately. He carried his boldness so far as to touch the diadem upon the forehead of the tsar. This happened on a feast-day, as Fyodor was going to church with the crown upon his head. Boris walked at his side. At a certain moment, he took the liberty of arranging the crown, even though it was not awry. Seeing this, the crowd was alarmed, for there has been from time immemorial among the Muscovites a custom whereby the person who dares touch the diadem, the sign of the tsar's majesty, must be put to death at once. He often allowed himself such acts of temerity in the presence of the people. For this reason, he was feared more than the tsar himself.

It was he who ordered the building of the great fortifications in Moscow known as the 'Imperial Wall,' of white masonry and following the line of the earthworks Tsar Ivan Vasilievich had ordered to be erected, as we have said before.[44]

He owned more estates than the greatest lords of the empire. The vast Vaga country, which is more than one hundred German miles across, was granted to him and his descendants in perpetuity. He had lands and magnificent castles everywhere, and spared no effort to acquire domains he wanted to add to his possessions. Among his country residences, one was situated on the heights a mile from Moscow, above the banks of the Moskva river. It was called Khoroshevo [Gorossova], that is to say, 'the beautiful.' He often resided there, and took pleasure in inviting foreign scholars and distinguished persons, whom he treated in a princely fashion, living with them in great familiarity, but without shedding any of his prestige.[45]

Boris seeks diverse means of destroying the noblest Muscovite families

Time does not permit us to describe all his actions. But the intelligent reader knows enough to understand the secret end that Boris was using every means to pursue. Having traitorously exiled to the depths of Tatary a great lord named Ivan Mikhailovich Vorotynsky, who had done no wrong, he also disposed of Ivan Petrovich Shuisky. The Shuisky princes were descended from the most noble families of the land of Suzdal, and there were three brothers, Vasily, Dmitry, and Ivan. The two last were allowed to remain at the court in Moscow, for Dmitry had married the sister of Boris's wife. But they dared make no move.[46] He behaved in the same fashion towards Ivan Vasilievich Sitsky, a lord of Polish origin, and the Belsky family. In short, he thrust aside all the principal great lords and princes, depriving the country of its most illustrious aristocracy and best patriots. In their place, he shamelessly advanced his own relatives, the Veliaminovs and the Saburovs, as well as the Godunovs. And since he was always close to the tsar, he found means of arranging matters so that Fyodor knew nothing of them whatsoever. The latter, being completely given over to religious practice in a somewhat unenlightened form of devotion, spent all his time in the monasteries and churches listening to the chanting and praying of priests and monks who were utterly in Boris's pocket; so it can be guessed how things went.

There is good reason to be astounded at the ability, finesse, and boldness Boris showed in his career, although he could neither read nor write. The source of all this was his prodigious memory. He forgot none of what he had seen or heard, and would remember a man many years later who had been in his presence only once. Apart from that, he was strongly aided in all his enterprises by his wife, who was even crueller than he. In my opinion, he would never have behaved in such a tyrannical or cunning fashion without the influence of this ambitious woman who, as I have already said, was a veritable Semiramis at heart.

If Boris was the factotum of the empire, he was helped at Moscow by Andrei Shchelkalov, the Grand Chancellor, a man of a finesse, audacity, and duplicity not to be credited. Boris had great affection for him, and believed him to be indispensible to the country. He was head of all the chancelleries of the empire, and nothing was done in either the towns or the countryside without his knowledge and his wishing to be informed. Endowed with great energy, he rested neither by day nor by night. He worked as unceasingly as a mule, always looking for more to do. Boris could not admire him enough, and often said: 'I have never seen a man like him. I truly believe that the earth is too small for him. He would have been very useful to Alexander of Macedonia.' This friend of Boris's died during the reign of Fyodor and was replaced by his brother, Vasily Shchelkalov, but he was not nearly as able as his brother.[47]

Punishment of several brigands

About this time, an ambassador sent from Persia to Moscow was robbed on the Volga by a band of nomadic Cossacks. But these pillagers were seized, and their chief impaled alive.

1598. Death and burial of Tsar Fyodor

Tsar Fyodor became ill and died suddenly on 5 January 1598.[48] I am firmly convinced that his end was hastened by Boris at the insistence and with the complicity of his wife, who was impatient to become tsarina. Many Muscovites agree with me. The tsar's funeral was conducted with great solemnity, amid the tears and sobbing of the people. He was particularly mourned by the magnates, who knew what was about to happen. His body was laid to rest in the church of St Michael the Archangel, the burial place of the tsars. Before his death, he had handed the sceptre and the crown to his nearest relative, Fyodor Nikitich, and also entrusted the empire to him.[49]

FYODOR IVANOVICH

As white to black, as shade to light,
The tyrant's cruel spectre thou hast put to flight
Who was, alas! thy sire; despising vanity
Thou loved'st piety and chastity.
Sad Russia flowered at thy behest;
In heav'n and earth thy name is blest.

BORIS FYODOROVICH GODUNOV

King, a different tyrant of your race;
A Janus with a double face.
To all your fairest face revealed,
Yet what dark secrets were concealed!
But your fair face hath not heav'n deceived,
As death's just punishment hath proved.

MARIA GRIGORIEVNA

What hast thou gained, pray, by the treacherous advice
Thou gav'st thy perfidious husband without cease?
Jezebel, Athalie and all their deeds,
The list of all thy crimes exceeds.
But by Heaven's punishment thou wert ensnared
In the trap for others secretly prepared.

1599

In all the preceding, there is no hint as to what the end of this history would be. I have given some foretaste, however, in relating the death of young Prince Dmitry, and it will be revealed completely with the beginning of the reign of Boris, who became tsar. For they began working against him, using the dead prince as a convenient instrument for the accomplishment of criminal designs, that is to say, the persecution of Christians and the holy church of God, but I hope these designs against others will fall on their own heads. I hope they will fall down from the height to which they have exalted themselves, they and their counsellor and queen, the old whore of Babylon seated on the seven hills, clad in scarlet and holding in her hand the cup of abominations so many men drain to the lees.

After the death of the pious Tsar and Grand Prince Fyodor Ivanovich, which we have related previously, the people, which is soon roused in this country, came in a crowd to the Kremlin, calling with a loud voice on Alexandra, the tsar's widow and sister to Boris. They wanted her to show herself and accept the government of the empire. 'Be gracious to us, and be our tsarina!' they cried to her: 'We will carry out your every desire!'

In answer to this stormy demonstration, and to prevent all misfortune and tumult, Alexandra came forward to the palace steps intending to speak to the people. Seeing her, the crowd let out such a clamour that one would have said heaven and earth were coming to an end. 'God save our sovereign lady!' Then they fell into a deep silence to hear the tsarina, who used these words:

The empress Alexandra expresses the desire to enter a convent; she declares her intention to the people

'Christian people, it has pleased God, St Nicholas and all the saints to gather my husband, our gracious emperor, from this world, and lead him to the heavenly kingdom where we all hope to come one day. Know that he made me promise with an oath that immediately after his death I would retire from the world and enter the religious life to devote my life, if I am worthy, to prayer for the repose of his soul, and those of our ancestors, and for all of us. And as I feel perfectly disposed in myself to comply with this wish, I beg of you most urgently to relieve me of the heavy burden of this vast government, and entrust it to him who is more deserving, and to whom it falls as of right.' (She named no one.) 'I beg of you, cease your insistence, for I will never consent to rule, and prefer to remain obedient to the wishes of my husband. I beg of you, compel me no longer, for I shall never agree. Send your supplications to the Almighty, that he may give you a virtuous and God-fearing sovereign who will govern the country with zeal, firmness, and justice. This will be the constant aim of my prayers, and I hope the Almighty will grant it to us.'

The people, hearing these words from the tsarina, began weeping loudly. They prostrated themselves on the ground and begged her not to refuse them; but it was all in vain. Seeing that her mind was made up, they begged her to name her brother, Boris Godunov. There was no one worthier, they said, for he had already governed the empire in Fyodor's lifetime, and sincerely loved the people. The tsarina half consented, but referred the decision to the will of the country, and recommended that everybody pray to God to guide their choice.[50]

Fyodor Nikitich hands the crown to Boris

Fyodor Nikitich, the late tsar's uncle, who had received the crown and sceptre from him, was also proclaimed by the magnates, who greatly preferred him to Boris. Yet seeing and hearing the demonstrations of the mob, and knowing all Boris's ways, Fyodor understood that he could not oppose the will of the people proclaiming Boris as favourite; moreover he did not wish to expose the country that was so dear to him to the horrors of civil war and blood-letting. He resolved, then, not to accept a position fraught with danger for himself, and handed the sceptre and crown to Boris, begging him respectfully to accept as being worthy to receive them.

Boris's hypocrisy

Boris did not wish to listen to him, and made a great show of astonishment. At last he voiced his refusal, saying: 'But who am I to take on the government of this immense empire? I, who am scarcely capable of governing myself!' – and begged Fyodor to urge him no more. For his part, Fyodor

Nikitich continued to plead his inability, and persisted in his refusal. The council broke up with the matter undecided.

Boris is elected tsar

The magnates and the courtiers, who did not leave off proclaiming Fyodor, were gripped by fear. Everywhere they heard the people's cry: 'God save Tsar Boris!' – and saw the crowd running to the palace to swear to serve Boris as behooved true subjects. It was Boris's uncle, Ivan Vasilievich Godunov, who received the oath. Fearing they would be seized by the people and punished as traitors, the boyars, and with them Fyodor and all his brothers, made haste in turn to swear allegiance and homage to Boris, recognize him as their tsar and Grand Prince, and proclaim his son prince and heir to the throne. Thus it was that the Godunov dynasty came to the Muscovite throne through the most adroit talents of Boris, who succeeded in thrusting the legitimate heirs aside in despite of the law of nations, justice, and reason, as I have plainly shown.

Although he had been informed of everything, and was not unaware that the people had taken the oath at the hands of his closest companions, Boris pretended to know nothing, and shut himself in his palace for several days, waiting for all this unrest to calm down a little.

When he emerged again for the first time, it was to visit, with a face affecting sorrow, the church where the tsar's funeral was being conducted. He took part in all the prayers and ceremonies. Dogging his footsteps, the people prostrated themselves before him and cried out once again: 'Praise be to Boris Fyodorovich, tsar and Grand Prince of all the Russias! May he be our gracious sovereign! Praise be to his son, Fyodor Borisovich, our prince!'

Seeing this spectacle, Boris paused, pretended to be afraid, and dissolved in tears. But they were crocodile tears. Then he addressed the people: 'Why, then,' he said to them, 'do you burden me with this crown? Who am I, that you have chosen me? I, the most incapable and humblest of your countrymen? Why are you in such haste to choose a sovereign? Let us pray first for the repose of the soul of our pious tsar; there will be time after that to think of finding his successor in a family which has a right to it, and is worthy of it. On the death of Ivan Vasilievich, the country fell into great distress because of numerous wars. At that time it was necessary to find a peaceful, virtuous sovereign as quickly as possible. Heaven granted us this prince. Under his healing government, and through my humble services, the country recovered, and today it is rich and prosperous. So do not be hasty.' This discourse was simply boasting, meaning: 'It is I who am the author of this prosperity, because it was I who governed.'

But the people would hear no more, and continued to proclaim him sovereign, and his son after him. This is what decided the magnates to acquiesce in the choice. It might even have been genuine. At this, Boris accepted.

It is said that Fyodor Nikitich, returning to his house, told his wife: 'Beloved, rejoice and be glad, for Boris Fyodorovich is now tsar and Grand Prince of all the Russias.' But she, full of terror, replied: 'For shame! Why have you given the sceptre and crown that belonged to our family to them who have betrayed our dear country?' Then she abused him and wept bitterly. Fyodor became so angry that he struck her on the chin, he who had never before offered her even one harsh word. It is said that after this scene, she conspired with Ivan and Alexander, her husband's brothers, and her relations, to have the tsar and all his family assassinated. But nothing could be more wrong. This was a calumny invented by some false witness to destroy her. As we will see, it was a new machination of the Godunovs.

Alexandra becomes a nun

During this time Irina, the tsar's wife, had taken the veil at the Novodevichy convent [Joncvrouwen clooster] on the Moskva about half a mile from Moscow. She was conducted there by the people, who wept and sobbed, and taking leave of her subjects, she bade them be faithful to the tsar and pray for her. Then she said farewell for the last time, as if she were leaving the world.

Boris's promises

Boris spent several days with his sister in the convent. There, in frequent interviews, she taxed him severely with all the crimes of which he was guilty, and entreated him with forceful argument and tears, before he had to account for them to God, to renounce the empire and do penance to win heaven's pardon. Having confessed to a number of things, he promised to govern the state in such a manner as to hope to avert divine wrath, but she went on condemning him on many counts. Persuaded at last of the uselessness of her pleas, however, she commended him to God's protection, enjoined him to reign in accordance with his promises, and, finally, pledged him the support of her counsel and her prayers. Then, they parted. After he had ascended the throne, Boris continued to see his sister frequently.[51]

According to custom, the coronation ceremony could not take place until 1 September, the New Year's Day of the Muscovites. During the summer, however, Boris wished to parade his power and his grandeur before the eyes of the people. He ordered his army to assemble and rally at the Serpukhov [Jirpag] camp beyond the Oka. He had sown the rumour that the tsar of the Crimea was near, so they must march to meet him and do battle with him; but his sole aim was to glorify his name and impress his subjects. In the month of May, troops in such numbers as no Muscovite prince had ever seen poured in from every side, adding to all those the tsar had brought with him from Moscow – lords, nobles, courtiers, officers, and musketeers, to the number of thirty thousand: there were five hundred thousand men there, all under arms. Their camp covered an area of twenty-five square miles all along the river Oka; vast artillery parks stretched out, and in the middle of the camp, a veritable tent city was erected, with chancelleries, banqueting halls, towers, stables, kitchens, and churches. All this had been built to receive the tsar. Catching sight of these cleverly constructed imitation buildings, those who came from far off believed themselves in a fine city, and as for the army that occupied it, this seemed to be without number. Tsar Boris arrived at the camp with all his court. He had left his wife and his daughter in Moscow, entrusting the care of the sanctuaries to Patriarch Job, and that of the imperial throne to Stefan Vasilievich Godunov.

The army spent several weeks parading in the countryside, every man taking pains to shine in horsemanship or the handling of arms in the tsar's presence. Thus they awaited the ambassador from the Crimea, for Boris knew that he was coming to congratulate him, present him with gifts, and also negotiate a several years' truce. Reaching the camp, the ambassador was filled with admiration at the sight of the rich costumes and accoutrements of the Muscovite nobles and soldiers. Thus was peace concluded for some years, and the ambassador departed.[52]

This expedition had as its aim, then, to show the Crimean tsar Muscovite power and instil fear in him; for in that year, the sovereign had no intention of moving beyond his own frontiers.

About six weeks after the tsar's arrival, all the clergy of Moscow were seen coming to the camp with crosses and banners to beg him to return to his capital. He consented to their petition and followed these emissaries, having first disbanded his army and permitted each man to return home. Then he sent out several foreign contingents of light cavalry to the Tatar frontier, to clear the country of rebel Cossacks; but these troops returned without seeing any rebels. The tsar promised all his soldiers a reward of triple wages on his coronation day, and then each went back to his home.

Boris returns to Moscow; his coronation

On 1 September of the year 1598, reckoning from the birth of Christ[53] – or, as the Muscovites say, the year 7116[54] from the creation of the world (although they cannot show why this number is many years greater than that given in the Bible of the Greeks) – Boris Fyodorovich was crowned tsar of all the Russias and his son proclaimed prince of Muscovy. The new sovereign's official title, similar to the one Fyodor Ivanovich had borne, was sent to all foreign governments. The ceremony took place with a great show of splendour. The imperial festival lasted eight days. The crown was set upon his head in the church of the Virgin by the Patriarch,[55] surrounded by bishops and metropolitans, with all the prescribed ritual and a host of benedictions, together with the burning of incense. All along the road the tsar was to travel on his way from the churches to his palace at the crown of the fortress, they had spread out crimson cloth and covered it over with cloth of gold; before the procession, gold pieces were thrown down in handfuls, and the crowd fell upon them.

At various places in the fortress they had placed great barrels filled with mead and beer from which all could drink. One of this people's greatest pleasures is to drink their fill, and they are past-masters at this particular diversion. But they prefer brandywine, the use of which is forbidden except to nobles and merchants. Without this prohibition, everybody would be addicted to this beverage until they died of it. But these details draw me away from my subject matter.

Amid the general rejoicing, the tsar ordered the distribution of triple wages to all those in the service of the state: senior commanders, captains, officers, soldiers of the guard, chancellors, and others. This remuneration was given for a threefold reason. First, in memory of the late tsar: this present was called 'pominania' or votive offering. Secondly, to thank them for having elected him their new sovereign; and finally, to commemorate the expedition, and also because it was New Year's Day. The whole country was glad and rejoiced, and everyone praised God for having granted the empire such a master. Everywhere, towns, convents, and churches sent public prayers to heaven.

Generosity to foreigners

Taking pity on the unfortunate Livonian merchants whom the tyrant had torn from their own country, led into captivity in Moscow, and several times despoiled of all they possessed, Boris summoned them to his presence, offered them a cup of mead with his own hands, promised to be a sovereign full of benevolence for them; and, inviting them to forget the injuries of the past, he granted them the full rights and freedoms of Muscovite burghers, with the same privileges as Muscovite merchants, and gave them permission to build a church according to their faith, which they promptly did. Finally, he lent them money without interest – some six hundred, others three hundred pounds – on the understanding that they would not have to repay the capital until they had made sufficient profit in commerce and speculation.[56] Thus did they remain in peace, as Boris had much love for the German nation. Moreover, there is a proverb current in Moscow which says: 'Who is wiser than a German or prouder than a Pole?'

His hypocritical promises

He also secretly spread the rumour that he had sworn not to spill blood for five years,[57] and in fact he kept this oath publicly with regard to thieves, brigands, and other base criminals. But when it came to people from the leading families, he condemned them on false evidence, then rid himself of them secretly by suffocation, drowning, or assassination, or by giving them the monkish tonsure, always with the aim of destroying the nation's high nobility and replacing them with his own relatives and creatures.

First, in November 1600, a number of wretched fellows came at his instigation to accuse Fyodor Nikitich, the very person from whom he held his crown, and his three brothers, Ivan, Michael, and Alexander, with their wives, children, and entourage, of having plotted to poison the tsar and all his house.[58] This accusation was aimed solely at lending a gloss of justice, for the benefit of the people, to the sentence of banishment and confiscation of goods that he had just levied against these exalted personages and their families. He had Fyodor arrested and sent him to a convent named Siisky [Chio] three hundred miles from Moscow near Kholmogory, where he was tonsured. Michael and Ivan were cruelly exiled, the first on the Volga and the other to the confines of Tatary. As for Alexander, for whom he had long harboured a violent hatred, he had him conveyed with Fyodor's young son to Beloozero, where he was suffocated in an overheated bath-house. The young child, who was there with him, hid in a corner where he could breathe a little air coming through a small vent. With the aid of Providence, he remained alive, and was saved by some people who took charge of him.

All those Boris hated met a similar fate. Some were drowned, and others strangled. Prince Fyodor Mstislavsky, a great lord of Polish origin and a man utterly above reproach, was twice deprived of all his patrimony, but thanks to popular demonstrations, his life was saved; otherwise he would have suffered death like all the others. Before his accession to the throne, Boris had offered this lord his daughter in marriage several times, but he refused her. Later, he was forbidden to marry any other woman, and Boris would no longer give him his duaghter. All this was so he would leave no posterity, for he would use any means to rid himself of those who had reason to complain of his deceit – out of fear that if they were left alive, they would one day overturn the government of the Godunovs.[59]

Secret tyranny; the tsar's chief henchmen

Also for this reason, he raised his uncle, Dmitry Ivanovich Godunov, to the dignity of first boyar, which made him the first personage of the empire after the tsar himself. Next to him came Ivan Vasilievich Godunov, who had a son called Stefan Dmitrievich. Simon Nikitich Godunov was treasurer,[60] and had jurisdiction over the doctors and the apothecaries of the court. Great was his tyranny in Moscow.

In short, all the high dignities and high offices of state were given to the Godunovs – to members of this dynasty and to those, such as the Veliaminovs and the Saburovs, who had alliances with their sons and daughters. Now the Shuisky, the Belsky, the Golitsyn, the Mstislavsky families, and many others who led irreproachable lives, along with others of high birth allied to the Godunovs, lived in retirement on the revenues of their estates and domains, discharging no public function except that they were named from time to time, and for three or four years, as governors of certain large cities. Finally, as I have already said, the first chancellor and the head of the chancelleries, which are many because of the great number of provinces, was Vasily Shchelkalov, brother of Andrei.

Boris desires to marry his daughter to a foreign prince

Boris had a daughter of marriageable age. He spared no effort to find a German prince for a husband – for he did not want to give her to a native lord, neither a Mstislavsky nor a Shuisky, since their lineage was nobler than his own. He regarded all the magnates of the country as his servants, and it seemed to him that it would be a dishonour for the tsar to give his daughter to one of his servants. He was obsessed, moreover, by the constant fear of being punished for his misdeeds by one of his own, and so lived in perpetual anxiety, like a thief who always fears discovery. To him, a son-in-law would be a sure protector, especially if he could find a German prince who would be devoted to him and fight in his defence.

He also had a son for whom he tried to find a wife from the other side of the empire, either a Cheremissian or a Persian, or from some other people, in order to be secure on two frontiers, for he was always afraid of some disastrous attack on the part of Poland. At this moment, his conscience let him foresee naught but misfortune. We will see later that these premonitions were justified.

At this time, there was a young prince, the son of King Eric of Sweden, who had fled his own country because of attempts on his life, as is well known. This Gustav had fled to Poland after a long residence in Danzig, in the house of one Christopher Kater, and had then placed himself under the protection of the Poles, but despite their promises, this prince, seeing little advantage there for his cause, sent someone privily to Muscovy to speak with the tsar. Boris was filled with delight. He hoped soon to satisfy his desire and find the man who would serve him well, and to whom he would give his daughter.[61] He was at the greatest possible pains to attract the prince to Muscovy, writing him letter after letter with instructions on how to steal away, and precise indications as to the place and the day when he was to come to the frontier.

Gustav escaped from Poland and reached the tsar's domains safely. Less than three hours after he had crossed the border a detachment of Poles sent in pursuit also came there and began exploring the territory around to inquire of everyone about the prince and his companions. But the matter had been so well organized by the Muscovites that the Poles were unable to learn anything at that time. Some lords of the court had been sent from Moscow to meet the prince, accompanied by German interpreters and a complete convoy of carriages, horses, princely accoutrements, and all kinds of munitions.

In honour of his journey, they even went so far as to repair the road between Ivangorod and Moscow. In fact, no greater honour would ever have been accorded a king. On 8 August 1600, Gustav made his triumphal entry into Moscow. He was mounted on the tsar's horse; most of the nobles, richly arrayed and forming his horse guard, led him to the palace that had been prepared for him, where he found horses, provisions, slaves, and menials – such a house, in fact, as if it had been for the sovereign himself. In addition, the tsar gave him rich presents, cloth of gold and silk for him and his entourage, and daily sent him dishes from his own table on plates of gold.[62]

On 19 August he was granted his first audience with the tsar, who was seated on his throne, the crown upon his head, sceptre and orb in his hand, and his son at his side. The tsar bade him welcome, sympathized with his misfortunes, and promised him the protection of the Muscovite government. The prince thanked Boris and was escorted back to his palace, where they brought more presents from the royal treasury for him and his servants.

On 21 November, during the winter, the tsar and his son passed Gustav's residence, accompanied by all the boyars. Boris's son presented his good wishes to the foreign prince, and the tsar's promises of benevolence were reiterated to him in the presence of all the noble boyars.

Prince Gustav presents himself again

On 23 August 1601, he had a second interview with Boris. At that time several young people, mostly sons of good noble families who had known Gustav well, came to join him. Learning of the favourable disposition of the court of Moscow towards him, they attached themselves to him, to follow his fortunes.

His mistress

But events did not come up to their expectations. For this prince, infatuated by the brilliant welcome he had received, so far forgot himself as to send to Danzig for the wife of his host, Christopher Kater, by whom he had had several children, to live publicly with him in Moscow.

This lady had taught him more than was good for him, and made him so proud that he ended by being utterly foolhardy. At the sudden impulse of his frantic brain, he often took it into his head to beat his gentlemen and servants, sometimes even Muscovites, and consequently it had to be recognized that he was half mad. He had his mistress taken around in a carriage drawn by four white horses and with a great escort of footmen, as would befit a queen. Finally, he committed many extravagances and stupidities, and believed that he would be permitted everything. If the tsar ever remonstrated with him on this subject, he regarded himself as a victim of injustice.

Boris despises Gustav

Boris, who saw or heard all this, came to understand what sort of man he was, and that the prince was unsuited to become the husband of his daughter, Xenia. He thought him quite mad, and incapable of furthering the designs he had conceived. He conveyed a warning to him one day that his actions were unworthy of a king's son. He upbraided him for living publicly with the wife of another, the regal train he had given his mistress, and, above all, for following a woman's advice in all things. He begged him, furthermore, to curb his impulses a little. Having heard these remarks and some others, the prince became very angry, but he did not mend his ways, saying that he was the victim of false accusations. As a result of all this, he was abandoned by his gentlemen and courtiers, who asked to enter the tsar's service. The latter received them very graciously, paid them well, and even gave them estates where they could live like lords. Only three or four of his courtiers stayed with the prince. The chief of these was a handsome young man named Wilhelm Schwartzhoff. Another, a Swede called Simon, remained faithful to him until his death.

Boris, however, for all that it was obvious there had been nothing remarkable about this prince, did not wish to send him away. He gave him the principality of Uglich and the town of the same name on the Volga, with all their revenues, and had him conducted to this residence. There the prince could build and construct at his leisure. He committed yet another host of eccentricities which would take too long to recount. Close to him, the tsar had settled a nobleman who was supposedly in his service, but was in reality instructed to spy on him. Even though his mistress was banished, the prince was still in Uglich at the time of Boris's death.

The Polish ambassador to Moscow concludes peace with the Muscovites

In the year 1600, a grand embassy from Poland was to come and negotiate several years' peace, live in amity with the new tsar, and bring gifts in felicitation.

These envoys arrived in Moscow on 6 October. They were richly dressed and made their entry escorted by all the nobility in raiment of the greatest magnificence, their horses caparisoned with chains of gold. The embassy was thus conducted to a palace prepared and well provisioned for it. It must needs be, as the embassy counted 903 men, two thousand superb horses sumptuously harnessed, and a large number of carriages.

On 16 November, the ambassadors were presented for the first time to the tsar. They offered their gifts, consisting of four Turkish or Hungarian horses, magnificently equipped. These horses were attached by their forelegs, but despite these bonds, they could scarcely be led. The gifts also included a little carriage adorned with silver pillars of most ingenious workmanship, and a quantity of plates, cups, and other precious objects. The leader of the embassy presented his credentials and pronounced a discourse. On that day, nothing was concluded. They simply confined themselves to the reception of these letters, and an exchange of presents and courtesies. The ambassador was invited to dine with the tsar.

This ambassador was called Lew Sapieha, and he was one of the principal counsellors of the Polish crown. He had more than twenty audiences with the tsar, in which the two negotiators parted sometimes as friends, sometimes as enemies. When the situation was amicable, the ambassador was loaded with honours, and all his expenses and those of his men and horses were paid. When, on the other hand, discussion took on a hostile tone, all the embassy was strictly guarded, had to pay dearly for the very water they got to drink, and could not communicate with anyone. Finally, on 22 February 1601, old style, a peace or truce of 22 years was signed between the crowns of Poland and Muscovy. On the day when it was concluded, the embassy remained with the tsar from morning until well into the night. He was present at a feast that was as splendid as one could conceive. Truly, it was not to be credited, but it would do no good to give all the details of it.

In the meantime, a courier arrived from Poland with some messages from the king to his ambassador. It seems that certain letters had been forgotten. Two days after the conclusion of peace, the ambassador sent this courier and two of his secretaries back with messages. Nobody knows what it was all about. The courier was called Elias Pilgrimovsky. Some inventive spirits later thought that it had to do with a message from the king of Poland warning the tsar of the appearance of someone claiming to be Ivan Vasilievich's son. But since nothing is certain, the matter rests, Boris not being concerned about it at this time.[63]

Sapieha leaves Moscow

On 1 March the aforesaid ambassador, Lew Sapieha, went with all his suite to take leave of the tsar. His expenses, both for men and horses, were paid in full. One can only imagine what such a body had consumed. On 3 March the procession left in triumph, and took the road for Poland.

Queen Elizabeth's embassy to Moscow

In the same year, good Queen Elizabeth of England, of happy memory, sent the tsar of Muscovy an ambassador[64] who came by sea on a ship belonging to the English merchant company trading with this land. This ambassador, a worthy and respectable old man, had a suite of 40 young gentlemen, all wearing scarlet cloaks. The post-horse system had been put at his disposal, and he was brought to Moscow, where he obtained an audience on 8 March. His gifts were a bed of very artistic workmanship, a quantity of cups and plate, containing elegant objects or fragrant spices, and cloth of excellent texture. Having delivered the queen's letter, full of protestations of friendship and congratulations, he was invited to the table of the tsar, who was pleased to converse with him amicably about the good queen and many other matters.

For a long time, the English have been trying every device to secure a trading monopoly with Russia, and making great efforts to supplant the Dutch there. Elizabeth's ambassador said this to the tsar plainly, and requested this privilege for his nation, giving the assurance that the English would furnish Muscovy with everything she needed, better and cheaper than various Dutch or other merchants.

But Tsar Boris, who had a very acute mind and sought to remain at peace with all powers, was able to handle himself in this situation quite well. Besides, he loved the German race, and from my faithful accounts knew of the memorable and extraordinary deeds of the Dutch, especially their victories under the command of our illustrious prince, Maurice of Nassau. Therefore, he replied that he had an equal affection for all the nations of the west, and desired to live in good friendship with every one. 'Their merchants,' he said, 'regularly pay the taxes and excise which constitute the revenue of sovereigns. They also have the same right as the English to do business. It should suffice the English to be exempt from these taxes in all the Muscovite empire, and pay nothing to the tsar's treasurer. Their proposal lacks wisdom, and they are wrong to wish to drive a people who are such close neighbours out of this market.' He objected to their proposal on still other grounds. The ambassador took his leave, and departed from Moscow on 17 April, returning to his country by way of Livonia. All the expenses of his stay were borne by the Muscovite treasury, and in addition, he received rich presents of furs.

For his part, Boris sent an ambassador called Grigory Mikulin to visit the queen in England, to renew a close friendship pact with her.

Scarcity in Moscow

At about this time, heaven afflicted the whole land of Muscovy with scarcity and famine such as history has never recorded. The descriptions of these times of privation by Albert, Abbot of Staden,[65] and other chroniclers, give us no idea of what that empire had to suffer from hunger and poverty. There were even mothers who ate their children. The peasants and other inhabitants of the countryside, having consumed all their resources, cows, horses, sheep, fowls, without observing the prescribed fasts, began to look for vegetables such as mushrooms and other fungi in the forests. They ate them hungrily along with husks and the winnowings of wheat, cats, and dogs. Then their bellies swelled; they became distended like cows, and died swiftly in great agony. In winter, they were prey to a sort of fainting. They doubled up and fell on the ground. The roads were encumbered by bodies that were devoured by wolves, foxes, dogs, and all kinds of wild animals.

Great calamity

The situation was no better in Moscow itself. Bread had to be brought to the market secretly for fear that it would be taken by force on the way. They had to organize teams of men who went every day with carts and sleds to gather bodies and take them outside to large ditches in the open fields. There they were thrown in heaps, as is done with mud and refuse at home. When the ditches were full, they were covered with earth, and new ones opened. Unfortunates who had not given up the ghost already were often found stretched out in the streets and roads, exhausting themselves trying to draw one more breath of life. Those whose task it was to pick up the dead also seized these unfortunates, who had merely fainted. They were lifted up by their arms and their legs, dragged hastily to their tombs, and thrown there indiscriminately like tufts of wool in a basket, so that they died there suffocated by corpses. If anyone had dared give anybody something in the streets, he would have been crushed instantly by the crowd throwing itself on him to get a share. One day, I myself wanted very much to take some food to a young man seated in front of our lodgings, whom I had watched for four days as he fed himself on hay, dying of starvation. Yet I dared not do so for fear of being seen and attacked. In the morning, if you went beyond the city wall, you would be sure to see dead bodies thrown on dunghills or else half eaten, and other things so horrible that the hair stood up on the heads of those who witnessed them.[66]

One Dutchman, Arent Claesen by name,[67] who had been the tsar's apothecary for a long time and had much credit among the magnates, told me as a true fact that one winter day, coming to an estate or village belonging to him, he happened to find lying in the snow in a deserted spot a child almost dead of hunger, cold, and weakness. Noticing the poor creature was still alive, he gathered it up and laid it between bearskins and furs in his sled. When he arrived in the village, which still had a few inhabitants, he placed the infant rolled up in his covers on top of a bath-house stove, and thus it recovered its bodily warmth. When the little girl came to, he made her take a little food and a hot drink. She was then able to tell in a feeble voice that all her family had died of hunger. 'Only my mother,' she said, 'survived, and she went wandering with me, but lacking the strength to watch me die of hunger, she fled into the forest and wilderness, leaving me there on the road in the snow.' That is all that could be gathered from her. Still having a long way to go, Arent Claesen left the child in these poor people's hands with some provisions for her upkeep, urged them to take good care of the little girl, and warned them that when he returned shortly he would take her with him. But when he did return, no one was there. All the inhabitants of the village had perished. He went as far as to think that when they had used up all the provisions he left, they had eaten the child, and died of hunger even so. Who could hear tell of such a dreadful thing without horror? However, he insisted that it is far from incredible, for there have been many stories of a similar kind, and no less dreadful. This grinding poverty aroused no pity in the hearts of those who had grain in abundance.

Others, who had provisions to last three or four years, wanted the scarcity to continue; they hoped to sell their grain at enormous profits, not thinking that the famine would overtake them in turn. Right up to the patriarch himself, the head of the clergy, a man regarded in Moscow as an exemplar of sanctity, there was no one who did not announce that he would hold on to his copious reserves until grain had reached an even higher price, and what is more, this man had neither wife, nor children, nor family to inherit from him. But in his gaunt body, bent with age and slipping quickly towards the grave, avarice reigned supreme. Yet God's punishment reached all these unfeeling hearts, and that punishment was so great and prodigious that no man, no matter how talented he might be, could possibly describe it. In fact, there was enough grain in the country to feed all the population for four years, but the people were hungrier than ever. When they did have food, they ate more than they were accustomed to; always afraid of lacking food, they ate incessantly, unable to restrain themselves. Lords, convents – which are very numerous – and many rich people had full granaries, so much so that being shut up there for years, their grain became mouldy. Nevertheless, they would not sell it. God so blinded the tsar that the one who could command his people failed to issue an edict which would have forced everyone to sell his surplus.[68] All he did was to open his own treasuries and distribute abundant aid every day. But this brought no relief.

Many rich peasants who had hidden great quantities of grain in cellars refused to sell it for fear that they would be suspected of possessing money from the sale, and people would rob and kill them. There were even some who were so tormented by anxiety after selling that they hanged themselves in their houses.

Good works which God does not value and are therefore of no avail

Moved by the best of intentions, the tsar ordered alms to be distributed at various places in the capital. Far from being effective, however, this measure made the situation even worse. For to benefit from this form of relief, all the peasants and serfs from more than 150 miles around, accompanied by their wives and children, came to Moscow, flocking into a city where people were already overcrowded and perishing in their thousands like flies on winter days. What is more, they abandoned their lands, forgetting that without cultivation they would have no crops. To the story of these ills, it must be added that the officers responsible for handing out the tsar's largesse were thieves, as moreover they are in all of this country. They told their nieces, cousins, and friends to come to the distribution centres. These came dressed in rags like the most destitute of beggars, and it was they who received the money allotted for alms. They even called their mistresses and a crowd of pickpockets and parasites, who came in the same group with the purpose of driving away all those unfortunates who were truly destitute. They crushed them in the crowd, and armed with cudgels and clubs, pushed them far from the doors. The poor, the lame, the blind, the deaf, who could neither walk, nor hear, nor see, fell dead like animals on the street. The last part of the victuals for distribution was also carried off by robbers or stolen by the servants who were supposed to guard it. With my own eyes, I have seen very rich secretaries, dressed as beggars, slip among those receiving alms.

From this one can estimate the state of affairs. Bread, which in that land had been baked without regard to weight, was ordered baked at a standard weight, and sold at a fixed price. But to evade the regulations, the bakers made their wares heavier by adding a half measure of water. Thus, the evil was worse than before. Some suffered the supreme penalty, but this was no use. Famine, poverty, and the dishonesty of men had all reached their height. Everywhere, one heard extraordinary stories of thefts and the cleverness of thieves. For example, it was said that in markets and crowds, horses had been taken from the hands of those leading them, leaving nothing but the halter. There are many such stories. The roads were infested by brigands and assassins, and where these were not about, there were hungry wolves that tore people to pieces. To all this were added serious illnesses or plague. In fact, no words could describe the extent of this scourge, and God's punishment was so prodigious that no one comprehended it; for people became daily more wicked, more inhuman, and more thieving than ever before, and nowhere in history could we find such obstinacy in evil. This disastrous period lasted until about 1605, and bread was scarce for four years.

Following on the heels of this famine and these epidemics came an internecine war that was certainly one of the strangest events to be recounted since the beginning of the world.

Boris's anxiety

Tsar Boris's conscience pricked him incessantly for his cruel tyranny and the unjust manner in which he had come by the crown. He lived in anxiety and fear, and was persuaded that a rival for his throne would still appear from somewhere. He trusted nobody, and hardly ever appeared in public except on great feast-days. His fears were only too well founded.

For at that time, rumour began to spread in Poland of the existence of Dmitry, the tsar's son, and this came to Boris's ears.[69] But it was too vague for him to know precisely what to make of it.

Thus, after careful consideration, the tsar decided he could do no better than marry his daughter to one of the brothers of the king of Denmark. It is said that he first made an offer to Ulrich, but when it was refused, obtained for her the hand of Johann, the other brother.

On this occasion, he renewed his friendship with this king, who was his closest neighbour. They divided the territory of Lapland, each taking his own share, and concluded a treaty of perpetual peace and solid alliance. To carry out this partition, he sent one of his courtiers, called Fyodor Boriatinsky, from Moscow. The ambassador charged with arranging the peace treaty and marriage was called Posnik Dmitriev. He carried with him the young princess's portrait, executed most artistically by a goldsmith called Jakob de Haen. He also had a fine gold statue carved of Christ, the twelve Apostles, and the Archangel Gabriel. The tsar wanted to put these statues in a great temple, for which a site had been designated in his fortress, and which he proposed to call the Holy of Holies. In this he thought he could imitate King Solomon, and act with sincere piety and true fear of God. He hoped above all to appease the divine anger. But he forgot that to honour the Almighty, it does not suffice to dedicate to him temples built by human hands, but what is needed above all else is to cleanse and purify that inner temple the soul, for which the son of God suffered death. He also forgot that the gold and jewels he had set aside for his offering came for the most part from goods confiscated and stolen from the noblest families in the country, those families he had exterminated in their hundreds, even though they were guilty of nothing. But his blinded eye received no light, and therefore he sat in darkness.

As I have already said, he had allowed the rumour to spread of an oath he had taken to abstain from spilling the blood of other than assassins, brigands or thieves for some years. Doubtless he wished to deceive God, but he succeeded only in deceiving himself, for while he did not actually spill their blood, he ordered people killed by being cudgelled to death and thrust under the ice. Thus did he deal with some of the most notable people of the realm. He also released a number of criminals, who went freely about the streets of Moscow listening to what people said of the tsar or the affairs of the empire. Those unfortunate enough to utter certain opinions on this subject were seized by these scoundrels at once, and on their testimony, sent to death after first being put to torture to make them confess what they had said about the tsar. And it often happened that, as a result of these torments, the unfortunates confessed to crimes they had not committed. These infamous informers were to be found everywhere. They penetrated into the taverns, houses, and wherever else people gathered. They were given the name 'donoshchiki' [danotsicken]. In the end, under this reign, everyone had to learn silence. Despite all their prudence, however, a large number of innocents became victims of this sad state of affairs, which lasted almost until the tsar's death.

While he did all these things, Boris's heart was often full of anxiety, as if he were pursued by the Furies, for he had learned too much through these denunciations and all these confessions – obtained, alas, by torture – and also by God's forewarnings, so that he was always awaiting misfortune, and cast about for any means of preserving himself from it.

The Danish herald comes to Moscow

Thus, as we have seen, the ambassador was dispatched back to Denmark. Soon afterwards, a courier arrived in Moscow from Denmark at night, secretly, on 27 May 1602. He obtained an audience the same night. He came to announce that the king of Denmark would send his reply and his decision by an ambassador. This courier was called Axel Brahe, and he was given leave to depart on 16 February of the following year, so long did he remain in Moscow.

The papal legate

On 15 August 1601, a legate from the pope came to Moscow to ask authorization to pass through the country on the way to Persia. This request was granted. But if Tsar Boris had known that this emissary's true mission was to observe the empire, study the character of the people, and make a report to his master the pope in order to set in motion the first stage of a projected conspiracy, he would undoubtedly have given this ambassador quite a different reply, and prepared a feast for him, the morsels of which would have stuck in his throat. But he did not know that a web was being spun to entrap him later on.[70]

On 14 March 1602, a courier arrived post-haste from Denmark to announce that everything had been concluded – the peace treaty and the marriage – and that the king's brother would be coming to Moscow with all his court. At this news, Boris was overcome with joy. He rewarded the messenger richly, and dismissed him on 14 April.

Prodigies in Moscow

At about this time, a series of terrible prodigies and apparitions occurred in Moscow, almost always at night and in the vicinity of the tsar's palace. These nocturnal phantoms frightened the soldiers of the guard to death, and sent them into hiding. Thus, they maintained stoutly that one night, they had seen a chariot in the sky drawn by six horses and driven by a Pole, who cracked his whip above the palace, crying out in such a terrible fashion that several soldiers of the guard fled to their quarters in terror. In the morning, the soldiers recounted these visions to their officers, who passed them on to their supreme commanders, so that all this came to the ears of the tsar, who grew more fearful every day. He greatly desired to see his plan bear fruit and was constantly afraid, without knowing why, that he would see something extraordinary come out of Poland; in effect, these portents all foretold of future misfortunes, misfortunes greater perhaps than famine and scarcity, those terrible punishments from heaven that the country had just suffered.

Preparations for the marriage

Nevertheless, he made busy preparation for the marriage, which was to take place immediately after the duke's arrival. To Ivangorod, the first town where the bridegroom was to stop, he sent a cargo of provisions, with such furniture as beds, chests, and all that was necessary to set up a kitchen, a stable, and a cellar. A great number of court officers awaited the duke's coming. The Grand Chancellor was charged with receiving him in the name of the tsar. This Grand Chancellor was called Afanasy Ivanovich Vlasiev

[Offonasy Ivanovits Blasof].[71] He was a man of spirit, very wise, very eloquent, who had many times been sent on diplomatic missions to the emperor of the Romans. He was assisted by Mikhail Glebovich Saltykov. All were impatient for the arrival of the Danish vessels.

On 23 July 1602, a courier came to announce that this fleet had set sail and that the prince was on the way. The messenger returned on the 25th, laden with gifts.

Duke Johann comes to Moscow from Denmark

The duke landed meanwhile at Ivangorod (or Narva) with several vessels and a suite of four hundred, a great many of them of noble rank. He was received with the greatest honour and magnificence by the lords delegated by the tsar as well as all the citizenry. They wished him welcome in the sovereign's name, and he was lodged with his suite in the best houses, which had been prepared for this purpose, and where they spent a happy time. Meanwhile, they unloaded the duke's baggage, furniture, wines, and treasure. All these objects were brought to Moscow by the tsar's post horses. Several carriages also came to the capital with the tsar's own, which was constructed most artistically in the antique manner. In every post relay they had placed horses to transport all these men, provisions, and baggage. There was a continual coming and going of dispatch riders, who brought hourly news to the tsar, and from the tsar to the duke. When everything was unloaded, after several days in Narva, the prince left for Moscow, accompanied by a magnificent procession of nobles and courtiers. He made his entry into the capital on 19 September 1602, with a great show of splendour in the Muscovite manner.

Tsar Boris had ordered all his German, Polish, Livonian, and other servitors to put on the most splendid garments of their respective national costumes, and furnish themselves with fine horses, richly caparisoned. Boris paid for all this, and all was done at his command. When the day came for the prince's entry, they sent out criers, that all the corporations, burghers, lords, noblemen, functionaries, merchants, and common people should clothe themselves in their best garments and come out of the town to meet the brother of the king of Denmark, and all work should cease for that day. Any who owned horses were to harness them in their best equipment and join this vast procession. Everything was so done. From afar, this multitude presented an admirable spectacle. One would have said that a mountain of gold had been scattered with flowers of all kinds. The magnates, nobles, and foreigners were each followed by thirty, twenty, ten, or five servants on horseback, as richly clothed as their masters. Among the merchants and people of all conditions there was the same enthusiasm to make the duke welcome.

In the morning, by order of the tsar, the Grand Master of the stables, Mikhail Ignatievich Tatishchev, a very well-educated and handsome man, came out of the town leading the tsar's horse, all covered with gold and jewellery. At a mile from Moscow, he was to wish the duke welcome in the tsar's name, present him with his horse, and preside over the duke's entry. All this was done according to schedule. At the aforesaid distance, the duke came out of his carriage and was placed on the tsar's mount with much respect and many bows. He was surrounded by thirty halberdiers and a number of musketeers in jerkins of white satin and breeches of red velvet. Behind him, on horseback and in the tsar's carriages, came all his suite. The duke wore a suit of black velvet with a cloak of the same, embroidered with gold and pearls.

Triumphal entry into Moscow

It was a marvellous spectacle to see this multitude going to meet him, and the strangers were amazed to see the splendour and magnificence of the Muscovites, all of whom were mounted. There seemed to be no end to the field outside Moscow; it was a huge army, almost all in cloth of gold and various colours.

The triumphal entry took place through the so-called Tver Gate [de Otphirse poort, alsoo genaempt]. The streets of the capital were thronged with inhabitants in their best raiment. They saw a host of ladies, sparkling with pearls and jewels. The duke was conducted thus to his palace, which had been provisioned with care, and had an army of servants, hewers of wood and drawers of water, menials, and horses, as though for the tsar himself.

The tsar placed his own uncle, Semeon Nikitich Godunov, at the prince's service. This Godunov was called 'the right ear of the tsar,' as the tsar entrusted him with his treasury and his secret business, and he too was a real tyrant. The duke had brought from Denmark one of the principal counsellors of that kingdom, Axel Guildenstierne,[72] an excellent man, full of spirit.

During the entry, the tsar and his son stationed themselves secretly on the ramparts of the citadel, where they could see the whole procession, for it had to pass in front of the Kremlin.

The duke's large entourage also included teachers, doctors, a surgeon, and even an executioner. Beyond these, he had been supplied with a great number of people in Moscow. His palace had a guard on it day and night, to preserve him from fire and all other misfortunes. In short, the duke and his people were treated in a completely royal manner.

On 28 September, in accordance with Muscovite usage, the duke and all his household, lords and servants, great and small, were invited to dine with the emperor. As custom has it, when someone is invited in this way, he brings with him several of his servants, who then eat together at the same table. They came with the invitation to the duke's palace, where the tsar's own horses had been brought, on which they made yet another triumphal entry. The duke was escorted by two great dignitaries, and all his suite and the nobles followed him as far as the great hall of the imperial palace. There, Boris and his son gave him an accolade and bade him a joyful welcome. The tsarina and the young princess could watch the duke through a small grille, without his seeing them. They were hidden behind the grille, for the Muscovites seclude their wives and daughters, and allow no one to see them.

Boris's feast

At the feast, Tsar Boris sat in all his majesty on a raised throne. To his right sat his son Fyodor, and beside Fyodor, the duke. These three persons alone occupied the high table. At many tables set a little below them and all around the room, all the guests were seated according to rank and quality. They were served by the lords of the land. The tsar, the prince, and the duke ate and drank from fine gold plate, and most of the other guests from silver plate. The feast was extraordinarily splendid, and the guests gave themselves over to celebration from midday until well into the night. In the fortress, great fires were lit in tall braziers prepared for this purpose. This feast was also attended by the clergy – that is to say the bishops, metropolitans, and the like – many powerful merchants, and foreign officers who served the tsar as soldiers or courtiers. The tsar spoke most affectionately with the duke about the king of Denmark and other monarchs. He drank three times to his health, each time placing around his neck, to honour him, one of the chains he himself was wearing. After the meal, when the duke had tenderly taken his leave, the tsar had him conducted back to his apartments under the escort of the greatest lords of the country.

The duke falls seriously ill

On 16 October 1602, Duke Johann suddenly fell ill, causing great affliction in the tsar's court and his own entourage. He was taken with a burning fever which gained hold and began to wear him out. The tsar became very anxious, and sent all his doctors, apothecaries, and surgeons [barbieren] to the patient, and they took turns watching over him day and night. On the 26th, he came in person to pay a visit. In this meeting, the tsar shed many tears and abandoned himself to profound grief. He feared God's will was against his plan to make the duke his son-in-law, and he was afraid he might see him die.

The Muscovites were very displeased with the tsar's conduct on this occasion. They murmured privily, claiming that the sovereign was lowering himself and had greatly compromised his dignity by visiting a pagan's sickbed. They even went so far as to say that in so doing he had lost his reason. For this people looks on its tsar as a god. Some of the magnates were violently opposed to the idea that a foreigner – a non-Christian, as they call all who are not their countrymen – should come to rule in their land and have the hand of the tsar's daughter. They wished his death, therefore, but were careful not to say as much.

He dies in Moscow on 28 October

However, Semeon Nikitich Godunov had dared say that the tsar must have been insane to accord a Latin, a man unworthy to tread the soil of the Holy Land – that is the name given to Muscovy – the honour of his daughter's hand.[73] This term 'latuys' is the most insulting one Muscovites can use to describe people of the Germanic race. It is a word that could not be rendered into the German language in any reasonable way. Semeon Nikitich's utterance would have meant death for him and many others had the duke regained his health. With his illness worsening from day to day, however, he died on 28 October. This unexpected death plunged the tsar and the many foreigners who lived in Muscovy into despair. These last had hoped to have in him one day a good lord or powerful advocate at the tsar's court. But I believe that the general sentiment among the Muscovites was one of joy, although they would not have let this show. Immediately after the prince's death, Boris sent a message to Denmark to tell the sad news to the king. The bearers of this message were the postillion Reinhold Dreyer, a certain Jurgen Buvar,[74] and several people from the duke's suite.

During this time, preparations were being made for the burial, which was to take place in the temple of the German suburb, a settlement about one English mile outside Moscow on the river Yauza, which flows into the Moskva. There dwell all the Livonians whom the tyrant Ivan once led into slavery, and who had now been freed with the stipulation that they must not leave the empire, though they could otherwise seek means of making a living in Muscovy. These colonists had a church where Luther's doctrine was preached. In that building, with the tsar's permission, a vault was constructed to receive the sarcophagus containing the mortal remains of the departed.

The duke's burial

His body, having been embalmed, was placed in a coffin of oak, which was enclosed in a great bronze casket decorated with bands and solid circles painted in black. This bier was placed on a great carriage, all decked out in black and drawn by four black horses caparisoned in mourning. Thus was the body taken to the aforesaid settlement on the bank of the Yauza. The procession was headed by eight horses, decked out alternately in velvet and black cloth. After them came three officers of the deceased, followed by three escutcheon bearers, one officer carrying the crown and another with the sceptre, twenty lords, each carrying in his hands a lighted candle of black wax decorated with the duke's armorial bearings, and three court functionaries on horseback, each having a standard decorated with three escutcheons. Behind them marched a troop of trumpeters and kettledrummers, their instruments draped in mourning. Then came the funeral car with the coffin. It was followed by the Grand Admiral carrying the great shield of the kingdom of Denmark, Norway, the Wends, and the Goths. After him marched all the lords and officers of the court of the deceased, all his entourage in mourning, and, finally, all the foreigners.

Tsar Boris and his son followed the procession along two streets of Moscow. On his return, the tsar wept greatly, and ordered his magnates, his chancellors, and all his court to accompany the body as far as the temple where it was to be buried. This command caused much agitation among the Muscovites, and they could not forget it. When the body was lowered into the tomb, the standards and coats of arms were unveiled in the church. The funeral oration was pronounced by Joannes Lundius, the duke's chaplain, and magnificent songs were sung by the minister, the schoolmasters, their pupils, and all the Livonians, who were rewarded generously for this. The ceremony all took place in the presence of the Muscovite lords and boyars, who were greatly astonished at it, for they held this cult in aversion. In addition to various gifts, the church received a sum of 2,000 reichsthalers.

On 7 May 1603, Reinhold Dreyer, who had had to take the news of the death to Denmark, returned to Moscow. He told us that it was generally believed in Denmark that the duke had been poisoned, and nobody had been more greatly afflicted than the duke's sister, who is now queen of England.[75] However it is improbable that he was poisoned, because the members of his suite, who had always been close to him, knew perfectly well what sickness he suffered from, and were witnesses that he maintained his coherence and presence of mind to the last.

He was a tall and handsome young man, with a large nose. He had a modest and quiet character. Boris had taken a liking to him, and went into great grief over him, and could not be consoled, because he saw this death as evidence that the Almighty was overturning all his schemes and undertakings. He no longer knew where to turn.

Embassy sent to Georgia from Moscow

He had also sent to Georgia, a land situated between the Caspian and Black seas, an embassy charged with asking the hand of a princess for his son. But this mission failed, as all his schemes to secure his state had failed, for nobody caused him so much fear or made him so wary as did his own conscience, which made him fear misfortune to a prodigious extent.[76]

The Danish courtiers leave Moscow

On 3 June Axel Guildenstierne took leave of the tsar and left with all his suite for Denmark. All of them, both great and small, took rich presents with them, and were conducted with great ceremony as far as the coast.

Some of the noblemen who had come with the duke desired to remain in Muscovy in the tsar's service. But he replied to their demand by urging them to return to their own country first and show themselves to their masters, telling how they had been received. After that, those wishing to enter the service of the Muscovite empire would be welcome, and receive honourable positions. 'If you remain here now,' he told them, 'they would think in Denmark that we had kept you by force.' This convinced them to depart. Later, a certain Matthew Knudson [Mattys Cnoetsen] returned to Muscovy, where he was cordially received. He became a captain of 200 horsemen and, beyond his salary, was rewarded with an estate that enabled him to live like a lord.

Hanseatic ambassadors in Moscow; their gifts

Amid all these events, some ambassadors from Lübeck, sent by the Hanseatic towns, came to Moscow. The aim of their mission was to obtain from the tsar and Grand Prince of Muscovy the privilege of doing business at Novgorod, where formerly these towns had their staple. They had lost the privilege because of the bloody wars in Livonia among the Muscovites, the Poles, and the Swedes. Apart from this, the Hanseatic towns asked for the restoration of their old exemption from tax. The tsar granted them everything, except that they had to pay tolls. 'Because these taxes,' said Tsar Boris, 'come to princes as of right, they constitute their resources for making war. It should suffice the towns to have liberty of conscience, freedom to trade, and other advantages throughout the empire. In any case, for them it is a thing of small importance to pay taxes.' The towns then accepted the concessions made to them, and in token of their gratitude, offered the following presents. First, a double-headed eagle of great dimensions. Its wings were spread, and in its talons it held a golden sceptre. Then, a lion holding a sword in its right paw and a globe in the other. After that came a single eagle, a rhinoceros, an elephant, a horse, a stag, a bear, a unicorn, a hare, a greyhound, an elk, a salamander, a dragon, a serpent, sculptures representing Hope, Love, and Fidelity, and others representing Venus and Cupid. All these objects were in vermilion and formed drinking cups, very cleverly worked. The tsar accepted them only because of their artistic beauty. Young men dressed in black brought them on sashes of white or red cloth. After obtaining an audience, the envoys were conducted to a lodging that had been prepared for them, and at noon they were sent 100 plates loaded with food from the tsar's table. All these plates were of pure gold, and each one of them was carried by a man dressed in scarlet. In addition, there were many vessels, goblets, and jugs, filled with all sorts of beverages. This procession was led by a lord on horseback who was charged to bring the envoys salutations on behalf of the emperor. They also received daily provisions for themselves, their servants, and their horses. Having finally taken their leave, they departed with an escort on 11 June, with all their expenses reimbursed.[77]

Persian embassy in Moscow

On 4 September an ambassador came to Moscow from Persia to congratulate the tsar and renew the friendship that has always existed between the Muscovite sovereign and the shah of Persia.[78] To offer him as presents, he brought magnificent tapestries, jewellery, and beautiful Damascene cloths, cloth of gold, precious balm in golden dishes, and, finally, aromatic plants. Having been treated royally for the entire winter, the embassy embarked in the spring in large boats on the Moskva, with a fine escort that took them down the Volga as far as Astrakhan. There they found ships ready to receive them and cross the Caspian Sea. They too had been relieved of all expense.

Robberies along the roads

In the same month, some serfs belonging to boyars and great lords, who had revolted in Moscow, joined forces and withdrew into the forests and wastelands, where they attacked and plundered travellers and made the road to Poland and Livonia impassable. Against these brigands, the tsar sent a corps of about one hundred selected musketeers under the command of a lord of the court, a very vigorous and active young man called Ivan Fyodorovich Basmanov. But the brigands, having been warned, took measures against him. They set an ambush for him in a narrow pass between two groves of trees, surprised the unfortunate young man, and pierced his body – his, and those of most of his companions. The tsar was greatly affected by the death of Ivan Basmanov, who had conducted himself heroically. He pursued the brigands with the greatest vigour, and when he had caught them, they were hanged from trees along the very same roads.[79]

At the end of the month of September, the old Tsarina Alexandra, wife of Fyodor Ivanovich of blessed memory and sister of the present Tsar Boris, who had become a nun, as I have said before, died. She died, it is said, from the grief brought upon her by the deplorable state of the empire, and the insidious and tyrannical conduct of her brother towards the great families. She prophesied many things for him, and foretold the misfortunes that would befall him. However, she was always full of devotion for him, and did not cease to give him excellent advice. Therefore, he felt her loss very greatly. But the Almighty took the virtuous princess from this vale of tears so that she might not see or experience the calamities that would occur in her country, and which she could not have survived. She was buried on 20 September, in the church of the Ascension in the Kremlin. The tears and sobs of the people accompanied her to her grave. The tsar and his son followed the procession in a sled with a crowd of people, women and children. This occurred on 20 September.[80]

Boris is unfortunate in all his undertakings

The famine still raged, as we have described before. Seeing that fortune was against him in all things, and God was overturning all his plans, as the simultaneous deaths of Duke Johann, the tsarina, and several virtuous persons had proved to him, Boris was seized with grave disquiet, and lost hope of ever realizing his ambitions. However, he resolved to make yet one more try. He hoped, if he could find anyone suitable, to give his daughter to one of the magnates of his court, to whom he would promise a large part of the empire for his apanage, thus acquiring a resource he could count on. As we have already stated, he sent an embassy to Georgia; it left Moscow in the spring and proceeded down the river Volga.[81]

This embassy was led by Mikhail Ignatievich Tatishchev, former Grand Master of the stables, a wise and honourable man. He had as his secretary Andrei Ivanov, a man both learned and virtuous, and his suite was made up of about forty lords of the court and servants. This mission, however, was fruitless. Despite their long stay, these envoys laboured completely in vain, for the land where they put forth their endeavours was, so to speak, full of little, insignificant rulers, given to pagan practices and living in a savage manner. In a word, they achieved nothing there, and returned to Moscow after Boris's death. They had taken precious furs and other objects with them as presents for the Tatar or Turkish governments. This embassy had been dispatched with the sole aim of discovering a princess of a good and powerful family to be a wife to Boris's son, the seal of friendship between her country and Muscovy. In case of attack, the tsar hoped to have the Tatars ready to fly to his side as allies, but all his plans were frustrated.

The ambassadors' journey to Georgia

This country, which the Muscovites call Gruzinia, lies between the Caspian and Black seas, two hundred or so German miles beyond Piatigoria. Some claim that the Caucasus mountains form part of it. Travelling there, the ambassadors encountered a large number of Tatars and petty princes with whom they concluded treaties of close friendship. But while they were crossing the mountains, it was learned that Turkish and Tatar bands indulged in murder and rapine among the peoples close to the Caspian Sea who were subjects of the Muscovite empire. Already, the inhabitants of Astrakhan and other towns had sent reports of this to the Moscow court. Boris sent fifty thousand men at once, including some Poles and Livonians, to defend them, but most perished, either at the hands of Tatars or Turks or from privation by losing their way, so that few ever returned.[82] There were some people in Moscow who could tell whole volumes about the marvels of the land of Gruzinia and the peoples that inhabited it, but still would not have told everything. They said that in many places there were men as strong as giants who never left their weapons behind, even when they were driving the plough or in their houses. They lived in vast caverns, for there are many mountains there; the heat there is very intense, and high up in the hills, the livestock is abundant. It is peopled by numerous tribes which attack and loot each other, and never live in peace or tranquility.

In a number of places, they revere the name of Alexander the Great, who, it is said, resided there for some time with his army – which is attested to by numerous ruins of marble walls, carved artistically and covered in Greek letters encrusted with gold and silver. They also honour a certain Timur-Askak, who is believed to be the same person as Tamerlane. I have already given these details in the life of the tyrant Ivan Vasilievich. He who told us these stories had been wounded by many arrows. He wandered a long time with his companions before reaching the shores of the Caspian Sea. When they had arrived there, they marched for about four more weeks before they came to Astrakhan, living on fish they caught and the flesh of wild horses that they shot and ate, and which are numerous there. During these four weeks they encountered neither towns nor inhabitants. They crossed green fields, heaths, and some exotic forests where superb plants grow. They found rhubarb, and other similar roots that were unknown to them. In short, the land seemed a veritable paradise to them.[83]

Thus, a few of them returned to Moscow without achieving anything, but no more was heard of the Turks, who were preoccupied with Persian affairs.

The Nogai submit to the tsar

The Nogai had always been tributaries of the Turks, but they now defected and recognized the authority of the tsar; he immediately sent one of his cousins, Stepan Stepanovich Godunov, a brave young man whom he commanded to receive the oath of fidelity from these peoples. He left with a large entourage and took rich presents for the chieftains of the Nogai. But his journey was impeded, and the young ambassador had to halt at Saratov, a town on the Volga. Many merchants from Astrakhan came to see him, complaining that the river was infested with brigands, all of them Cossacks who had pillaged vessels of a thousand tons and killed the crews; for which reason, nobody dared sail on the Volga, and most of the merchants stayed in Astrakhan. Those who were in Saratov thought it better to make their way across the great steppe, and reached Moscow after a journey of twelve weeks. Stepan Stepanovich could not continue, for the Cossacks were stirring up the whole country. This was the prelude to the advent of Dmitry.

A renegade monk flees from Moscow to Poland, claiming to be the dead Dmitry

Everything going on in Muscovy was known in Poland. Some brigands, escaping from Moscow, had put themselves at the disposal of Polish lords – the Wisniowiecki, the palatine of Sandomierz, and others. Among them was a young man who had at one time been the servant of an abbot or monk in the Chudov monastery, or the monastery of the Miracles at Moscow. Intended to wear the cowl himself, this young man had been employed at copying books, or even writing those of his master. In this manner, since he was very intelligent, he acquired a perfect knowledge of the secrets of state.

He knew of all Boris's actions, how he had ordered the assassination of Dmitry, and the measures taken to erase the memory of it, as we have previously related. He ingrained these things deeply in his memory, and then, laying hold of various objects he needed, and stealing some secret papers from his master, fled the monastery, crossed the empire begging alms, and came to Poland. There he learned the language of the country, and some time later returned to Muscovy, disguised sometimes as a farm labourer, sometimes as a beggar. In the year 1600, when the 22-year truce between Poland and Muscovy was concluded, he accompanied the Polish ambassador in the quality of a gentleman, and was thus informed of the most secret business of the empire, as of all that had gone on there. For a long time in Poland, he had given himself out to be the son of Ivan Vasilievich, the Dmitry who was believed to have been assassinated at Uglich. He produced much evidence to establish how he had escaped with the help of a number of court personages whom he could name, though all were by now dead. He recounted point by point, without omitting any detail, all the incidents of his deliverance, and how a young boy who resembled him in every way had been clothed in his garments, substituted for him, and assassinated. In short, he stuck resolutely to his story.

The Jesuits in Poland take counsel how to provide help for the pretended Dmitry in Muscovy

He was put to rigorous questioning by the adherents of the Jesuits in Poland, but he held fast to all his claims with the most solemn oaths. He told the hour of his birth and his alleged death and burial. With these details, which he had learned in his master's books and memoirs, he was able to convince his listeners. The lord of Sandomierz and several of his followers, all of them Jesuits, sent this information to the pope and asked for his advice. After he had carefully examined the question, he authorized them to attempt an enterprise upon Muscovy. First, he sent a legate to Moscow on the pretext of asking permission to cross the empire to Persia, but in reality to study the country's situation, the character and condition of its people, and the extent of their credulousness and poverty. When he had received a good report on all these points, he imagined that it would be easy for him, acting vigorously and promptly, to seize the country by using the name of Dmitry, son of the deceased sovereign. The common people, in fact, are very partial to a change of prince, hoping to get a better one. Besides, the Muscovites would appear to be getting back their lawful hereditary ruler, and so the undertaking could not fail; it was bound to succeed.

This Dmitry, then, began growing in importance and boldness day by day. He addressed the estates of Poland and the lords of the kingdom, asking their assistance in recovering his inheritance and punishing the traitor who sat wrongfully on the throne of the tsars of Muscovy. In addition, he promised to marry the daughter of the count of Sandomierz and crown her tsarina as soon as he had been restored to the throne of his ancestors. Finally, he requested the help of the king of Poland, revealing all to him.[84]

A warning from the Holy Roman emperor to the tsar, brought by an ambassador

This intelligence was sent from Poland to the emperor of Germany and other sovereigns, and it was added that there was no doubt of the Pretender's authenticity. The emperor had always lived in amity with the tsar. He resolved to warn the latter that he should be on his guard and take precautions. To this end he sent him a solemn embassy. This embassy was preceded by a courier, who came to Moscow in the month of May 1604 with letters from the ambassador asking for free passage to Moscow. Being granted this, the courier departed.[85]

On 15 July the ambassador himself made his entry into Moscow. He was a man of small stature but great intelligence, a knight of Malta.[86] He was received with great honour. He was mounted on the tsar's horse, attended by an escort of 30 halberdiers dressed in white and blue velvet. On the 19th, he was admitted to the tsar's presence, delivered his credentials along with several presents, and made a fine speech in his master's name, praying the tsar to take prompt precautions, for this so-called Dmitry already had numerous adherents in Poland waiting to lend him vigorous armed assistance. This could result in great disasters for the German empire, as the Poles, those eternal enemies of the Muscovites, asked nothing better than to do them as much harm as possible. For these and other reasons, Boris paid no attention, saying that he was well able to chase this ball with one finger, and did not need his whole hand to do so. Nevertheless, he thanked the emperor, whom he called his brother, for his affectionate attention, and sent in writing the true story of Dmitry's assassination and burial. He who was now usurping Dmitry's name, he said, was an evildoer and a traitor, and his enterprise drew most of its support from the Poles, who were simply trying to stir up the country. He gave this document to the ambassador to transmit to the emperor, and the same day the ambassador and all his suite dined with the tsar. Being granted yet two more audiences and given many presents, this envoy left on 13 August with his suite. The tsar defrayed all the expense of their stay.

In Poland, there was no lack of activity. With the formal support of the pope and all the company of Jesuits in Poland, this Dmitry concluded a treaty with the palatine of Sandomierz, whereby he promised to marry his daughter and make her tsarina as soon as he was seated on the throne of his father. He also promised to repay the Polish lords and various Jesuit houses the sums they had lent him for his cause. He also promised to give Sandomierski[87] the principalities of Pskov and Novgorod, Mniszek's son the town of Smolensk, and to other lords, the land of Severia [Sibiria]. But above all, he promised the pope to use all his efforts to change the country's religion at the earliest opportunity, and submit it to the Roman Catholic faith. He also had to promise to reform the rites of the church according to the ordinances of those whom the pope would charge with this mission, and allow them to establish schools in the towns and villages like the ones in Poland, so that the Muscovite youth, sunken in ignorance and barbarism, might be raised and educated in what they considered the proper manner. In short, the Pretender promised everything. He was firmly persuaded that all his program would be accomplished. But Providence placed an obstacle in the way.

The Cossacks go over to Dmitry, and proclaim him the true Tsarevich

After these events, there were great efforts elsewhere to bring the Cossacks on the river Volga and in other areas over to Dmitry, thus greatly enhancing his strength and prestige.

These Cossacks are an ill-assorted miscellany of peoples – Muscovites, Tatars, Turks, Poles, Lithuanians, Karelians, and Germans. Most of them are Muscovites and speak the Muscovite language, but among themselves they also use a slang which they call 'otvernitsa.'[88] For the most part, their hordes are made up of individuals who have abandoned their masters' service – serfs, thieves, swindlers, and rogues of all kinds. They are almost all to be found in the wildernesses of Tatary, around the Volga, the Don, and the Dnieper, moving constantly from one place to another. Among themselves, these Cossacks maintain a severe code of justice and observe good discipline. Their chiefs, whom they choose themselves and obey unconditionally, are called 'hetmen.' It is in them that the Ottomans have their origins, as can be read in their annals.[89]

These hordes most often put themselves at the service of princes offering pay, or even those who in place of pay merely promise pillage. Up to the present, it has always been the Muscovites who employed their assistance, as defence against the numerous incursions of the Tatars. But suddenly, such was God's will, without knowing why themselves, they turned against the subjects of the tsar, and began to pillage and kill merchants going to trade in Persia, Armenia, Shemakha, or on the shores of the Caspian Sea.

From Poland, Dmitry sent them some secret agents to whom he had given letters telling of his enterprise. He swore that he was the true heir to the Muscovite throne. He adjured these peoples to help him vindicate his just rights, and promised that they would be greatly rewarded for the signal service they were about to render him, and expressed like sentiments in many similar speeches and letters.

When they received these proposals, the Cossacks met with their hetman, to the number of eight thousand. After lengthy deliberation, they decided to send delegates to Poland to find out the truth of the matter that had just been brought to their attention. If it could be shown to them that the Pretender was truly Dmitry, they would give him aid and assistance. If not, they declared, they would treat him as an enemy. The eight thousand Cossacks there assembled were too great a number to remain in a single region where they had to seek their subsistence in the countryside. Therefore, they fixed a term within which the delegates would have to return. Until this time was up, the assembled host would remain camped where it was. But if the delegates did not return, everyone would be free to go home. After this declaration, the delegates, who were chosen by lot, set off immediately.

Coming to Poland, they perceived that they could not return to their companions by the time set. Seeing this, they sent some of their number back to the assembly to ask for an extension of 15 days. They thought that after this time, they would be able to return with a complete report. This is in fact what happened.[90]

Dmitry's first incursion into Muscovy

In Poland, after the most exhaustive investigation, they could come to no other conclusion than that he was truly Dmitry, the son of Ivan Vasilievich, who was believed to have been murdered at Uglich; and seeing that a number of lords, notably the palatine of Sandomierz, were already making great preparations for war, the Cossacks recognized Dmitry as their sovereign, offered him their services, and at once acclaimed him Grand Prince of Muscovy. Thus, they rejoined their companions and reported the whole matter, and declared for Dmitry, setting off with all their forces for the Muscovite frontier, towards Chernigov, which they first besieged and then took by storm. They bound the governor hand and foot, and all through the country proclaimed: 'God save Dmitry Ivanovich, tsar of all the Russias!' This was the beginning of the affair, towards the month of October 1604.[91]

They seized a large monastery with the villages surrounding it and marched in the direction of Putivl, a populous commercial town situated in the same region. This town embraced Dmitry's party with cries and acclamations, and proclaimed him tsar. Dmitry came, made it his residence, and passed most of the winter there. All his war council was assembled in Putivl. He made this place his storehouse for munitions and provisions. Traitors and deserters from Boris's army were brought there, and, finally, Dmitry established his seat of law and justice in this place.

Boris, the tsar of Muscovy, soon had reports of this Dmitry, as I have just recounted. He enjoyed even less tranquillity than before hearing of Dmitry's appearance. Tormented by his conscience, he seemed to have foreseen everything in his imagination. But he had not expected to see it all come about so quickly. He believed that it would take some time for his enemies to organize and set in motion such an enterprise. He had also hoped that the king of Poland would at least give him some warning. Deceived in his expectations, he passed from astonishment to consternation. He ordered his informers, of whom we have already spoken, to spread out among the people and sound out the spirit of the masses; and if they discovered someone who had even pronounced Dmitry's name, this unfortunate paid for the crime with his life, as well as his relatives, wife and children.

Constantly, night and day, they gave victims to torture, burning them alive on slow fires, or pushing them under the ice. In a word, these calamities were immeasurably great; the land was full of famine, madness, plague, war, and uneasy conscience, for nobody dared speak the truth, no matter what the occasion, as whosoever had enemies must needs fear ruin by false accusation for the sake of a single word, for people were condemned without being heard. The tsar had lost all hope. He withdrew from all eyes, and caused the petitioners who tried to approach him when he showed himself in public on feast-days to be driven away with cudgel blows. As for his officers, they were rogues who rendered justice to nobody, so that desolation was general.

Boris makes a declaration concerning an unexpected calamity, and prepares his defences

Boris dispatched a number of messengers into the countryside so that he would be informed early of events. In Moscow, he spread the rumour that a group of Cossacks had mutinied and invaded the land of Severia. He ordered all his army commanders to prepare for an expedition, and gather their troops in all quarters. Even the monasteries were obliged to send great levies of men. Thus, nearly two hundred thousand men were under arms. They had as commanders the following dukes and lords, all relatives of Boris: Prince Ivan Ivanovich Godunov, Princes Vasily and Dmitry Ivanovich Shuisky, Prince Vasily Golitsyn, Prince Vasily Morozov, Prince Andrei Teliatevsky, Peter Basmanov, and Mikhail Saltykov.[92]

Mstislavsky as chief commander of the Muscovite army

After these princes or dukes, who were the chief commanders of the army, came commanders of the cavalry, captains, and other officers, almost all men of the court or else illustrious by their deeds. Then Fyodor Ivanovich Mstislavsky was sent from Moscow to take chief command of the army. Mstislavsky was a lord of royal family, originating from Hungary. He was a man of proven virtue and, like his father, he had served in all the wars. Boris had always kept him apart, and would probably have wished to have him disappear in the same manner in which he had rid himself of the greatest families. But he could find no charge against him, as his life was irreproachable and modest, even his servants living better than he did. However, he was forbidden to marry, so that he would have no heirs. He had also forced his sister, a charming young girl, to enter a convent so that she might not have a husband.[93] The tsar now chose Mstislavsky to command the army and promised to give him his daughter in marriage, with the kingdom of Kazan and all the land of Severia, if he came back victorious and succeeded in depriving Dmitry of his life. Mstislavsky swore that he would do his duty and be faithful unto death, and then went to join the army.

The whole land of Muscovy knew that the Cossacks were not the cause of the war, and knew what the true cause was. The people in the army spoke of Dmitry, describing him by the name 'rastriga,' which means 'the untonsured.' For, they said, he took the cowl from his head and was shaven once again, since he had been a monk. They regarded him as a traitor and sorcerer, sold out to the Devil. In the end, he was given several other such epithets, by which he was described in various documents, as we shall see, but they called him nothing but 'the Renegade Monk.'

Boris also had a German interpreter named Hans Angelaer, whom he sent to Sweden with instructions to discover what was being said in Sweden, Germany, and other countries about the pretended Dmitry, and sound out the feelings of those peoples with regard to him. He was also instructed to find out whether there was a prince to whom they could entrust the command of the Muscovite army in the event that matters grew worse. But Hans Angelaer never came back from Sweden, and it was thought that he had been thrown in prison by King Karl and put to death, for what motive it is not known.[94]

Boris sends an ambassador to Poland, accusing the king of violating his oath

Boris also sent the king of Poland an ambassador named Posnik Ogarev, accompanied by the secretary Zakhary Yazykov. In the letter they were instructed to deliver to this monarch, the tsar said that the Muscovites could never believe that a king set so little store by the oath he had sworn, and could turn perjurer, giving aid, not to an open and avowed enemy of the empire, but to an unfrocked monk, an impostor prompted by the Devil to trouble the land. Boris asked Sigismund whether he had not signed a treaty by which he promised to live in peace with the Muscovites for 22 years, and lend assistance to none whom the Muscovites considered enemies. Finally, he showed by live witnesses and written depositions that Dmitry had truly been dead for a long time; he told how, and on what occasion, he had been assassinated; but he did not say that he himself had been the cause.

The Polish king makes excuses

To excuse himself, the king of Poland replied: 'If this is the true Dmitry, as has been affirmed to me by the most solemn oaths, his cause is just, and the hand of Almighty God will suffice to make him triumph. If he is not the true Dmitry, and an impostor, as you say, his kingdom will not last, and for him there will only be the punishment of the Almighty.' The king added, moreover, that he had not given aid or protection to the Pretender. He even sent the names of all those who had embraced his cause, and were supporting him; they were all independent lords. 'Dmitry,' he said finally, 'has contrived to attract all the Cossacks to him. This is a fact of which we were completely unaware. We will remain friends of the Muscovites as before, so long as they give us no reason to become their enemies.' Receiving this reply, the ambassador took his leave.

Dmitry's victories; all submit to him

Dmitry, or the Renegade Monk, as he was called in Moscow, pursued this success vigorously. He marched into the land of Komaritsk, a country fertile in grain, honey, wax, linen, and hemp, and populated by rich farmers. His army crossed this country without the slightest misconduct; he took only what he was given out of the generosity of the peasants. This behaviour was extraordinary in a man who had come to conquer Muscovy; rather than acting as an enemy, he refrained from causing the least harm, but on the contrary, protected the people. This astonished the inhabitants, and they said among themselves that this man must be the true heir of the empire, because if he were not, why would he treat the land with so much respect? But they did not perceive, alas, that in behaving thus, Dmitry was drawing all hearts to himself; and when, on the other hand, they saw the Muscovite army sowing desolation in its passage, sparing none whom they were supposed to be protecting and defending against invasion, they flocked in their hundreds to Dmitry's banner, and accepted him as their legitimate sovereign.

Boris's cruel decree and the devastation of the Komaritsk district

Hearing of Dmitry's passage through the land of Komaritsk, and that the inhabitants had taken the Pretender's side and sworn him allegiance, Boris called to his side the Kasimov tsar Semeon, the son of the king of Kazan, the same one mentioned in this book in the part dealing with the life of the tyrant, and who had married the sister of the commander-in-chief, Mstislavsky. Boris commanded this Semeon Bekbulatovich to gather the Kasimov Tatars, of whom he was leader, on a war footing. They formed a contingent of forty thousand horsemen. With these forces, he was ordered to report to the Komaritsk region and lay waste, burn, and destroy everything he found. The men and old women were to perish by the cruellest of torments. As for the young women and children, they could be sold or else carried off to bondage in Tatary. All this was done, for the Tatars are past-masters at this type of reprisal. After them, there came Muscovites and others who ravaged the country to such an extent that not a hedge or a stalk was left standing. They hanged men by their feet from the branches of trees, where they burned them alive. They stretched women, whom they had first dishonoured, on red-hot stoves, and impaled them on burning spits or wooden stakes. They threw children into the fire or the water and sold young girls for twelve stuyvers each;[95] but the more the executioners went about tormenting the inhabitants, the more these persisted in recognizing Dmitry as their legitimate master. No suffering could induce them to deny him. They remained staunch and unshakeable unto death. The neighbouring populations, who saw or learned of these horrors, said: 'If our own army and our own sovereign of Moscow begin treating us in this manner, we have no recourse but to throw ourselves with all speed into the arms of Dmitry, who will protect us.' And all those who could reach Dmitry or join his army hurried to swear allegiance to him. Nobody wished to hear anything more about Moscow. The Muscovite army was powerless to prevent this, and during all the winter, it did nothing but steal and pillage. As for Dmitry's army, it advanced steadily, and seized all the land it could.[96]

Boris's advisers

Boris sometimes held counsel with those bishops and abbots in whom he had the greatest confidence. But not knowing what course to take, this council began seeking, by various means, to procure traitors to dispose of Dmitry. The tsar, in fact, was in such a dilemma that although he was quite convinced that the true Dmitry was dead, he began to have doubts to the point where he frequently lost his reason. He was sometimes moved to ask if such a man, who has committed such a crime – and he specified acts without, however, naming himself – could be saved. If they answered that he could on condition that he confessed his misdeeds, begged for pardon, and did penance, he replied that this was impossible, and began to doubt utterly the mercy of God. He even went so far as to believe that there was no salvation. In short, he had become completely irrational.

Often he would go to visit a prophetess whom Moscow considered a saint, named Elena Urodliva. This woman lived underground near a chapel, with three, four, or five nuns, of whom she was the superior, and she lived in great poverty. She prophesied to everyone who came to her, and did so quite freely without fear of either tsar or king. And all she predicted came to pass. On the first visit Boris paid her at about this time, she did not allow him to enter, and he had to go away. Then he came back to consult her, and she made him bring a square beam of small dimensions into her cavern. Then, having called in three or four priests carrying censers, she commanded them to sing the office of the dead over this beam and cense it. She wished to convey by this that the same ceremony would soon be said for Tsar Boris. That is all Boris could draw from her, and he went away with his heart full of sadness. Were I in the tsar's place, you can imagine what I would have said to these fooleries, this incense and so on. This woman was, as I have said, considered a saint, which is hardly surprising, since this people still lives in darkness. May God send them the light.

Despite its numbers, Boris's army had not met with success. Its operations were confined to burning and killing the inhabitants of the country it was supposed to be defending, pursuing deserters, and moving hither and thither to indulge in pillage. Its deeds are not worthy of mention. Every time Dmitry seized a town, Boris's troops hurried to invest it with no preparation. During this time, the Pretender followed the course of his conquests. Boris's soldiers deserted in crowds to Dmitry's camp. A great number of lords and some chancellors followed their example, among them Vasily Mikhailovich Mosalsky, who was faithful to Dmitry to the end, and Mikhail Glebovich Saltykov, who took every opportunity to pass from one party to the other, blown by the wind of fortune, and ended up being thrown into prison. A certain Bogdan Ivanovich Sutupov, who had been sent from Moscow to the army with part of the military treasury, hastened with these funds to Dmitry's camp at Putivl, the town which was still the capital of the lands conquered by the usurper. The latter had seized a number of towns which he had manned with good garrisons – Briansk, Rylsk, Chernigov, Karachev [Caratzou], and several more. Besides, he had cast his eyes on the land of Seversk, of which the capital is Novgorod Seversky, a magnificent region rich in livestock, grain, wax, honey, furs, flax, and tallow. The Muscovites were most fearful of losing this territory. They made haste to send an army there under the command of Peter Fyodorovich Basmanov, a valiant captain. He entered Novgorod Seversky, surrounding it with solid defence works, and set up his headquarters there. But before these defences were complete, the enemy arrived below his ramparts with a group of Poles and Cossacks, and invested the town on all sides. This was in the middle of winter.

Dmitry conquers the Severian land

Seeing that to go farther, he had first to seize the land of Severia, which was one of the best provinces of Muscovy, Dmitry resolved to come before Novgorod Seversky himself. Leaving some of the men in whom he had the greatest confidence at Putivl, and safeguarding the towns he already possessed against attack, he left with a body of troops for Novgorod Seversky, which his army was besieging.

There, he found several Polish commanders, lords, and a corps of cavalry already yielding to discouragement. 'It is impossible,' they said, 'for us to conquer a land as great as the world with a handful of men. We cannot even seize this little town, and must here await the impetus of the entire Muscovite army. How will we do when we are before great cities? For up to now, the lands we hold have almost all surrendered to us of their own free will. We have poured all our resources into this enterprise, and there is no prospect that we will be compensated for it.' Dmitry was very upset when he heard this murmuring and saw the discouragement. He begged his companions not to lose courage or fear to expose their own lives while he was risking his. He had the firm hope that he would soon be seated on the imperial throne of Moscow. He begged them not to abandon him, if they wished to reap the fruits of so much effort. Having spoken in this manner, he took the chain he wore around his neck and gave it to some of them. They all were persuaded, and promised to follow his destiny. The little town was besieged more closely. Basmanov was soon reduced to feeding on horseflesh. One day, he pretended that he desired to open the gates and surrender, as though he had been reduced to the last extremity, with all his ammunition spent. Seeing this, Dmitry's soldiers rushed into the town, but as soon as some had entered, a large number of artillery pieces, hidden in houses near the gates, were suddenly uncovered; terrible salvoes were let fly on the assailants, who were driven back and the gates shut behind them. Nearly all were left lying on the scene of the encounter. At the same time, a group of the besieged sallied forth from the town and ran towards the enemy camp, where they found great booty, which they brought back to the town, entering by another gate. Dmitry was elsewhere at this moment, and did not return until after the engagement. This bold stroke occurred on 21 December, and was credited to Basmanov, who received warm congratulations from both Boris and the troops.

Dmitry wins a victory over the Muscovites

The next day, Fyodor Ivanovich Mstislavsky came before Novgorod with a hundred thousand men. Wishing to destroy or scatter Dmitry's army completely, he surrounded and trapped it between the town and himself. Great was the terror among the Pretender's troops. But he knew how to breathe courage into them by his assurance, and at the moment when the Muscovites were making ready for combat, he threw himself upon them at the head of his men, put them to flight, and obtained victory. The commander-in-chief, Mstislavsky, was grievously wounded; however, he recovered from his wounds.

Dmitry fought with such bravery that after the battle, they could scarcely remove the lance from his hands; it seemed to have been nailed to them. This amazed everybody.

Despite this success, a number of Poles went home. They complained that they had received no pay, and saw no prospect of conquering the kingdom or being able to hold out against the opposing armies. But by his prayers and supplications, Dmitry succeeded in retaining some of them. The Cossacks were faithful to him to the end, and never thought of leaving him. They always fought for him like heroes, and they are in fact heroes.

A large number of wounded arrived in Moscow, and doctors, surgeons, and apothecaries were sent from the city to the army to take care of the wounded and sick. Finally, the town of Novgorod, oppressed by famine, opened its gates to the besiegers, who left a fine garrison there and continued their advance.[97] Dmitry had returned to Putivl to attend to some matters, and during this time, his troops did nothing in his absence.

On 1 January 1605 a number of prisoners, both Polish and Cossack, were brought to Moscow with plenty of equipment and a number of banners and arms, to convince the inhabitants that victory had been won – what a victory, alas! – and show them that they should not lose courage. Boris already feared, I think, that the inhabitants of the capital were ready to be persuaded in their turn that Dmitry was the true heir to the throne, and already saw them submitting to him. It was to change this situation that he led detachments of prisoners into the city from time to time. It is said that about five hundred came at a time, or even more.

Another day, Boris sent an order from Moscow that no person was to be spared in the land of Severia, and that they were to be treated in a manner similar to those of Komaritsk. This order was executed in such an inhuman way that even to tell of it brings on a chill of terror. How many innocent people were sacrificed there! How many women, girls, and children were outraged to death! Those who were spared the Tatars sold for an old garment, a half-bottle of vodka, or the like. At the outset of this pillage, they were selling steers in the camp for half a florin, sheep for a few pence,[98] and so on. The soldiers were so weighed down with booty that they no longer knew what to do with it. The country, which was very rich, had offered them good quarry. For Dmitry, as I have always said, took nothing from anyone, and protected everyone's property. The barbarous conduct of the Muscovites had the immediate effect of pushing the inhabitants into Dmitry's arms. They repudiated the tsar of Moscow, and despite intensified tortures, they would maintain to their dying breath that Dmitry was their true sovereign. Even some who had never seen him affirmed that they knew him, and held to this despite the most terrible torments, so great was God's punishment.

Pack of wolves in Moscow

In the same month, fearful noises were heard at night around Moscow. These were caused by packs of wolves passing by, making this din. Also in the town, near the tombs of the Kremlin, they captured a number of wild foxes which had come there from the forests after crossing the river. There were other sinister prodigies as well.

The adversaries exchange insults

While Dmitry was at Putivl, several detachments of troops occupied the towns recently taken; others were still on campaign. The two sides exchanged insults. The Muscovites called their adversaries traitors in the service of a renegade monk. The others replied: 'It is you who are traitors and scoundrels. We are the soldiers of the legitimate heir to the crown, of him the perfidious Boris believed had perished, but was saved by a miracle of Providence. And if we were not convinced of this, how could we, who are children of the same country and have lived under the same sovereign, resolve to make war against you, who are our fellow citizens? Yes, our leader is the true Dmitry.' This conviction, which they buttressed with the most solemn oaths, spread among their adversaries. With every passing day, they rallied in swelling numbers to Dmitry's banner, and neither the sword, nor fire, nor tortures could dissuade them.

Battle near Dobrynichi, in which Dmitry suffers a defeat[99]

On 10 January of the aforesaid year, the Muscovite army, under the command of its principal leaders, was camped around Dobrynichi, a large village situated on a vast plain surrounded by numerous hills, some of them quite high. At dawn, a troop of about four thousand horsemen came out to forage, looking for anything they could find, chiefly oats, hay, and straw for their horses. After travelling three miles, they came near a wood. Scarcely had the Muscovites entered it than a squadron of Polish cavalry fell upon them, attacking with such fury that they took flight full of terror, leaving five hundred men on the field. The rest managed to get away, as they were not pursued very far. The Muscovites had not expected to meet the enemy so close to their camp. From the reports of spies, they had believed them to be at least thirty miles away. During their flight after this rout, the Muscovites seized a single Pole whom they brought to the camp. He was drunk, and asked only for more to drink; for two or three cups of wine, he promised to divulge important secrets concerning Dmitry's army. These proposals were brought to the one of the generals, who ordered that the prisoner be given nothing to drink, but that he be closely guarded until he had slept off his drunkenness, in the hope of interrogating him thereafter. But this boyar forgot the proverb, 'In vino veritas,' for scarcely had the prisoner been placed on a bed when he fell asleep, but he did not wake up, for he died by the will of divine Providence; if they had made him talk in his stupor, they would without a doubt have drawn useful revelations from him. It is even claimed that Dmitry might have been taken prisoner. However, nothing resulted from this incident.

After he had returned from Putivl, Dmitry judged that if he was to advance, he must offer the Muscovites a pitched battle. The land to be conquered was so vast that his successes were not known everywhere. For some time, he had been assured of the fidelity of the conquered country's inhabitants, because of their resentment of Boris's supporters. Therefore, he gathered all his troops and advanced to within three miles of the Muscovite army camped near Dobrynichi. Coming there, his soldiers began to drink and feast, each taking whatever he could find, for they believed they were sure to have the victory. On the night of 20 January, Dmitry set forth with his entire army. They had with them not only Prince Vasily Mosalsky and the chancellor, Bogdan Sutupov, who had fled Moscow, as I have related before, but also the Polish lords and magnates who had always been of Dmitry's party. In a word, all the army was there, except for the corps garrisoning the fortresses.

Through their spies, the Muscovites had been well aware of the enemy's impending approach, but they were not expecting them until a day later. They were filled with alarm when they heard the tumult of this advancing mass. Their preparations for defence were hasty and disorderly; they divided their forces into three corps, but without designating troops to guard their flank, or thinking to give them the support of a good reserve. This rabble was somewhat like a herd of cattle, and stricken with fear. But the Germans and the Livonians in Boris's service, commanded by a Frenchman, Captain Jacques Margeret, pulled together, placed themselves at the head of the army in the face of the enemy, and began skirmishing with them.

Dmitry was approaching meanwhile, but his entire army could not be seen because of the number of hills that broke up the plain; he had taken care to hide his troops behind them to dissimulate the strength of his forces. He had divided them into several corps, but at the beginning of the action he brought only three detachments of two thousand men each into the line. These detachments, composed of cavalry, took up their positions behind a high hill. When they got under way, they gave the appearance of trying to outflank the Muscovite camp; they advanced to the sounds of trumpets, fifes, and calumets; the Polish officers galloped bravely through the ranks, getting up the courage of their soldiers, who in turn uttered cries of joy and triumph, as though they had already won the victory. Seeing this, the Muscovites waited calmly. When these three squadrons of the enemy emerged from their concealment, the Germans and the tsar's army advanced on them, firing their weapons. After them came three or four hundred Muscovites who engaged the skirmishers. During this time, from behind the mountains and hills, sixty or seventy banners were seen, around which there were little detachments that threw themselves impetuously on the Muscovites, making a great noise of trumpets and timbrels, and uttering cries. The Muscovites, who had noticed only the first three detachments, had not expected the onset of this multitude. They were seized with fear, and their ranks fell into disorder. The Poles glanced at the lines at the centre of the Muscovite army and crossed them. At this point, one Arent Claesen, a German still living who fought there under Captain Margeret's command, cried out that they should fall upon the Poles, who, already believing themselves assured of victory, would be thrown into confusion. He said that it would be easy to exterminate them all. He told this to Ivan Ivanovich Godunov, who commanded the vanguard, but he was not heeded. This Godunov was as though petrified in the saddle of his horse. His fear was such that he dared not look in front or behind, or advance or retreat. At a finger's touch he would have fallen to the ground.

Pushing through the enemy centre, the Poles came behind the village of Dobrynichi. There the 'streltsy,' or Muscovite musketeers, to the number of six thousand men, had built an entrenchment of sleds stuffed with twisted straw, and taken up their position behind these. The Poles came up to this obstacle and made ready to force it. At this moment, the musketeers let fly a general volley from their artillery, about three hundred battle cannon. This volley was followed by concentrated musket fire that sowed fear in the assailants. Some turned back in utter confusion. In their flight, they were hotly pursued by the Muscovites, who had regrouped into numerous bodies, and pushed them back two miles having made a great carnage of them. The ground was strewn with their dead.

Dmitry had placed himself with some troops in the dry roads. There he awaited the opportunity to pursue a victory that he believed assured. But when the fleeing Poles arrived he was dragged along in their wake, and barely managed to escape. His black horse had been killed beneath him. Fortunately, Vasily Mosalsky, who was present, made haste to dismount and offer Dmitry his own horse. Mosalsky then took his squire's mount, and braving a thousand dangers, the Pretender and he managed to slip from the enemy's hands. To reward this devotion, Dmitry heaped high dignities on his rescuer, as shall later be seen.

During this encounter, the Poles, to the number of about five hundred, rallied around two artillery pieces abandoned on the road and tried to put up a resistance. But greatly outnumbered, they nearly all perished. Had the Muscovites been able to continue the pursuit, they probably would have captured Dmitry. But heralds recalled them to camp, and they all returned there towards evening. There was great joy in Boris's army. According to custom, each man was given a gold coin to mark the occasion.

The Muscovites have no trumpets in their army, and they display only three standards, of such weight and size that they must be carried by horses. These standards are very rich, sparkling with gold and pearls. On them are seen embroidered figures of the Virgin, St Nicholas, and other ornaments.

For the call to arms, they use only kettledrums. They wage war without tactics, and they obtain victory only by chance, superior numbers, or against the Tatars, who have no conception of order.

During the flight of the Poles, they captured a bugler. Stripping him of his clothes, they led him to the camp, where they placed him, completely naked, on an artillery piece, heaping raillery and sarcasm upon him. A moment later, they realized that he was the bugler of their German auxiliaries, who had been pursuing the enemy along with them.

The Muscovites thirst for plunder

There was also a Scotsman in their ranks who in the same encounter had seized a Polish flag, which, even as he was charging at the enemy, he waved in the air, instead of dragging it after him or rolling it up. Now it happened that his companions, believing that they saw a Polish standard-bearer, fired on him and hit him. He managed to escape, however, by a miracle, dropping his prize on the ground. This feat, and others of the same nature, give us an idea of the way they behave in war.

Furthermore, the Muscovites killed one another like dogs while fighting over the booty. In this encounter, the Muscovite losses amounted to six thousand men, and those of the Poles were reckoned at eight thousand, though it is said that their casualties were in fact greater. Truly, had the Russians carried on with their pursuit, the Poles would all have been slaughtered, and the Russians would also have captured Dmitry, who was not very far away.

After this victory the chief general, Mstislavsky, put all the Muscovites' Cossack prisoners to the sword, hanged them from the trees, shot them, or pushed them under the ice. As for the Poles, they were brought to Moscow with the trophies, trumpets, kettledrums, flags, and Dmitry's lance, which had been found near their camp at the place where the Pretender had his horse killed under him. This lance was gilded and decorated with three white plumes; it was very heavy. The general entrusted these spoils to a young officer of the court, whom he recommended to the tsar for a promotion in rank.[100] In one combat, this young man had saved Mstislavsky's life. I saw these prisoners and trophies enter Moscow on 8 February.

Dmitry had returned to Putivl, where he gathered great sums of money coming from the conquered towns and the people of Komaritsk. Much aid in men and money also came from Poland. He took courage again, therefore, and put a fine army back into the field.

Boris summons his forces from all quarters

Boris continually ordered greater and greater levies to increase his army. I saw large detachments of them go through Moscow every day. The monasteries also furnished large numbers of men. The towns of Totma, Ustiug, Kholmogory, and Vychegda, and all the other towns as far as the sea, which until then had enjoyed exemption from military service, were obliged to equip soldiers, and the army grew from day to day in a formidable manner. For all this, they could accomplish nothing.

On 14 February Peter Fyodorovich Basmanov and Prince Nikita Trubetskoi made a triumphal entry into Moscow on the horses and sleds of the tsar. They were given honours for their heroic conduct at Novgorod, as has been mentioned before. In addition, they received rich presents and estates from the tsar, and remained in Moscow until after his death.

Dmitry and his army once again set out on campaign

At the head of a great army, Dmitry set off once more in pursuit of the Muscovites, intending to attack them more carefully than he had done at Dobrynichi.

Boris's army set up camp in one place after another without attempting anything, either in open country or against towns occupied by the enemy. On 14 March it halted in the middle of a large plain, near which there were numerous swamps. The ground was frozen solid, and at this place there is a hill crowned by a wooden fort with several houses in and around it. This fort was called Kromy. In the summer, it has only one exit, very narrow and on the side of the hill, for it is protected all around by marshes. A captain of cavalry had thrown himself into this fort with his squadron and there raised his standard. This captain was called Las Viugo, and he was one of the German officers who live in Tula, for the most part Livonians, Kurlanders, or former prisoners who are not German. But the commander-in-chief, Prince Mstislavsky, told him to abandon this place, set fire to it, and fall back to the ranks of the army. Nobody knows why he gave this order.

Courage of the Cossacks

Dmitry's army, marching in search of the Muscovites, had as its vanguard a corps of two thousand Cossacks on foot, armed with long muskets. As soon as they noted the enemy's presence these Cossacks advised Dmitry. When they saw flames consuming the fort of Kromy, and the Muscovites abandoning it to rejoin their army, they at once thought of taking up residence in this place themselves, being familiar with it and realizing how important it would be in summer.

They capture Kromy in the face of the Muscovites

They seized it promptly by a bold stratagem. They had with them a large number of sleds loaded with victuals. On top of each of these, they placed another sled filled with twisted straw, and the two were bound tightly together. They pulled these sleds forward in such a way that they were like rectangular chambers open at the front and carrying half the vanguard. Escorted by the boldest, who marched with their muskets loaded, this convoy scaled the hill rapidly and entered the fort despite concentrated fire from the Muscovites, which caused them no harm. As soon as they entered, the Cossacks, who found the interior of the fort provided with entrenchments, began to dig trenches all around, so that in a short time they were protected and feared no one. The leader of these Cossacks was called Korela. He was a mangy little man, all covered with scars, and a native of Kurland. Because of his great bravery he had been chosen, even in the steppes, as hetman of this horde, and after he entered Kromy, his behaviour was such as to make everyone tremble at his name.

Judging how important this fortress's position was, Korela hastened to inform Dmitry of the feat he had just wrought and ask for reinforcements of men and munitions. Several convoys managed to get through, braving great odds. He hoped that the rigours of the winter and spring would dissipate and destroy the Muscovite army blockading them. During this time, Dmitry was busy strengthening his best strongholds and protecting them against attack. Wherever he happened to be, he was constantly sending help to the besieged in Kromy. He and his supporters also sought the best means of winning the hearts of the Muscovites. He wrote various messages to the inhabitants of Moscow, but not one could be delivered. The brave messengers to whom he entrusted them never returned. They all fell into the hands of the spies Boris posted at every crossroads and were hanged on the spot. Dmitry also addressed letters to the tsar's army and its commanders, Mstislavsky and others. But he addressed none to the Godunovs, Boris's dynasty. These he described as traitors and destroyers of the empire.

In his missives to Boris, he promised to show him clemency if he came down from the throne he unjustly occupied. In addition, as the true son of the late tsar and Grand Prince Ivan Vasilievich, he promised to grant Boris and his son estates where they could live in regal style. But it would have been impossible for Boris to thus yield his crown to someone he had never seen or known. He therefore replied to Dmitry with letters full of sarcasm. He called him a child of the Devil, a rebellious thief, and a sorcerer, and used other such epithets, refusing to pay him heed.

Dmitry writes to the Muscovite commanders declaring himself the true tsarevich

Dmitry's missives to Mstislavsky were full of benevolence and friendship. In them he gave numerous proofs of the authenticity of his claims, and insisted it was not possible to doubt that he was the true Dmitry. He pardoned the army commanders for all that they had done against him up to then, because they had only been acting by virtue of the oath they had sworn to Boris. He begged them in friendship to believe his letters. But all this was in vain. Later, however, it was learned that several commanders had entered into relations with him and replied to his letters in such a manner that he was informed of all their actions and movements. He did not write to any of the Godunovs, who, he said, were traitors, and the authors of all these calamities.

Sometimes, from the heights of the Kromy ramparts, he had the Muscovite army harangued, or messages thrown among the besiegers, in which he demanded to know how much longer they would continue in blindness and fail to see that all the country had embraced his cause, and that ere long they themselves would be forced to come and place themselves under his banner. 'For shame!' he told them: 'For you cannot see that you are soldiers of a traitor to the fatherland, a man who came by the crown most unlawfully, who has caused the deaths of my relatives and destroyed the great families of the land in the hope of delivering himself from fear, having massacred everybody about him.' He also said to them: 'Bring me before Mstislavsky and my mother, who I know is still alive, though unfortunately in the hands of the

Godunovs, and if they affirm that I am not the true Dmitry, then cut me into a thousand pieces.' By these words and others of the same kind, he managed to win the majority of the soldiers to his cause. The very commanders, at least those not allied with the Godunov family who knew the tsar's past and the depths of his character, said among themselves: 'Oh, if only we had Dmitry for our emperor!' They dared not declare themselves openly. They did not believe that he was the real heir to the throne, but they already saw him as a rising sun. Thus, every day, a large number of them passed over to the Pretender's banner.

The Cossacks as skilled marksmen

The besieging army camped around Kromy soon amounted to three hundred thousand men, thanks to the reinforcements coming in daily. They remained a long time below this fortress, which had no more than four thousand defenders. Not a day passed without the Cossacks making sorties in detachments of two or three hundred infantrymen armed with long muskets. These marksmen advanced towards the enemy and aggravated them. Then, from the Muscovite camp, to show their valour, horsemen would advance, seeking to surprise the Cossacks. But the latter waited for them on firm ground, and as they are the most capable people in the world in the use of the musket or arquebus, they let fly when the Muscovites were within range, missing not a man or a horse. In these encounters, the Muscovites lost from thirty to fifty men every day, in particular a large number of young noblemen, whom the love of glory always carried too far. During all the time the hetman Korela was active, the Muscovites did not have a moment's rest. They were attacked, fired upon, and provoked incessantly. Every day, a new stratagem was devised against them. On one occasion, they set upon the hill's summit a stark naked woman who sang satirical ditties about the Muscovite commanders. At other times there were even grosser insults, but my pen would be ashamed to write them. All this pushed the besiegers to the limit. They used their heavy artillery unrelentingly, but all in vain. They did no harm to the besieged, who were forever sounding the trumpet, drinking, and giving themselves over to revelry. In short, there was treason in the Muscovite army, and it was noticeable that the commanders had no stomach for the siege. It was obvious that there were relations between them and Dmitry, but they did not dare act openly in his favour. Very often, for example, on dark nights, they brought sacks of powder, which were concealed, right up to the gabions. There the defenders of Kromy came to take them away secretly, carrying them off even in the presence of the sentinels. Other facts of this kind can be cited.[101]

Brave resistance at Kromy

Sometimes also, arrows were fired from the Muscovite camp into the besieged fortress with letters attached telling of all the happenings in Moscow or the tsar's army. In this manner did Dmitry inform the defenders of the place of the state of affairs in the capital, Boris's movements and actions, his anxiety, the murmurings of the people in Moscow – for the majority of this people had begun to believe in the existence of the true Dmitry – and, finally, of the Pretender's confidence that he would achieve the conquest of the empire. This is why he left the army besieging Kromy in peace. The garrison of that place remained quiet for a period of time. They were content to repel the attacks, which were never very formidable. Their inactivity was caused by a severe wound Korela had received, for he alone was capable of advising them on what means to use for unsettling the Muscovites. As soon as he had recovered, things went back to normal.

Boris falls into despair

Tsar Boris saw that fortune was against him, his army making no progress, because everything was going in Dmitry's favour, and all were embracing his cause. He also learned, by what he could see himself and the reports of his innumerable spies, that even the people of the capital were beginning to be persuaded of the true Dmitry's existence, and that all the other towns were already wavering and showing ill will in the dispatch of recruits for the army, with their contingents incomplete and much delayed. Boris even began to wonder whether his rival for the throne was not truly Prince Dmitry. In a fit of despair, he wanted to destroy the town of Uglich entirely, with all its inhabitants, in punishment for letting Dmitry escape. But hearing the solemn oaths of the patriarch and the bishops, and hearing Prince Vasily Ivanovich Shuisky swear that he had put the true Dmitry in a coffin and buried him with his own hands, he abandoned his terrible plan. Besides, he was told that by ordering the slaughter of the innocent, he would push his people into revolt, as was evident from what had happened in the Komaritsk district and the lands of Severia, where he had also seen fit to take reprisals against his own subjects. He wanted to punish them because they had submitted to Dmitry, but it was not by exterminating the innocent along with the guilty in a barbarous manner, as had been done, that he would make them understand.

It was as a result of these observations that he abstained thereafter from sacrificing any more victims. At that time, he scarcely ever came out of his palace, and very frequently sent his son to the churches in his place. He had almost lost his spirit, and in his bewilderment did not know whether he should believe in Dmitry's existence or not. He decided, however, to make a final effort, and had resolved to commit suicide if he did not succeed.

Basmanov is made commander-in-chief of the Muscovite forces; Boris promises him his daughter's hand if he defeats Dmitry

He called to his side Peter Fyodorovich Basmanov, a valiant hero who had behaved well at both Severia and other places, as I have reported. Even though Basmanov was of humble birth, Boris promised him his daughter's hand and, as his apanages, the kingdoms of Kazan, Astrakhan, and all the land of Siberiá. He had made the same promise previously to Mstislavsky, the chief commander of his army, but seeing that the latter had not made good his promises, even though this was not his fault, he had begun to distrust him, and regarded him as not only negligent but even traitorous.

Thus, Boris recalled him to Moscow at the same time as Shuisky. Basmanov accepted Boris's proposal and swore to lay down his life or deliver the Pretender to the tsar dead or alive, if he was a false Dmitry. But if he was dealing with a true son of Ivan, he would never resolve to make war against him, much less kill him. To this declaration Boris and many others replied with the most solemn oaths that his rival was not the true Dmitry but a renegade monk, namely the monk we have already described. Given this assertion, Basmanov withdrew.

In the antechamber, on leaving the tsar's apartments, he met Semeon Nikitich Godunov, the first man in the empire after Boris himself, the one who was called the tsar's right ear, and a great oppressor of the people, as I have already said. Godunov asked what promises the tsar had made him. Basmanov, well knowing that he could not refuse to say, even though he would not have told anyone, recounted his conversation with Boris. 'Oh,'

Godunov replied, 'do your very best to deliver us from this Dmitry, for I have just dreamed that he is genuine, and I fear he might be so. If you succeed, you will have every right to become the closest relative of the tsar.' Basmanov did not forget these words, and said to himself: 'Whatever success I may have, it will be no use to me later, for I will get none of what has been promised me.' He knew full well, in fact, that Boris had already made the same promise to more exalted lords and not kept it. He would act otherwise, he thought, if he feared God. All this confirmed in him the idea that Dmitry could well be genuine. But he held this idea very secretly, and remained in Moscow some time longer.

Boris's cruel-hearted wife

In his terrible anger against this country and people, the Almighty sent dreams and ideas which led men to believe in things they knew full well could not exist. God so acted in the case of Boris and his wife, who was the prime mover of most of the tsar's tyrannical actions. They had summoned the mother of Dmitry, who had been assassinated at Uglich. This former tsarina was the seventh wife of Ivan Vasilievich, and for a long time, as we have already seen, had been a nun in a convent far removed from Moscow. When the first rumours of Dmitry's resurrection began to spread, she was taken to a great wilderness where never a living soul was seen, and strictly guarded by two wretches so that she might communicate with no one. From there, Boris had her brought secretly to Moscow and conducted to his own bedchamber, where he and his wife subjected this unhappy woman to a severe interrogation to find out her thoughts concerning the existence of her son. At first, she answered that she did not know whether he was dead or alive. Then, Boris's wife, wild with anger, cried: 'Do not hide what you know, whore!' and pushing a lighted torch at her eyes, would certainly have blinded her, so tyrannical was Boris's wife, had the tsar not interposed his own body. Then Tsarina Martha replied without hesitation that her son was still alive, that he had been led secretly out of the country; and that this had been done without even her knowledge, but certain people, who were now dead, had reported it to her. She said these things with God's permission, for she knew very well that her son was dead and buried. Boris had her taken at once to another wilderness. There, she was the object of even stricter surveillance than before, but if Boris's wife had had her way, she would have been put to death on the instant. Despite the mystery surrounding this interview, news of it reached Dmitry. God alone knows who told him. Some people desiring to show their insight go so far as to say that the evil spirit, who favoured him in all things, gave him this knowledge.

Boris sends to Sweden for aid

Boris had sent an embassy to demand aid from King Karl of Sweden, but since the tsar came to die shortly afterwards, the ambassador did not leave the country, and went no farther than Novgorod, whence he returned to Moscow after Boris's death.

In addition, the first chancellor, Afanasy Vlasiev, was sent to the army with great sums of money which were to be distributed to encourage the troops and make them take the tsar's interests more to heart. This emissary was also the bearer of the letter by which the king of Poland had denied that he had supported Dmitry's cause, of which he said he knew nothing. He ordered this letter to be read to the camp before the soldiers. All this fell on deaf ears. The next day, the defenders of Kromy knew everything, and were gloating about it. They were in communication with the commanders of the Muscovite army, and the two sides were only awaiting a propitious time to join and blend into one.

In Moscow meanwhile, couriers were coming every day, and all of them brought bad news. One would come and say such and such a region had submitted to Dmitry, another that great forces were gathering in Poland to march on them, a third that the Muscovite commanders were all traitors. In addition, the people of Moscow were murmuring more loudly each day, and neither sword, nor fire, nor torture could curb their obstinacy. The situation appeared so desperate to Boris that he resolved to kill himself rather than fall into the hands of Dmitry, who, he thought, would dishonour him, and at the time of his triumph drag him in his train, to be subjected to the jeering of the multitude.[102]

Boris takes poison and dies

On 13 April, according to the old style, Boris was especially jovial, or at least pretended to be so. At dinner he ate copiously, and surprised everyone present with his unaccustomed good humour. After the meal, he went up to a high gallery from which all the city and the surrounding countryside could be seen, and it is believed that it was there that he poured himself some poison, for as soon as he had come down into the lower room, he summoned the patriarch and the bishops, and ordered them to bring him a monk's cowl, and tonsure him. He said he was close to death, and in fact scarcely had these birds of evil omen chanted their prayers and accomplished their office when the tsar gave up his soul at three o'clock in the afternoon.

His consort and her son ascend the throne

Two hours or more passed before rumour of this event went through the court or the city, but immediately afterwards, a great tumult was heard. This was made by the magnates, who were hastening, mounted and armed, towards the Kremlin. They were followed by musketeers, also under arms. Nobody said anything, and none knew why they were rushing to the Kremlin. We assumed that it had to do with the tsar's death, but nobody dared say so. It was only the next day that the magnates and courtiers were seen once again as they proceeded in mourning to the castle, where conjecture was transformed into certainty. The news then spread everywhere. The doctors had noted afterwards that the cause of the tsar's death had been poison. They told this only to the tsarina, and no one else. The people were summoned at once to the Kremlin, there to take the oath of fidelity to the tsarina and her son. The magnates, nobles, merchants, and burghers went there in person to perform this duty. Couriers were sent to all the towns that had remained faithful to carry out the same formality. The towns taking the oath were Pskov, Novgorod, Ivangorod, Rostov, Pereiaslavl, Yaroslavl, Vologda, Perm, Kargopol, Ustiug, Totma, Kholmogory, Kondinsk, Obdora, and Siberia, Lapland, and the rest of the country. As for the regions bordering on Poland, the lands of Severia and Astrakhan, they remained with Dmitry. But Kazan recognized the government of Moscow. Thus did Maria Grigorievna become empress, and her son Fyodor Borisovich tsar of all the Russias, on 16 April 1605.

Description of Boris's deeds

Boris was a man short in stature, fairly corpulent, with a somewhat round face. His hair and beard were greying. He walked with difficulty owing to the gout that frequently tormented him.¹⁰³ This infirmity, quite common among Muscovite lords, afflicted him because he was always standing or walking. The magnates lead a fairly unhappy life in this country. Obliged to be at court continually and remain standing for days on end before the emperor, they scarcely have one day of rest in three or four. The more they are raised in honour, the wearier they are out of anxiety and fear, and yet nevertheless they are constantly seeking to mount higher.

Boris was very partial to foreigners, and he indulged them very greatly. He had an astonishing memory, and although he could not read or write, he knew all things better than some who labour greatly with the pen.¹⁰⁴ He was 55 or 56 years old, and, had all gone right for him, would have done great things. He had greatly improved the city of Moscow, and given it good laws and fine privileges. He had established watchmen at all the crossroads and ordered the streets closed by large barriers, which were lowered in such a fashion that each street formed a separate community. One of his ordinances called for a fine of a thaler for going out at night without a lantern.

His administration

In short, he knew the art of ruling. He loved to build. Under the reign of Tsar Fyodor he had the capital surrounded by a wall of masonry. He did the same for the town of Smolensk.¹⁰⁵ He also built a strong town on the confines of Tatary, naming it Boris-gorod after himself.

How he encouraged informers

But he put his trust much more in priests and monks than in his most faithful lords. He lent his ear overmuch to flattery and denunciation, and it was in allowing himself to be led by scoundrels and his cruel wife that he wrought so many tyrannical acts, and sacrificed the country's leading families, as we have already seen. By himself, he would never have committed these crimes.

He was the declared enemy of those who had been guilty of extortion, accepting presents and bribes. He had great lords and chancellors who were convicted of this crime punished by public execution. But these examples did not stem the evil.

He is buried, and alms are distributed

He was buried in the Church of the Archangel in the Kremlin, the burial place of the tsars. According to custom, his funeral took place amid the weeping and sobbing of all the people. Shortly before that, the tsar's uncle, Dmitry Ivanovich Godunov, the eldest of the dynasty, had died. The body of this Dmitry Godunov was taken to Kostroma, a town on the river Volga, where it was buried in the Godunov vault.

In the six weeks following Boris's death, more than seventy thousand rubles – 490,000 florins in the money of Holland – were distributed as alms to the people. During the same period of time, there were services in all the monasteries for the repose of his soul.

Basmanov is sent to the army as commander-in-chief

Only then was Peter Basmanov sent to the army as commander-in-chief, to announce Boris's death to them officially and have them swear allegiance to the young tsar, the new sovereign of the empire.[106]

Even before Basmanov arrived, the Muscovite army had news of Boris's death through Dmitry's soldiers, but they did not wish to believe it until Basmanov appeared with the same news.

On the tsar's order, Fyodor Ivanovich Mstislavsky and the two Shuisky princes gave up command of the army to Basmanov, who received it, and then they returned in shame and secrecy to Moscow, where they lived thereafter in obscurity, even though they were the principal lords of the country. Only the Godunov family remained with the army to assist Basmanov.

Restlessness of the Muscovite populace

After Boris's death, Moscow was in utter disorder, and the people grew bolder every day. They ran to the palace in bands, sometimes loudly demanding the return of the lords who had been sent into exile in Boris's reign, sometimes wanting the return of the old tsarina, Dmitry's mother, so they might place her at the town gates where everyone could learn from her whether her son was living or not.

There was great division among the lords. The Godunovs, though half-defeated, still looked with envy on all those who had escaped the proscription of the ancient families. They were already afraid that they would see them in the highest offices if Dmitry succeeded in seizing the throne. Semeon Nikitich Godunov even tried to get rid of Mstislavsky, and he would have been successful in this but for the intervention of someone or other, for he had denounced Mstislavsky as, among other things, a traitor to the country.

The people murmured more and more every day, and relentlessly demanded the return of the old tsarina and the exiled lords. They were forced to promise that all survivors of the proscriptions would soon be allowed to return to Moscow; but as for the old dowager tsarina, it was impossible to wring any concession from Boris's wife. On the contrary, she had her guarded more closely than ever in the wilderness where she had been taken. It was feared that, to be delivered from her prison, and take revenge on her enemies, she would simply assert loudly that Dmitry was still alive; but the people did not tire of demanding their former sovereign lady, and their words became menacing. The court was gripped by intense fear. Vasily Ivanovich Shuisky dared come out of the palace then, and speak to the crowd. He spoke well, beginning by saying that divine anger had been visited on the people in punishment for their sins, as could be seen well enough in the evils afflicting the land. He was surprised, therefore, to see the people obstinate in their perversity, sighing after a revolution that would necessarily bring ruin on the country, the overthrow of religion, and the destruction of the sanctuaries of Moscow. He swore with the most puissant oaths that the true Dmitry could not exist. He showed his hands, which had put Ivan's son into his coffin at Uglich. He added that the rival for the throne was a renegade, unfrocked monk, inspired by Satan, sent on earth for the greatest punishment of the people's crimes. He adjured his listeners to mend their ways, and pray God to have mercy on them, and finally, to remain always faithful, assuring them that events would have a happy outcome.

These words calmed the popular unrest a little. The unfortunates whom Boris had exiled were returning daily to Moscow. Among others, Ivan Mikhailovich Vorotynsky, who had been banished for more than twenty years by Boris's order, was seen to return. He was of noble birth and ancient family.

We have already related how Peter Basmanov was sent to join the army, and on 21 May he assumed the chief command. He was assisted by several of the Godunovs, Ivan Ivanovich, and some others, and also by two Golitsyn princes.

Basmanov then ordered the official announcement of Boris's death, and called on the army to remain faithful to the young tsar and obey him, and to obey himself also, who had been made their leader. He also ordered the reading of letters from the king of Poland, of which we have spoken; but one of his first tasks was to scatter spies through the ranks of the army to listen to what was being said and report to him about this every day. He discovered in this way that there were more supporters of Dmitry among the soldiers than there were of the Muscovites. After pondering this revelation, Basmanov resolved to pass with all his troops to the side of the Pretender, using every means of achieving this with the least bloodshed. He sent letters to Dmitry secretly to take counsel with him on what measures should be taken to this end.

Basmanov is convinced that the Pretender is the true Dmitry

In order to justify his resolution, Basmanov declared himself convinced that this was the true Dmitry, the conviction being reinforced by the words Semeon Nikitich had used to him in Boris's antechamber. He justified himself further by saying that the resolution he had taken should be considered, not an act of treason, but the action of a man seeking the welfare of his country. He justified it also by recalling Boris's cruel tyranny, which had wiped out the ancient families, and, using the misfortunes of his reign, by asserting that these stemmed from the unjust occupation of a throne that had a legitimate heir, as divine Providence was showing him at this time. He and his army wished, therefore, to devote themselves to the service of the true successor of the tsars. All these negotiations took place with such ease that no one on either side could later have said who had begun them. Nobody even knew where Dmitry was – neither those in Kromy nor the Muscovites. Apart from some sorties from time to time, the besieged in Kromy remained for the most part inactive. For at the time of the thaw, neither side had any business other than to find protection from the invasion of the floodwaters. Unable to approach the fortress because of the marshes, the besieging army used up all its ammunition keeping up an incessant but harmless bombardment, wasting powder and lead. A crowd of Muscovite defectors came into Kromy by night with news of what was going on in their camp, and the councils being held there to take the entire army over to Dmitry's side during a great, unforeseen attack.

Having agreed with Dmitry in everything, Basmanov set the date of the plot for 7 May, according to the old style. On this day, the Kromy garrison was to make ready for the attack. On his side, early in the morning, Basmanov would order the commanders and captains of his army to be seized and bound in their tents, after which the two parties were to cry out together: 'God save Dmitry, tsar of all the Russias!' However extraordinary, however incredible this feat may be, it is nevertheless very true; but it is evident that it did not succeed but by God's will. Basmanov and his accomplices knew full well, moreover, that more of the army were on Dmitry's side than remained loyal to Moscow. Until the appointed time, it seemed, every day was to be marked by some skirmish. Thus, some detachments were continually kept ready for combat; but on this day, that precaution was neglected.

Basmanov perfidiously surrenders the entire Muscovite army to Dmitry

At about four o'clock in the morning of 7 May, the besieged in Kromy, as well as Basmanov and his accomplices, stayed close together. At a certain moment, one of the conspirators left the Muscovite camp mounted on a black horse and went almost up to the ramparts of the fortress. That was the signal. At this, the besieged rushed out like a whirlwind and poured into various sectors of the camp, without a single sentinel or soldier uttering a cry of alarm. In an instant they had seized the commanders, whom they bound and dragged into the fortress while the Muscovite conspirators set fire to their own camp. The Muscovites who were not part of the plot were seized with such terror that they fled in all directions, abandoning their arms and garments – an amazing sight to see.[107]

At this time, Dmitry's supporters went over to the other side in their thousands. They did so with such haste that their weight broke the bridge across the river close to Kromy, where there were three or four priests empowered to receive the people's oath of allegiance which is done by presenting a crucifix to kiss. The entire crowd was plunged into the waters. They all tried to save themselves, some by swimming, some by finding a ford, others by clinging to their mounts, but several lost their lives. In short, there was such confusion that it seemed heaven and earth were coming to an end. In this disordered flight, some made for their home country and others for their villages: some returned to Moscow and some took refuge in the woods. All fled without knowing where or why, killing one another with swords or muskets like animals with rabies. Some cried, 'Long live Dmitry!' and others, 'Long live Fyodor Borisovich!' while a third call was, 'Long live whoever seizes the throne!' The majority of the army, however, rallied under the banners of Dmitry; the rest broke up in disorder. Such was the terror that pursued them in their flight that they abandoned their chariots and other vehicles on the way, making haste to unhitch the horses so as to get away more quickly, in the belief that the enemy was still at their heels. The fugitives passed through Moscow for three whole days. When they were asked the cause of their panic, they did not know what to reply. To the lords of the palace who questioned them with authority, they answered boldly: 'Go there and see for yourselves!' The population of Moscow also began to grow menacing; without declaring themselves openly, they would certainly have opened the gates of the city at that instant to anyone who came.

Some Germans, about seventy of them, who had also fled, came to Moscow. They were received by the young tsar, who thanked them profusely, and spoke to them with tears in his eyes of the misfortunes that were about to rain on him. Several lords who were present began to laugh up their sleeves at the prince's words, but the Godunovs presented a completely different face; anticipating vengeance, even death, at every step, they were quickly distributing to the convents the estates and treasures they possessed.

During the great tumult stirred up for Basmanov's treason, the latter had undergone the fate of other commanders, and like them had been bound to give countenance to his action and the appearance that everything was taking place without his knowledge; but when he had arrived in the enemy ranks, he was unbound on the instant along with his followers. On the other hand, Ivan Ivanovich Godunov, with many other commanders, was left in his bonds in the middle of the field, like an animal. At his side, there was a young page chasing flies away with a fan.

Andrei Teliatevsky, a relative of the Godunovs, was the last to stay by the artillery, crying to his followers: 'Stay firm, my friends, do not betray your tsar!' But on this side, the attack was so sharp and so sudden that he and those around him could not remain at their posts, and they sought safety in flight.

Basmanov sent his helmet, adorned with insignia, to the commander of the German cavalry, which had reassembled still almost intact around his banner, and he begged them to change sides and swear allegiance to the true tsar; at first, the captain refused outright, but after further persuasion, he ended up joining Dmitry's soldiers with a number of his men, though about seventy of them were faithful to their oath of allegiance and fled towards Moscow.

These Germans related to us that nobody could possibly have understood the things that were happening. They could not distinguish between friend and foe. The one ran from here, the other from there; they mingled like dust blown by the wind. One could see from that whether or not it was God's will that this Dmitry should reign for a certain time, as the rod with which the divine wrath chastised the Muscovites.

The next day, everything went more quietly. The soldiers of the fort and the besiegers, who formed but a single army, said among themselves: 'Oh, if only we could see him, Tsar Dmitry, to whom we have sworn allegiance without knowing him!' To which someone replied: 'Dmitry is at Kursk, thirty miles from Kromy, and he will soon be here.' A second answered: 'No, he is at Rylsk, fifty miles from Kromy.' The next day they found out that he was still at Putivl, and the day after that, they went so far as to say that he had fled to Poland; he was nothing but an impostor who had set the whole country in turmoil. All these rumours spread new unrest in the army, but the commanders dispelled them, saying to the soldiers: 'Await the conclusion, and be silent.' Despite these assurances, however, many were seized with fear; they thought of their wives and children, and regretted a thousand times that they had not taken flight for Moscow. They were now ashamed of being defectors, having had so little regard for the oath they had sworn first to the tsar of Muscovy. In short, they awaited the outcome of this affair with anxiety.

Three days later, a Muscovite gentleman called Boris Lykov brought a letter from Dmitry. In this missive, having thanked the soldiers, the Pretender notified them that everyone was free to return to his home or else remain in his service until the day when he made his entry into Moscow. A large number took advantage of this leave and did return home, while still recognizing Dmitry as tsar and Grand Prince.

At Moscow, everything seemed to go on as though nothing had happened. Fresh troops passed through daily, having the appearance of reporting to the army; but when they had gone five or six miles beyond the city, they chose another direction. Some made their way home, while others made for Dmitry's camp.

Dmitry conquers nearly the whole country, and sends letters to the populace of Moscow

Accompanied by the body of soldiers he had with him, Dmitry himself appeared below the ramparts of Kromy. There, he formed a guard composed mostly of Poles and Cossacks, with a few Russian troops in whom he had confidence, and then sent all the others farther on, some to Tula and some to

Kaluga, a town on the river Oka even closer to Moscow. One group seized this place and pushed on to Serpukhov, another town about eighteen miles from the capital. Below Serpukhov there were many 'streltsy,' or Muscovite musketeers, who fought for Moscow, faithful to the last; this encounter took place on 28 May. Then a great fear seized Moscow, where it was believed that all was lost. To everyone's great astonishment, Moscow remained in a deep calm.

Dmitry had come to Tula, where he stayed for several days. He dismissed and paid off a number of troops, Poles and others, but retained the Cossacks and some Poles, promising to pay them at Moscow, as soon as, by the grace of God, he was seated upon the throne of his fathers.[108] From there, he addressed proclamations to the whole land, and sent messengers everywhere to announce his successes and ask the people whether they still doubted that he was the true heir to the crown. Hearing this news, the towns began to waver, though Dmitry's envoys were not welcome everywhere, for several were killed.

Quietness still reigned in Moscow; but the common people continued to agitate silently, and were ready to surrender to Dmitry as soon as any of his supporters appeared.

About ten o'clock in the morning of 30 May, two young men came into the city by the Serpukhov gate, saying that on the road they had perceived distant clouds of dust, raised as far they could tell by a large number of chariots or a body of soldiers on the march. They themselves had no doubt: this was the enemy. Thus, as soon as they had entered the town, they began to cry, 'Liudi! Liudi!' – that is to say: 'An army! An army!' At these cries, the inhabitants were persuaded that the enemy was at the gates, and began pouring in from all sides, repeating in turn: 'It is the enemy host!' They pushed, they jostled in the street, and everyone ran as though he had an army at his heels. It was an indescribable tumult, as if a swarm of bees were in motion. Some hastened to their lodgings to look for arms, while others went to the market to buy salt and bread, intending to offer it to the conquerors entering the city, so that they would be treated favourably. This is a Russian custom, in fact, to present bread and salt to those they desire to make welcome.

In short, the agitation and panic were general, though nobody made any preparation for defence, and everyone was making ready to open the gates to the enemy. The lords of the court, and even the tsarina and the young tsar, did not know what was happening, and were half-dead of fear. They sent several messengers from the Kremlin to gather information, but hearing all this uproar, they were filled with fear themselves, and turned around. The first were convinced that those behind had been killed. It was only after things had quietened down that they noticed nothing had happened. No enemy had arrived, nor was there any way of telling who had contributed most to the agitation. As for the two young men who had been the first cause of it all, they were punished. Then everything went back to normal.

Thereafter, a number of lords came out on to the great square before the Kremlin where there was a great gathering of people, and asked them what was the purpose of these daily disturbances. Did the people not have a sovereign whom they had chosen, and sworn to be faithful to him unto death? And as good Christians, should they not obey him, whose willing subjects they were? If they wanted to ask for some change that might benefit them, could they not do so without recourse to all this agitation, which could not be justified? Then, in the manner of a peroration, they urged everybody to go back to their homes, and announced that henceforth the instigators of disorder would be arrested and punished as they deserved. After that, everyone went back to his own house.

It was announced the next day that hetman Korela had camped with his Cossacks six miles from Moscow. On hearing this, they made haste to prepare the defences, and brought the artillery on to the ramparts and walls; but they worked at it in such a careless manner that the people were scornful. As for myself, I think all this activity had no aim other than to keep the people in check, because they greatly feared the populace, reduced to poverty and so violently threatening the merchants of Moscow, the nobles, and a number of rich persons with pillage that they were more afraid of the inhabitants than of Dmitry's soldiers. For the most part, the city's leading people were in contact with Dmitry, but they took good care not to let this show; and before giving any orders, they were waiting for Dmitry's arrival or his manifestos to the people. But the Godunovs had intercepted a great number of letters, and put those who brought them to death, so that not a single missive reached Moscow for the people to hear.

I do not believe that there was a single piece of money or article of jewellery in the town, for everything was hidden in the ground. For in moments of danger, it is the general custom in Muscovy to bury one's money and precious objects in the woods, cellars, and other waste places. In this manner, a number of things are lost. They often remain there for a long time, and those who had hidden them do not tell their secret to anyone, and end up by forgetting it themselves.

On 1 July 1605, at about nine o'clock in the morning, two of Dmitry's couriers were first spotted boldly entering the town. They brought letters addressed to the inhabitants of Moscow, to be read publicly to the people assembled in the square. It was certainly very bold to dare come thus into a city that was still unconquered, the capital of the country where the tsar still sat in all his power; but without any doubt, they knew that they could rely on the disposition of the majority of lords and inhabitants, for they came with the utmost assurance. Neither could they have been unaware that the young tsar had thought of going to meet Dmitry, throwing himself at his feet and begging for pardon and mercy, but had been prevented from doing so by his mother. For this reason, all the lords in Moscow were uneasy, and had no care for either the tsarina or the Godunovs, but inclined increasingly to Dmitry's side, except for some good patriots who were few in number and dared not speak for fear of losing their lives.

These two couriers, therefore, arrived on horseback in the square, and were in an instant surrounded by thousands of members of the populace. They were recognized as two gentlemen, Muscovites by birth, named Gavrilo Pushkin and Naum Pleshcheev, who had been among the first to rally to Dmitry's party. There, before the assembled people, they read their message, which was couched in these terms:

'Dmitry, by the grace of God, tsar and Grand Prince of all the Russias, and true heir of the late Tsar Ivan Vasilievich of blessed memory, true successor to the throne, wandering so long in the saddest of exiles because of the Godunovs' high treason, as is well known to all – to all Muscovites health and prosperity! This is the twentieth letter I have addressed to you, but you are still obstinate in rebellion. You have also slain my messengers, desiring not to heed them, and remained deaf to the many manifestos in which I have acquainted you with the truth. But I know and understand that this has been not your fault, but that of the traitor Boris, the Godunovs, the Saburovs, and the Veliaminovs, all of whom are traitors to the fatherland, and who have oppressed you to this day. I later learned that my letters have not reached you, since the tyrant intercepted them, and put to death those who brought them. That is why I pardon all you have done against me. I am not bloodthirsty, like him you have so long recognized as your tsar. Everyone knows how he has treated my unfortunate subjects, whom I love as the apple of my eye, and whom he put to death in the cruellest manner with dagger, rope, and gibbet, and sold as slaves to the savage Tatars. From this, you should have understood that he was not the protector of his people, and did not reign lawfully over the empire; but once more, everything is forgiven you. Seize all the Godunovs and their supporters as traitors against me, and hold them in prison until I come to Moscow, so that I may inflict on each of them the punishment he deserves. Beyond this, let none lift his hand against anyone, but watch over everything, and be faithful to God.'[109]

After the reading of this manifesto, all the people prostrated themselves on the ground, begging his pardon, excusing themselves for all the crimes they appeared to have committed, and wishing good fortune to Dmitry Ivanovich, tsar and Grand Prince of all the Russias. Then they stormed the Kremlin, seizing with great fury those who belonged to the Godunov family. They also seized the tsarina, her son, and her daughter, placed them on a water-cart, and took them from the palace as far as the house the tsarina had occupied before Boris became emperor. This house was also in the citadel compound. It had remained unoccupied because Boris thought no one worthy to tenant it. The crowd at once set about the work of destruction. On the pretext that the tsar's dwelling had been polluted by tyranny, it was looted from top to bottom. Nothing remained intact; everything was pillaged and sacked. From there, the crowd spread throughout the city, attacking all the Godunovs' houses, where they did likewise. They did not leave a nail on the wall; pearls, clothing, silver, furniture, all was taken away. All who were hostile to Dmitry were thrown in jail. Some innocent people, such as the doctors, apothecaries and surgeons of the tsar, were robbed but not harmed, except that their enemies took advantage of the situation to settle scores with them; but those lords who were not of either party acted swiftly, and order was restored, though they did not restore to the innocent the objects taken from them in the pillage. It would have been impossible, moreover, to discover into whose hands they had passed, for the entire multitude was guilty of these excesses. So the Godunovs were all taken and thrown separately in prison. The same was done to all those of the Veliaminov and Saburov families as well as their followers. Their houses were put to the sack, and the pillage was so quick and furious that the pillagers killed one another over their booty. Some had reached the wine cellars. Standing the casks upright, they staved them in to get at the wine, some drinking from their hats, others from boots or shoes. They were so desperate for drink, as they usually are in this country, that about fifty were found dead of their bout. In this devastation, everyone carried away all he could to his own house. The pillagers found no money – or at any rate very little – for the victims, apprehensive of their fate, had taken care to bury their riches or else give them away to the monasteries in the hope of buying their way into heaven with these pious endowments. This orgy of destruction did not end until about noonday. A large number of people who were completely innocent, both men and women, were robbed of everything, even their clothes. Their sufferings can only be imagined.

About midnight, there was another disturbance. The bells sounded, and the tocsin was rung. This was a move by some troublemakers who hoped they could resume pillaging by taking advantage of the disorder. Some cried to the others that certain of the Godunovs had forced the gates of their prison, that they were on horseback to the number of about four hundred, and were trying to flee through the city gates. All this was but a tall tale and false alarm; but nobody could discover the originator or his accomplices.

Shortly afterwards, Dmitry sent couriers through the country to all the towns with manifestos ordering the people to take the oath of allegiance to the legitimate heir, so miraculously saved by divine Providence, and telling them all the circumstances of his return. The people, alas, believed all his words, recognized him as the true Dmitry, and went to pray in all the churches for Dmitry Ivanovich, tsar of all the Russias.

Dmitry dismisses his army, and sets out for Tula, whither many things are sent to him from Moscow

A large number of people left Moscow and proceeded to Dmitry's camp at Tula, about thirty-six miles from the capital, to offer the new tsar presents, implore his clemency, and express their desire to see him in Moscow. He promised to come shortly, but first he had to dismiss a large part of his troops at Tula. Horses, carriages, victuals, and other supplies, as well as large sums of money from the state treasury, were brought for distribution to the people at the behest of the emperor.

Oh, how blind they were, and in what deep darkness God's wrath had cast them! They did not see that they were preparing the rod that would strike them one day.

Meanwhile, strange things were happening in Moscow. The body of the late Tsar Boris was exhumed from its tomb and carted scornfully out of the city. He was buried in the earth, close to a small old monastery, for he was not thought worthy to rest beside the tsars.

Having made us witness to all these events, God sent this nation another blindness. Suddenly, most of the people began to believe that Boris was not dead, even though they themselves had buried him twice. Some said that he had fled, and someone else had been put in the tomb in his place. Others said that he had gone to Tatary. Yet others claimed that he had left for Sweden, but most were convinced that the English merchants had taken him with rich treasures to their own country.[110]

In the great tumult, some of the rioters discovered an angel carved in wax, the model for a statue which the late tsar had planned to have cast in fine gold, with twelve statues of the Apostles, for the projected church of the Holy of Holies [Sweeta Sweeti]. Those who brought this statue out, never having seen such an object, cried: 'Look! See what we have found in the coffin where they said Boris was laid! It is now quite certain that he has fled!' They swore to this statement, which made everybody believe it despite themselves. There were even some who swore they had seen Boris seated behind barrels in the cellars of the Godunov house, with food and drink before him. In sum, it can be said that people had become mad, prattlers, and prey to the most ridiculous blindness.

Dire punishment visited on Muscovy

This blindness was so great that numerous couriers were sent along all the roads, to a distance of three or four hundred miles from Moscow, to warn the people of Boris's flight. Thus, these tidings were believed in all this country, and caused such commotion that Cossacks were seen ransacking the villages and forests beside the Volga, bent on the search for the alleged fugitive. Even we foreigners were for some time in the greatest fear of being pillaged and massacred. We were travelling to Archangel to do our business and await the arrival of our ships. Everywhere, people came to warn us that we were being pursued. The rumour had spread that we were transporting Boris's treasure, and that he himself had already been carried away. So we were expecting attack at every hour of our journey; but by the grace of God we miraculously escaped all danger. It can be seen by these details how heavily the arm of heavenly anger was weighing on these people. It would even be impossible to tell everything that happened in Muscovy at this time.

While all the country had thus fallen into Dmitry's power, the town of Astrakhan still held out against him, resisting the Cossacks who were surrounding it whom Dmitry had sent there in the winter to lay siege. They could not conquer it, and the governor of the town, who was a Saburov and a relative of the Godunovs, answered their summons by refusing to surrender, saying that he still wished to wait and see, and would not place the powerful kingdom of Astrakhan in the hands of anyone but him who was in possession of the throne of Moscow. These proud words earned him clemency from Dmitry, who excepted him from the punishment suffered by all his relatives. The Cossacks left this region and returned to their respective homes.

Every day, Dmitry came nearer to the capital. His daily progress was only about a mile because of the multitude that followed him. They came from all sides to see him and implore his favour. Lords, priests, bishops, monks, all came from Moscow to offer him presents. It is from there also that all his court's needs were brought daily. He made frequent speeches to the people who came to see him. He recounted his adventures in such a manner as seemed best and most pleasing to his listeners, and he did not fail to impose upon their credulousness; but they were prepared to believe everything he told them, and if there were some who were better informed, they did not say 'Amen!' any less than the others.

All the noble families fall into disfavour, and are exiled by Dmitry as traitors to the fatherland

At that time also, all the great families allied to Boris's were exiled from Moscow, and with them a large number of their followers.[111] Ivan Vasilievich Godunov and his followers were banished to the confines of Tatary; Stefan Godunov was banished to some other place; they all suffered the fate to which they had formerly subjected others. As for Semeon Nikitich Godunov, who had committed so many acts of tyranny towards the people during Boris's reign, he was taken to Pereiaslavl and thrown into a dungeon. When he demanded food, they brought him a stone, and he died in a torment of hunger. They had delivered from the same prison some unfortunate whom this tyrant had caused to be put there unjustly six years before. How astonished he was, seeing him who had put him in prison, the first lord of the empire after the tsar, coming to take his place! Thus, each receives his just reward in this world. The poet was quite right to say: 'Few rulers depart this life without murder or bloodshed; tyrants all succumb to dusty death.'[112]

Murder of the empress and her son

Meanwhile, Dmitry had sent a certain Andrei Sherefidinov to Moscow, a disreputable person who was one of the first to take sides with the Pretender and was given the task of getting rid of the tsarina, Boris's wife, and her son, but in a manner so secret that nobody might find out that they had been murdered; and the rumour was to be put about that they had poisoned themselves. As for Boris's daughter, he was to leave her alive and keep her until Dmitry entered Moscow. And so Andrei Sherefidinov seized the tsarina and her son, a handsome and well-built young prince who had promised to become an excellent sovereign, suffocated them between two pillows, and thus piteously took their lives.

Calamities of this earthly life, and the inconstancy of fortune

Hence we may see the uncertainty of good fortune, and how our existence here below is a matter for tears. How profound is the wise man's saying: 'Vanity of vanities; all is vanity.'[113] May I be permitted to recall here the fine verses of Eobanus Hessus on the instability of fortune. 'And they who are now born will die at their appointed time; and what we see planted now will be carried away in the next hour. Once there was a sapling, that we now see as a tree, which we now destroy before it is fully grown. What we have brought into this troubled life with many tears, we destroy with immoderate laughter. All will be taken away; nothing is eternal; and nothing remains constant amid eternal flux.'[114]

Straightway after they had carried out the assassination – leaving the daughter alive – they brought a number of townspeople to see the bodies, and told them that the mother and son had just poisoned themselves; but they said that the daughter, whom they wanted to save, had not drunk enough poison from the cup to die of it. At the sight of this mother and child lying in each other's arms the witnesses gave credence to all they were told, and at once informed the entire country that they had poisoned themselves. The two bodies were taken without ceremony to the small monastery where Boris had been buried, and stuck into the soil like animals. Then many hearts were oppressed, not knowing of this murder, but deploring the country's unhappy state, and seeing clearly that all was going ill, they bewailed their misfortune and the fall of the country day and night. Their feeling was also very great for the young hero, Fyodor Borisovich, whom they could never forget. But all these things came about through God's will.[115]

Dmitry had come very close to Moscow, but he did not wish to enter until he was assured that all the country had accepted him as sovereign. This solemn entry took place on 20 June. He was surrounded by eight thousand Cossacks and Poles. Many troops followed him as well, but they went off in various directions when he had come into the town. The streets were so crowded with people that they could be crossed only with very great difficulty. The crowd swarmed over the roofs and walls around the gates by which he was to enter. All the people had put on their best attire, and greeted with tears of joy him whom they believed to be their legitimate sovereign. When he had passed through the third wall and crossed the Moskva river, he came to the church of Jerusalem, which is the name of a church on a hill close to the Kremlin. There, he stopped and told all his escort to halt, and being mounted, removed the imperial cap from his head to put it on again straight away, and gazed at the magnificent ramparts all about him, the city, and the innumerable crowds filling up all the spaces. Then he began to weep bitterly, at least in appearance, and thank God for letting him live long enough to see Moscow, his native city, and his dear subjects, whom he had carried in his heart. As he pronounced these fine words he shed tears, causing many people to do likewise. Alas, if they had known that these were but crocodile tears, they would have restrained themselves from doing the same, and behaved quite differently. But God's will had to be fulfilled in this manner.

While he stopped there, the patriarch, bishops, priests, and monks, carrying crosses, banners, and sacred relics, came to meet him to lead him in procession to the Kremlin, and gave him to embrace and kiss an image of the Virgin which, according to their rite, can be presented only to tsars. Dismounting, Dmitry embraced the image, but he certainly did not perform this ceremony to the satisfaction of certain monks who were watching attentively, for these seemed to doubt whether he was even a genuine Muscovite, much less the legitimate tsar. Though they did not dare say much, he was perfectly aware of their inquisitive looks, and, perhaps knowing them, had them killed secretly and thrown into the river the next day. The procession made its way to the Kremlin to the sound of bells and general shouts from all the people of: 'Long live our Dmitry Ivanovich, tsar of all the Russias!' They led the new sovereign to his palace. There he was placed on the imperial throne, and the magnates came to kneel before him, and recognize him as tsar. The Cossacks and the other soldiers were posted in the enclosure of the Kremlin, their muskets loaded and fully primed. This soldiery responded with insolent words even to lords, being very brutal, with no respect for anyone.

Changes in the Muscovite state

Great changes took place in the tsar's court. The officers of the former court, such as the chancellors, secretaries, grooms, stewards, major-domos, cooks, and chamberlains, were dismissed and replaced by others in whom the new sovereign had more confidence. In the same manner, the governors of provinces, towns, dominions, and other places, were also changed. For his chamberlains and pages he took on Poles, who are more adroit, more alert, more learned, and more valiant people than the officers of the court and the nobles of Moscow. The latter, in fact, have never left their native land, and for the most part do not know how to read or write. This ignorance, moreover, remains very common among the Russians, who live like animals.

Meanwhile, Dmitry's alleged mother had been sent for. As I have reported before, this lady was closely guarded in a hermitage by order of the Godunovs who, as their ruin approached, had ordered her killed, but she had been saved. In all the towns through which she passed, the people greeted her with the honours due their former tsarina, the seventh wife of Ivan Vasilievich. She was now a nun.

When she came within two miles of Moscow, she stopped at Taininskoe [Taninsco], where there is an imperial residence. It is there that Dmitry came to meet her with a crowd of lords and people. The interview was a scene of sobbing and tears. The people were given to believe that mother and son, descendants of their ancient monarchs, were meeting for the first time in many years, and people wept and sobbed with them. It was not surprising, alas, that she recognized Dmitry as her son, even though she knew full well that he was not. She lost nothing thereby; on the contrary, she was thereafter considered a tsarina, treated magnificently, and led to the Kremlin, where she was given the convent of the Ascension [Vosnesenie of hemelvaert Cristi] as her residence. There she lived as a sovereign.[116] Every day she received a visit from the young tsar, or from the nuns who lived with her.

As Martha re-entered Moscow, reaching the city gates, Dmitry dismounted from his horse with his suite of lords and walked bare-headed beside her carriage as far as her lodgings, to the great astonishment of all the population. Oh, the perfidious snares of Satan!"[117]

Dmitry makes preparations for his coronation

He then had the arrangements set in motion for his coronation. Although according to Muscovite custom this ceremony could take place only on 1 September, he wanted it done before that date; this seemed very strange to a great number of people, though nobody said anything about it. He was crowned, then, in accordance with that nation's ritual, and with the same magnificence as his predecessors, on 20 July 1605 in the church of the Virgin in Moscow.[118] The bishops placed the crown on his head with many genuflections and great ceremonial. Gold coins were strewn before him, and he walked upon cloth of gold. Couriers were sent into all the towns to announce that this inauguration had been carried out. As for the towns, they offered presents to the new tsar in token of their recognition.

He dismisses his troops

The halberdiers and a great number of other soldiers were dismissed, having received their money, and were ordered back to Poland. Among the commanders dismissed at the same time there were several who displayed scant satisfaction. A certain Adam Wisniowiecki, a boyar of White Russia [Alba Russia],[119] complained that he had spent several thousand crowns from his patrimony for Dmitry's cause and had not been reimbursed or compensated. He refrained from telling why he was being treated thus. It could be, however, that he deserved no better. But we have no time to elaborate on that.[120]

The Cossacks, when they were given their leave, received rich rewards. Though this did not prevent some of them from murmuring also. Each of these malcontents would have liked to have been tsar himself!

He kept hetman Korela in Moscow with a group of Cossacks, and wished to heap the highest honours on him. But Korela cared little for the greatness of this world. He did not value the treasures, and did not want to be one of the lords of the empire because he disliked the duties the title imposed. He led a disorderly life and had one care only, to have a good time every day.

Dmitry had the old patriarch, Job, deposed, and handed him over to the curses of the people, giving him the name of Judas, and accusing him of being the cause of all Boris's crimes. He was relegated to the little monastery of Staritsa [Nastaretza], where he lived in poverty.[121] In his place they named as patriarch a Greek by birth, a perverse and artful man, a sodomite and whoremonger, whom the people of Moscow detested; but he was there by the will of the tsar.

Everywhere, he installed officials and officers of his choice, men on whom he believed he could rely. He dismissed above all those who were full of presumption and knew too much, and some were even banished.

Many perish at Dmitry's behest

The leading lords and patriots of the land were greatly afflicted seeing all these things, and they began to point out that the new sovereign was not the legitimate sovereign. Several individuals – for the most part ecclesiastics and monks, who knew the secrets of state – went so far as to commit some indiscretions in this regard. Some of those on whom suspicion fell were executed or removed. A number of people from the populace and citizenry suffered this fate in Moscow. Every night was taken up with handing these unfortunate people over for torture and putting them to death. Despite the secrecy surrounding these executions, it was impossible to prevent people from talking. All words offensive to the tsar were punished instantly by death or the confiscation of goods.

Conspirators against Dmitry are apprehended in Moscow

Given the deplorable state of affairs in Moscow, a conspiracy was hatched to dispose of the tsar. It had as its chief instigator Vasily Ivanovich Shuisky, who knew full well about the authenticity of Dmitry, and had, as I have already said, always given the most categorical testimony on this matter. Shuisky was continually holding secret meetings with various conspirators, both lords and merchants, in whom he believed he could have confidence, seeking the means and the opportunity to kill the tsar; but their plot was denounced by some traitors, though they did not know very much and could produce no proof to support their allegations. A number of conspirators were seized nevertheless, and put to torture. Several confessed, while others were unshakeable. Shuisky was arrested, and found guilty of treason and attempting to murder the tsar. Brought to judgment, he was condemned to death, and his execution set for 25 August. On that day, he was brought on to the square before the Kremlin. The vast square was occupied by eight thousand[122] 'streltsy,' or musketeers, well armed and commanded by Basmanov. Seeing the spectators saddened by Shuisky's fate, Basmanov went around on horseback addressing groups of people, telling them that the only aim of the accused had been to overthrow the empire once again, and that his machinations had given rise to terrible evils. 'Our tsar,' he said, 'is full of clemency, and he only has those executed who have doubly merited death.' With these words, he managed to turn the people's sentiment against the unhappy Shuisky, and yet Basmanov could not help remarking that their affliction was truly great. The executioner came and began to undress the condemned, who stood before a large log on which the axe lay ready. The executioner was also taking off his rich shirt, embroidered with gold and pearls. It was an object which he coveted, but Shuisky refused to be deprived of it, and wished to die with this garment on. He waited a few moments more, to see whether a message of pardon would come. This delay was against the wishes of Basmanov and several others, who wanted the execution done forthwith.

Finally, a chancellor brought the rescript whereby the tsar let him live. He made no great haste, as he himself desired Shuisky's death. At this news, the multitude of the citizens and inhabitants of Moscow were overwhelmed by joy. Then Basmanov began to ride about the square once again, crying out: 'Oh, what a gracious sovereign heaven has given us! See? He even pardons traitors who seek to kill him!' This act of clemency was doubtless intended to reach the hearts of the people, and convince both poor and rich even more compellingly that the tsar really was the true Dmitry, and that this act of mercy had resulted from the intercession of the old dowager tsarina.[123]

In reality, it must have been inspired by Jan Buczynski and his brothers. These were very intelligent men Dmitry had brought with him from Poland, and one of them was his first secretary, going with him everywhere. They constantly advised the tsar to pardon the small number of lords still surviving, treat them with kindness, show them friendship, and assure them that by this means he would obtain more than by tortures, which, in point of fact, would only sow suspicion and doubt in the people as to their sovereign's legitimacy. These Buczynski brothers were of German origin, and one of them belonged to the Reformed Church.

Thus pardoned, Vasily Ivanovich Shuisky and his two brothers, Dmitry and Ivan, were sent into exile or prison at Viatka, but towards Christmas, on the repeated insistence of the Buczynski brothers, they received yet another commutation of their penalty and returned to Moscow; but they persisted in working for the good of the country, strongly opposing the flood of heresy that they felt was spreading, and they conspired in secret, with the same energy as before, to kill Dmitry at some opportune time. Every day, in various places, ever larger numbers of people were going to execution. At this same time, God gave Dmitry a plain warning, but he was blind to it. He did not care about the Muscovites, saying that they would not dare do the things that were being reported to him.

I must now say a few words about his way of life and his domestic habits. He sent great sums of money to Poland to pay his debts and reimburse everyone from whom he had borrowed. Poles also came to Moscow in great numbers, and carried away a large amount of specie, selling their rich jewels and other precious objects the merchants brought, which the tsar sought eagerly. All that was rare or curious aroused his interest. All those who offered him these goods quickly got their price and could go away content.

New palace built by Dmitry

He had a magnificent palace built on the Kremlin ramparts, from which he could see all the city, for these ramparts are situated on a large hill with the Moskva flowing at its foot. This palace was composed of two adjacent lodgings, and formed an angle. One of these lodgings was intended for the future tsarina. Here is an approximate drawing of this palace built on the Kremlin walls in Moscow. Thus, the palace stood on walls of triple thickness.

In the interior of the apartments, he had splendid gilded baldaquins; the walls were furnished with precious tapestries in gold and embroidered velvet. The nails, hinges, and other ironwork on the doors were covered with thick gilt; the stoves were works of art. On the windows hung draperies of cloth and crimson velvet. He also caused magnificent baths and fine towers to be built. Although there were already vast stables in his palace compound, he had a special stable built close to his new dwelling. These new buildings had a number of hidden doors and secret passages, which proves that he was following the example of the tyrants, and that like them, he lived in perpetual fear.

His love of hunting

He also ordered the strongest and most ferocious dogs to be sought throughout the empire. On Sundays, he had cages of wild bears brought into the rear court of the palace, and took pleasure in pitting these animals against the dogs. Often, he would even command the first noblemen of the country, who are able hunters among other things, to enter the arena armed with simple spears and do combat with the bears. I have seen this extraordinary spectacle with my own eyes. Several times, I saw a man attack an enormous bear which sprang forward with spirit, and pierce it in the neck or chest with a spear with a skill truly not to be credited. For the most part, these courageous men come away from the struggle with hand wounds, though they usually also win a victory. The greatest danger to their lives comes if they happen to misplace their blow; but then hunters armed with pitchforks rush upon and stab the bear. In any case, these games are horrible to watch. Dmitry wanted to fight wild bears in person several times, but he was always prevented from doing so by the magnates.

He also went out of Moscow to hunt in the open fields, where bears, wolves, and foxes were set free at his command. He loved to pursue them with great ardour. In one day, he would wear out several prize horses, and change clothes frequently. He was truly a horseman of extreme boldness. He tamed all mounts, no matter how fractious they were, and in this exercise astonished even the Russians, who are all good horsemen, and go about on horseback from infancy to death.[124] In fact, there is not a merchant in Moscow, no matter how poor he may be, who does not own horses, and they go on errands from one street to another only on horseback. Horses, besides, are cheap there, as is their fodder. In good years, a horse's upkeep costs barely four pounds.

Dmitry was also able in the art of government. He made all the laws, and made them good and above reproach. The officials themselves found fruitful instruction in them.[125]

Dmitry's greatness

Finding that Muscovy did not suffice him for his empire, he would have liked to have added Tatary to it, and even Sweden and Denmark. This project did not appear difficult to him, but he limited himself at first to Tatary. He was a brave warrior and loved to see blood spilt, though he hid this inclination, keeping it up his sleeve. Beyond this, he was endowed with great physical strength.

He learns to know the Muscovites, and organizes a strong bodyguard

Having learned to know the Muscovites, he clothed himself with precautions and doubled the guard of his palace. Choosing three hundred men, the biggest and strongest, from among the Germans and Livonians, he formed two corps, one of two hundred halberdiers and the other of one hundred life guards. He gave them brilliant uniforms in the German style, good pay, and great privileges. This troop formed his personal guard, and escorted him on all his excursions. The life guards were mainly Swedish and Livonian gentlemen. Their leader was Jacques Margeret, formerly captain in the German corps. Their uniform was of velvet and cloth of gold, with rich cloaks. They carried gilded battleaxes mounted on staffs covered in velvet and silver thread. The halberdiers formed two companies, each having its own hundredman. The first company, clad in violet cloth embroidered with green velvet, was led by a Scotsman called Albert Lanton. The second company, who wore a uniform of violet cloth embroidered in red velvet, were commanded by Matthew Knudson, a Dane who had remained in Boris's service after the death of Duke Johann. These three officers and their lieutenants, in addition to the highest marks of esteem, had received gifts of villages and estates. Life guards and halberdiers always surrounded the tsar, even at night. They mounted guard in turn on the heights of the palace. When the tsar went out with his suite, the life guards accompanied him on horseback, but the halberdiers led him only as far as the door, and there awaited his return. The life guards carried loaded pistols at all times.[126]

The bodyguard of previous sovereigns

All this entourage seemed most extraordinary to the Muscovites' eyes. Accustomed to see their tsars go about with a simple guard of Muscovite musketeers, they did not see why Dmitry had to add this foreign guard to the two or three thousand men armed with long muskets who were protecting him already. He had large numbers of cannon cast, even though the town of Moscow was quite well supplied with them. From time to time, he built forts which he had bombarded by the heavy artillery. He himself took part in these exercises as a common soldier, and spared nothing to instruct the Muscovites in the science of war.[127] On another occasion, he ordered a sort of engine or mobile fort on huge rollers, bearing several field pieces and completely filled with artifices. He intended it for use against the Tatars, desiring to sow fear among their horses. This device was truly ingenious. During the winter, he set it up on the ice-bound river, and ordered a company of Polish cavalry to attack and bombard it. From the height of his palace he could observe the exercise in detail, and it seemed to him that it had succeeded according to his wishes. This machine was of very remarkable construction, and entirely covered with paintings. The doors were in the shape of elephants, and the windows represented the mouths of furnaces spewing flames. Above these other apertures, serving as embrasures for small artillery pieces, were openings in the form of the heads of demons. In truth, its appearance was so fearful that if it had been carried into the middle of the enemy, such as the Tatars, it would have thrown their ranks into disorder and put them to flight. Even so, the Muscovites called it 'the monster from hell,' and said after Dmitry's death that he, whom they considered to be a sorcerer, had long housed the Devil within it; so they burned this contraption along with his corpse.[128]

Exaltation of Mstislavsky

He had numerous mortars built to fire grenades and often tried them out. He frequently took pleasure in mock attacks and military exercises with his gentlemen as a form of recreation, but sometimes he exposed himself too much; for conspirators had resolved to kill him in the course of one of these diversions, though fear stopped them from carrying out their design. He heaped honours on Fyodor Ivanovich Mstislavsky and made him a gift of the entire palace of the late Tsar Boris; and when Mstislavsky excused himself, saying that he did not deserve such favours, he said: 'You are more worthy of them than Boris, because Boris was nothing but a scourge of the country.' After this, he gave him the hand of a daughter of the Nagoi family, to which the old tsarina, his pretended mother, belonged. Having also restored to their former rank and dignity those whom Boris had reduced to poverty and exile, he arranged numerous alliances between these lords and the daughters of the same Nagoi family, or between the sons of the Nagoi family and the daughters of the victims. He honoured their weddings with his presence, and gave them feasts and hunting parties. His aim in this was to promote alliances between the members of his presumed dynasty and the families of the magnates, who still formed a neutral party, in the hope of weaning them from the disbelief with which they regarded him.

He sent an ambassador to Poland meanwhile with the mission of announcing to the king and others there his divinely-favoured accession to the throne and bringing from that country his betrothed, the daughter of the palatine of Sandomierz, Jerzy Mniszek. This ambassador took the palatine great treasures of jewels, pearls, precious stones, and gems set in gold, and also great sums of money, so that he might prepare a trousseau worthy of a sovereign lady. The old tsarina also added numerous presents for her future daughter, as she called her. The betrothed was called Maryna. I will detail later in this book the contents of these presents sent to Poland.[129] In the distribution of this largesse, the king of Poland was not forgotten. In Moscow, Dmitry ordered the treasures of the empire to be put in order, and new strong-boxes made. The jewels were sorted in various chests according to their kind. Precious antique objects hidden for centuries were brought from their hiding places and sorted and stored according to his instructions. He also bought a large number of precious objects from the English, Dutch, and other foreigners. Jews from Poland sold him many rich jewels.

Having had his will of Xenia, Boris's daughter, he had her hair shaved off and sent her a hundred miles from Moscow to the monastery of St Cyril [Kirilowa], where there were still many nuns of high birth.[130]

Vasily Mosalsky – his best friend, whom he gave marks of high esteem for being the first to join him, and who remained with him to the end – was sent to the duchy of Smolensk on the frontiers of Poland with magnificent presents and gilded sleds, to be offered to those who came to Moscow that winter in the young bride's party. During his stay in Smolensk, Mosalsky was treated like a king. He became owner of the best lands he could find, and acquired great riches there.

After Mosalsky, Dmitry's two most intimate and trusted friends were Peter Basmanov, whom he had created commander-in-chief of his armies, and one Mikhail Molchanov, who had joined his party in Poland and always given him great support. He was a rogue and a flatterer, one who feared neither God nor man. These three persons committed dishonourable acts, indulging in much scandal and whoremongering. Molchanov filled the office of procurer. Through his agents, he sought out the most beautiful girls, inducing some by offers of money, others by force, and taking them by secret passages to the tsar's bath-house; then, when the latter had sufficient satisfaction of them, he passed them on to Basmanov and Molchanov. When Dmitry's eyes fell on a beautiful nun, of which there were many in Muscovy, she could not escape his passion. At his death, at least thirty were discovered with child as a result of his activities. Such was his private life. Beyond this, he was a warrior and a hero in all things. There was not a chancellor or officer who failed to experience his anger. More than once, he broke sticks across their backs to teach them court manners and humble them. This did not make them very happy, but recalcitrants had only to wait patiently for better times.

Embassy from Poland and the Polish nobles

On 16 October an ambassador arrived from the king of Poland to offer his sovereign's congratulations, with presents of fine horses, a chain of gold, and a large cup. This emissary left in the course of the same month. He was accompanied by a papal legate, commissioned to renew with Dmitry the treaty concluded beforehand in Poland. This legate received presents.

About this time, the Shuisky family obtained pardon and came to Moscow, but they began their conspiracy afresh – this time, however, more secretly.

In December, the Cossacks stationed along the Don close to Azov brought to Moscow a Turkish captain named Dus Bakhmet [Doesbagmeth], who had committed great ravages around the Don.

He takes people into his service

The tsar kept by him a Polish troop commander who had served him faithfully in the conquest of the empire. His troop consisted of valiant young men, all of them gentlemen of good family. Dmitry inspected these horsemen personally, and gave them great tokens of esteem, even though they had nothing to do but stay in Moscow and accompany the tsar, armed and in dazzling array, whenever he went on his hunting expeditions or outings. The commander of this troop was called Matthias Domaradzki.

A great number of young Polish nobles came to Moscow to present themselves to the tsar, whom they had known in Poland when his circumstances had been quite different. They had no occasion to regret the kindness they had shown him at that time. A cousin of his betrothed, Kazanowski by name, arrived in the capital and was assigned a special palace. He was a young man, but full of pretensions. All these young lords and others joined Dmitry's hunting parties and diversions, and had no thought but to amuse themselves.

In the fall, the tsar ordered preparations so that they could attack the land of Narva with great forces during the winter, but the leading lords argued vigorously against this expedition, so he gave the idea up for some reason or other.

From Uglich, he summoned the son of the king of Sweden, young Gustav, with whom I have already dealt sufficiently in the history of Boris. Dmitry sent him orders one day to swear allegiance to the Muscovite crown and promise to serve the tsar faithfully whenever he was required to do so. But Gustav, who was touched in the head and stubborn, replied that he also was a king's son, and would not tolerate anyone's speaking to him in this manner, and that Dmitry would do better to be friendlier to him and help him recover the kingdom of Sweden which rightly belonged to him. On hearing this reply, Dmitry flew into a violent rage. At his order, the prince was arrested and with a Swedish servant named Simon thrown, bound hand and foot, on a sled, and taken to prison at Yaroslavl, fifty miles from Moscow, where he died; I think his death was hastened by poison.[131]

Every day, couriers were travelling, either from the bride, or from the palatine her father, or from the pope or his legate at Krakow, or from Moscow to Poland.

On 8 January 1606, a great tumult broke out at night in the Kremlin. It appears that a number of persons had come there from the apartments of the tsar. The latter was obliged to take up arms, and stationed himself in a vast room with two captains of the guard who were on duty that night. These two captains were called Fyodor Brenzin and Roman Durov; but nobody could discover the cause of this tumult. Two or three individuals whom they seized and put to torture would reveal nothing, and suffered death. Truly, the Almighty protected Shuisky, who was both the head and the arms of all the conspiracies.

After this affair, the guard was further increased by large numbers. It seems that Andrei Sherefidinov had been bribed to assassinate the tsar. He was the same person who had earlier, at Dmitry's command, suffocated the tsarina Maria and her son with pillows; but he disappeared, and nobody knows what happened to him. For my part, I believe that he too was assassinated.

Every day, in fact, people who had talked too much were put to death. These were monks, for the most part. I still say that it is quite astonishing that the conspiracy was not brought to light. Without doubt, God had blinded the tsar.

Even among the musketeers, there were some who had dared to say that the tsar could not be the true Dmitry. Basmanov, the commander of this troop of eight thousand men, becoming aware of these sentiments, reported them to the tsar and warned him to be on guard, claiming that his person was in great danger. After a severe and secret inquiry, seven musketeers were singled out and apprehended without anybody's knowing about it. At dawn the next day, all the musketeers were summoned to the rear court, where bear baiting customarily took place on Sundays. They all gathered there unarmed, and very anxious to know the reason for the summons. A moment later, the tsar came out of his palace, escorted by his life guards and halberdiers and accompanied by Basmanov, Mstislavsky, some of the Nagois, and several Polish lords. He stood on the great staircase of this court and ordered all the gates shut. Seeing the tsar, the musketeers all prostrated themselves on the ground, according to their custom, and began to look upon him with their heads bared. Dmitry could not help laughing when he saw all these uncovered heads bowed to the ground, and said: 'Oh, would to God they were all filled with wisdom!' Then he gave them a stirring speech. First, he spoke of divine Providence, quoting from the holy Scriptures. He then reproached them for their obstinacy and disbelief. 'How long,' he said to them, 'will you seek discord and evil consequence? Is it not enough for you that the land is infected right to the marrow? Must it be destroyed to its very foundations?' Then he reminded them of the crimes of the Godunovs, their tyrannical conduct towards the leading families of the land, the manner in which they had usurped the imperial throne. 'There,' he continued, 'is the reason why the land has suffered so greatly. Even though God has delivered me from the mortal snares with which I was surrounded and singularly preserved me, you are still not satisfied. You seek any pretext for hatching new treason, and already you want to get rid of me. What have I done to you? Who among you can show that I am not the true Dmitry? Let him come forward, and I will let myself be struck down at once here before you. My mother and all the lords here present can vouch for me. And how could it have been possible for someone almost without troops to complete the conquest of this powerful empire, had he not been sustained by his true rights? Would God have permitted it? I have exposed my life to danger, not to raise myself to the supreme power, but through pity of you, to deliver you from the depths of misery and fearful slavery into which you were about to be plunged by these traitors and oppressors of the land. It is through God's inspiration that I have accomplished my mission; it is with the support of the arm of the Almighty that I have come into the possession of a throne which belonged to me. Why, then, do you conspire? Here I am! Tell me, without fear, and frankly, the reasons for your disbelief.'

Piteous deaths of those who had allowed themselves to say too much about Dmitry

At these words, they were struck with astonishment. Nearly all of them prostrated themselves on the ground and swore to their innocence. With tears, they begged for the tsar's clemency and implored him to tell them who had falsely accused him. The tsar then ordered Basmanov to bring before them the seven persons who had been arrested. This was done instantly. 'Here they are,' cried Dmitry, 'those who maintain that you are conspirators, and hatching criminal designs against your legitimate sovereign and master!' They all threw themselves at once upon these seven wretches, seized them, and tore them to pieces in a manner so horrible that nobody would believe the telling of it. It must be remembered that all this multitude of soldiers, who had no weapons or staves, rushed on the seven victims and tore them into a thousand pieces with their bare hands so that their clothes were stained with blood as though they had just been slaughtering oxen. There were even some who, like dogs pursuing a stag, had torn lumps of flesh out with their teeth. One of them, having torn off an ear, was so ferocious that he kept it between his teeth until it was reduced to small morsels. Hungry lions would not have committed such atrocities on young lambs as did these men on their fellows. Finishing the execution, they cried out: 'May all enemies of the tsar and traitors perish in this fashion!' Tyrannical as he was, Dmitry could not bear to watch this frightful spectacle. He withdrew into a room where he walked up and down all the while this was going on. When it was all over, he returned, gave his troops yet another speech concerning his identity, and once more affirmed that he was their legitimate sovereign. Then he dismissed them. They all prostrated themselves once again on the ground, asking pardon, and then each returned to his home. The remains of the corpses were gathered into a cart and thrown to the dogs in the open field. The sight of this cart on which these human remains had been placed on view, and which thus crossed the city, made the hair stand up on the heads of all beholders.[132]

This event spread such terror throughout Moscow that little was said of it, and everyone curbed his tongue more closely. There were, however, some obstinate persons who were troubled by neither death nor torment. As for these seven unfortunate victims, I do not believe that they were guilty as Dmitry persuaded his soldiers they were. His only aim in sacrificing them was to inspire fear in the masses.

The tsar resolved to mount an expedition with all his forces against the Crimean Tatars straightway after his marriage. Over the entire winter, he had been sending great quantities of war supplies to Elets, a town on the confines of Tatary. At the beginning of the year, he had gathered enough flour, lard, powder, and lead to suffice an army of three hundred thousand men. All these munitions were to await his arrival there. As a preliminary to this expedition he sent a message to the Crimea, telling the chief of the Tatars to give the tsar back all the tribute the Muscovite empire had formerly had to pay them, with the threat that if he refused, he would make him and his people as bald as a fur he was sending him, shaved to the skin.[133] But the courier who carried this message never returned.

Spring was near, and according to reports reaching Moscow with each day, the arrival of the palatine and his daughter, the tsar's bride, was to be expected. The tsar had made all ready to receive them. All the nobility, following his example, were supposed to spare no pains to impress with the magnificence of their costumes and equipment. His entire guard received new uniforms and mantles of crimson velvet, and they were told to keep on the alert for the moment when the tsarina made her entry. He also had the apartments which his mother occupied in the monastery elegantly decorated. It was there that the bride was to be brought first, to remain there for eight days so that she could be initiated into Muscovite customs. The palace that she was to occupy, as well as his own, was completed and decorated with much artistry.

A large number of rich merchants arrived in Moscow from Poland, bringing jewels and precious objects of all kinds to offer for sale to the tsar on the occasion of his marriage. Here are the names of the most notable of these merchants: a Polish gentleman called Niemojewski, sent by Princess Anna, a sister of the king of Poland, who had jewels to the value of two hundred thousand crowns, and wished to sell some of them to the tsar; Wolski, a cousin of the marshal of the king's court, who possessed precious tapestries and tents which he sold to the tsar for about one hundred thousand crowns; a certain Nicholas Polucki who brought with him a large quantity of objects; a native of Milan, Ambrogio Cellari, had about sixty-six hundred florins' worth; two agents of Philip Holbein of Augsburg had about thirty-five thousand florins' worth; Andrew Nathan of Augsburg brought jewels to the value of three hundred thousand florins; a certain Nicholas Demist, from Lvov in Russia,[134] was as well furnished. Apart from those mentioned, a great number of Polish merchants and Jews had arrived with a large quantity of merchandise. All this was bought at very high prices. The sellers would certainly have been well off had they been paid in cash. Happy were those who received it; but they were very few.[135]

Great preparations for the marriage

The tsar also caused very rich pavilions and barges to be built. He gave sums of money to the captains, cavalry commanders, and officers of the guard, so that they could dress their men in the most splendid manner. Messengers went with requisitions to all the tsar's villages and estates. Rich villages were required to supply fowls, eggs, oxen, sheep, and other foodstuffs, which each had to send to Moscow daily according to its assessment, for a large number of persons were coming from Poland. As many as six or seven thousand were expected. The lodgings assigned to them were also to be furnished daily with hay and straw. Inspectors and commissioners were appointed to supervise these details. Several Moscow merchants were obliged to give up the best apartments of their own dwellings for a time to accommodate the Poles invited to the wedding. All this caused a great deal of consternation.

Secret conspiracy against Dmitry

All this time the conspirators were preparing, on their side, quite a different type of celebration. They gathered in large groups, and, binding themselves by powerful oaths, plotted to kill the tsar during the marriage feast after all the Poles had arrived in the capital. This was, in their opinion, the best way of recovering the treasure that had been sent to Poland. These conspirators were almost three thousand in number in Moscow, Novgorod, and elsewhere. It is quite surprising that this conspiracy did not come to light. It was led by Prince Vasily Ivanovich Shuisky, who was always full of ardour for the defence of his country and religion.

The Muscovite ambassador, Afanasy Ivanovich Vlasiev, was charged with fetching the bride and taking her presents from her future husband. He arrived at Krakow in Poland with the lady and her father, the palatine. There, the king and his sister received them with the greatest honour. The ambassador stood proxy for his master at the wedding. The bride was placed before the king. The wedding took place in the presence of the legate, or agent, whom the pope maintains permanently at the king's court. After this ceremony, the young king and his sister left the town.

Arrival of the palatine of Sandomierz in Moscow

The palatine or governor of Sandomierz continued on his way to Muscovy and came to Smolensk, where he was received in splendour by Prince Vasily Mosalsky, who brought him in great state to Moscow with the ambassador,

Vlasiev. He made his entry into the capital mounted on the tsar's horse, in the midst of the magnates, the nobility, and all the populace. This entry was just as triumphant as that of Duke Johann of Denmark in Boris's time. As his lodging, he was given Boris's palace, situated close to the tsar's, and he was treated royally. Every day, Mass was celebrated there; he had with him those clowns who were expert in the art of celebrating it.

After his entry, which took place on 24 April, the palatine was received by the tsar. At this interview, the two men were profuse in their mutual tokens of respect and wishes for prosperity.

The next day, Dmitry had a great number of splendid pavilions erected on a beautiful plain about a mile from Moscow. Tapestries were spread all around, giving the whole scene the look of an embroidered town, and they brought food of all kinds, and wine. It was there that the future tsarina was to halt and rest before her triumphal entry. Dmitry went out, accompanied by the governor of Sandomierz, who rode on horseback behind him and to the right of Prince Vasily Shuisky, who had once again been restored to favour. They were followed by the lords and all the guard. Despite the great heat of the day, the halberdiers were obliged to run to this tent city, which caused great discontent among them, as they were not accustomed to such exertion. When he had come there, after his meal the tsar organized a bear hunt. He himself pursued these wild animals valiantly on horseback, and killed an enormous one by his own hand. Had his horse not been perfectly suited for this hunt, Dmitry would have been in great danger. For despite his ability as a horseman and his skill with arms, he frequently exposed himself to risk through his incredible boldness. Having spent an entire day at these amusements, the tsar and his guest returned to Moscow, where the marriage preparations went ahead without respite.

Elena Urodliva, the Muscovite prophetess

During these days, the hellish soothsayer, Elena Urodliva, of whom I have spoken in the life of Boris,[136] began to prophesy Dmitry's death, and this caused great consternation among the conspirators. Luckily for them, Dmitry laughed at these oracles and was not disturbed by the babblings of idiots and possessed persons who, if matters had been pressed farther, might possibly, in their evil doings, have revealed the names of several conspirators. The prophecies they made against the tsar were few, and they repeated again and again, like the poet: 'While the marriage bed is being prepared, fate prepares death for you.'[137] But for Dmitry, this prophecy was fulfilled.

On 1 May the bride was received in the aforesaid tents.[138] Early on 2 May, heralds went about the streets of the capital announcing the order for the dukes, princes, boyars, chancellors, nobles, knights, merchants, and common people, all to don their finest attire to attend the tsarina's entry, and leave off all work and all business. In addition, all horsemen were told to ride out of the city at two o'clock in the morning. All this was done in a brilliant fashion. New bridges had been built over the Moskva on the side where the bride was to enter. In the meadows close to the river, they raised vast and sumptuous tents under which the reception of the future bride would take place. There she would leave her carriage to mount the triumphal chariot of the tsar.

Solemn entry into Moscow of the tsar's bride

The nobles and lords rode out of the city in magnificent costumes gleaming with gold and pearls. Their horses' saddles were gilded or inlaid with silver, their harness covered with gold and silver chains and decorated with precious stones. A host of valets followed them on foot and horseback. Their costumes were almost as resplendent as their masters'. The imperial chariot was brought; it was of antique design, somewhat resembling a stage, very artistically built, all gilded and hung with cloth of gold. Inside were cushions embroidered with pearls. Even the wheels were gilded. On this carriage was seated a pretty little Moorish boy playing with a monkey, which he held by a golden chain. The conveyance was pulled by 12 white horses, dappled with black markings which seemed to have been painted. However, I can affirm that they were natural, because these horses had been brought thus from Tartary to Moscow. A hundred life guards, richly arrayed, served as escort to the carriage. They were commanded by a captain of horse; two other captains, also mounted, commanded companies of halberdiers, each of a hundred men, who marched flanking the carriage on each side, and also before it. Two Muscovite boyars of high rank, covered with pearls and jewels, held to the right and the left. Thus was the carriage led to the aforesaid tents. There, the halberdiers were drawn up on both sides in their German-style uniforms, with the life guards behind.[139]

Basmanov, accompanied by numerous pages on horseback, had a train as magnificent as that of the tsar himself. The company of Polish cavalry, under the orders of its commander, Domaradzki, was distinguished by its lances and vari-coloured banners. They marched to the sound of trumpets to meet the bride, and joined up with two companies of the tsarina's cavalry.

When the whole procession had arrived at the tents, the king's ambassador was the first to enter the enclosure in ceremonial array, followed by all the nobility, and those who had come of their own accord from Poland with the bride. They had old-fashioned carriages, pulled by six, eight, or ten horses, all of the same colour.

Just as the entrance was getting under way, the tsar rode out incognito, clothed in poor garments and wearing a wretched little red cap. He was accompanied by Vasily Shuisky and a Polish valet, both of them on horseback as well. He had taken care that no one should do him honour, so that he would go unrecognized and pass through the ranks of soldiers and Poles without anyone remarking it. He positioned his noblemen and musketeers, to the number of about four thousand, mounted on horses from the imperial stables and dressed for the most part in red velvet with distinctive liveries, their muskets slung from their saddles. The musketeers were placed in good order from the river to the city walls in such a way that from afar, they looked three times as numerous as they actually were. He ordered them to move quickly into the second great enclosure, using another gate, as soon as the tsarina had entered the city, and form up in the same order there. This is what was done. Having inspected everything, he went back into the city, still unrecognized except perhaps by a few people. As for myself, I saw him perfectly, as did all those who were riding in this area to watch the entry.

As soon as the tsarina, or the bride, reached the tents, she was greeted with the greatest honour in Dmitry's name and placed in the imperial coach, which brought her to Moscow slowly and carefully, so that the progress lasted an entire day.

At the head of the procession two banners of haiduks, or Polish musketeers, marched on foot in good order, carrying muskets or arquebuses on their shoulders and Turkish scimitars at their sides. Some also had battleaxes. Their uniform was of blue cloth with silver insignia. They wore white plumes in their caps. They were all men of fine bearing and the same height. Their standard fluttered among them, surrounded by fifes and pipers, who alternated joyously with the trumpeters in the march.

After them came two companies of Polish cavalry, holding pointed lances, decorated with flags, in their hands. The company commanded by Domaradzki joined forces with them. For the most part, the soldiers of this last company wore antique costume; for weapons, they had great gilded Persian and Turkish bucklers depicting all kinds of dragons and serpents, and bows and quivers of great value. They were all young men and good soldiers. They marched boldly to the sound of trumpets. But what I could not admire enough were the magnificent horses on which they were mounted, cantering all the time and splendidly harnessed. Several of them had painted wings, so it appeared that these horses flew rather than walked. Most of them were from Hungary.

Then came two horses that were certainly the most beautiful I have ever seen, and I have seen many. Each was led by a Turk holding large gilded reins. Despite the gold chains attached to their legs and the efforts of their grooms, these horses did not stop rearing and neighing, so that foam streamed from their gilded bits. They carried saddles of the richest workmanship, covered in turquoise. A great number of the horsemen had their mounts dyed in a highly original fashion – red, orange, and yellow. These colours were very solid, and did not fade even when the horses walked or swam in water. This dye, commonly called 'China,' comes in fact from Persia. The nobles and the lords who followed, accompanied by their servants, competed in the beauty and good taste of their costumes. They preceded the imperial carriage, which was escorted by the halberdiers and the life guards marching with their captains at the head. On both sides of the carriage, the four boyars maintained their positions bare-headed, flanked by six lackeys clothed in green velvet with gold trimmings and wearing chains of gold and mantles of scarlet, also trimmed with gold. A crowd of nobles accompanied them close behind the carriage, like an army – Muscovite boyars, lords, officers, and nobles, all with their servants. Finally, the merchants and others came behind. The streets were crowded, and, as everyone was turned out in his best attire, they looked like beds filled with the most beautiful and varied flowers.

When the tsarina, coming through the third city wall, reached the great square before the Kremlin, musicians posted on platforms built for this purpose and on the city gates made the air ring with the sound of their flutes, trumpets, and many kettledrums.[140]

The princess wore a dress of white satin in the French manner, sparkling with jewels and pearls. Across from her sat two old Polish countesses of her family. After her came several carriages filled with ladies and girls of noble lineage. These carriages, their floors supported by gilded pillars, were magnificent, and nearly every one had a team of six or eight horses. Thus the procession entered the Kremlin. There, the carriages were unhitched and the ladies taken away to the lodgings assigned to them. A number wept bitterly on parting from the bride, who was conducted to the convent of the Ascension where the old tsarina, Dmitry's mother, lived. Dmitry himself hastened incognito to bid her welcome.

Then they all went to their own lodgings. The people were notified that the princess would be lodged in this convent until she had learned the Muscovite usages. They said this to make her popular, but I believe that Dmitry taught her something quite different.[141]

For all the time I was in Moscow, I made great efforts to procure a faithful representation of the city, but had never been able to obtain one. There are no painters in this country; nor would they be held in esteem, seeing that nobody has any knowledge of the arts. In fact there are some sculptors and fashioners of idols [godemaekers], but I would never have dared propose to any of them that he do me a drawing of the town, because they would have quickly seized me and delivered me over for torture, thinking that in making such a request I must be contemplating treason. This people is so suspicious in this regard that nobody would have been so bold as to undertake the task. At this time, there was a gentleman in Moscow who had received a leg wound in the battle of Kromy that confined him to his house. Having a great passion for drawing, he had in his service a sculptor of idols who taught him to draw, and he produced, among other things, a view of Moscow done in pen. The merchant at whose house I learned business knew this gentleman, and would send me to his house sometimes with damascene cloth or satin. Frequently, however, the old soldier quizzed me on the customs and religion of my country, and about our princes and statesmen. I gave him the best information on these points, and also a gift of several engravings representing the battles of His Excellency our prince, such as the battle of Tournhout[142] and the Flanders campaigns, with sieges of towns. He found this present so agreeable and astonishing that he did not know what he could offer me in return to express his gratitude. 'Ask me whatever you want,' he said, 'and I will give it to you. And if I can render you some service by my credit at the court of Moscow, do not hesitate to ask.' In his enthusiasm, he called his wife and showed her to me. This lady gave me an embroidered handkerchief. The greatest honour the Muscovites think they can do anyone is to show them their wives, who live secluded in private apartments where nobody can see them. But since he very much liked to have me by him because of the accounts I gave him of all I could find out, and as he wanted very much to offer me something in return, I was so bold as to ask him for a view of the city of Moscow. On hearing this, he swore that if I had asked for one of his best horses he would have given it me more willingly. But as he considered me his best friend, he gave me this drawing, on condition that I swore I would never say anything about it to a Muscovite, and never reveal the name of him from whom I had it. 'For,' he said, 'I would be in danger of my life if anyone knew that I had made a drawing of the town of Moscow, and that I had given it to a foreigner. I would be killed as a traitor.' I have placed the drawing here in this book, done by pen with such exactitude that truly, you have the town before your eyes. I offer it from the bottom of my heart, with this little work, which is but a trifle, to my best friend after almighty God, with the urgent plea not to destroy it, but rather accept it as a token of the tender affection and devotion I bear to your worthy person, which may God keep always in good health and grant long life and eternal salvation.

Dmitry's anger with the Polish ambassador

During the three or four days that followed the entry of the future tsarina, the city of Moscow was extremely quiet. The Polish ambassador had had an audience with the tsar and bestowed presents of two fine horses, plate, gilt cups, and a large, magnificent hound. After his address he delivered the king's letter, in which Dmitry was given no title but Grand Prince of Muscovy. Seeing this, Dmitry flew into a rage and returned the missive, whereupon the ambassador replied on the king's behalf that the tsar would first have to conquer the empires of the Tatars and the Turks, and then he would be given the titles of tsar and autocrat, but not before. This reply so irritated Dmitry that he would have thrown his sceptre at the ambassador's head in his rage had he not been restrained by the lords and the palatine of Sandomierz, who trembled for fear of disaster. The ambassador went away, and was confined to his house until the day of the marriage.[143]

To the titles his predecessors as sovereigns of Moscow had assumed, Dmitry had added that of 'monarch' and the adjective 'invincible.' It was the Lithuanian lords who had suggested this idea, as, out of hatred of the king of Poland, they hoped for a chance to submit that kingdom to Dmitry's yoke. This was their desire, but not the will of God.

Early in the morning of 6 May, a fine carriage came to take the tsarina from the convent and conduct her to the magnificent lodgings that had been prepared for her. Before the banqueting hall within the Kremlin, scaffolding had been put up for the trumpeters, flute players, and drummers. The musketeers, to the number of eight thousand, received the order to remain under arms in the castle for the duration of the wedding feast, and the greater part of the German life guards and halberdiers were on guard there under their captains with loaded pistols.

Celebration of Dmitry's marriage in Moscow

On 8 May all the bells pealed, all work was suspended by order, and everyone was dressed again in his best; the magnates, the nobles, and the young gentlemen rode to the palace once more in their ceremonial costumes of cloth of gold, embroidered with pearls and laden with gold chains. Heralds announced everywhere that this day was one of celebration; that the tsar and Grand Prince of all the Russias was celebrating his marriage and would show himself in all his splendour. The Kremlin was crowded with lords and nobles, both Muscovite and Polish. The latter were nearly all wearing sabres according to their custom, and they were accompanied by infantrymen with muskets. The fortress was surrounded by eight hundred 'streltsy,' or musketeers, in uniforms of crimson cloth and armed with long muskets.

All along the road the tsar was to travel from his palace to the various churches he would visit they had spread a carpet of crimson cloth, on which were stretched yet two more thicknesses of cloth of gold. The patriarch and the bishop of Novgorod, clothed in white robes decorated with pearls and jewels, were the first to descend, carrying between them a high imperial crown which they placed in the church of the Virgin. They then carried into the same church a ewer and basin of gold. Straightway afterwards Tsar Dmitry came, preceded by a young gentleman bearing the imperial sceptre and orb, and another young gentleman, named Kurliatev [Coerletof], holding a large bared sword right before the tsar. The tsar could hardly move under the weight of pearls, diamonds, and gold that covered his vestments; he was led by Prince Fyodor Ivanovich Mstislavsky and Fyodor Nagoi, and wore on his head the great imperial crown sparkling with rubies and diamonds. After him came his bride, the princess of Sandomierz, her hair parted, all covered with gold, pearls, and precious stones. These cost fabulous sums. The little diadem garnished with gems that adorned her brow was alone worth 70,000 rubles, or 490,000 florins, according to the estimate I myself heard from the imperial jeweller. She was escorted by the wives of the two lords who conducted the tsar.

Before the emperor, on either side, walked four men in white costumes bordered with pearls, each carrying a large gilded battleaxe on his shoulder. These four men, along with the sword-bearer, halted at the door of the church and waited there for the tsar to emerge. The marriage ceremony was conducted in the Muscovite rite by the patriarch of Moscow and the bishop of Novgorod in the presence of all the clergy and the Russian and Polish lords.

Oh, how vexed the Muscovites were when they saw the Poles enter the church with plumes on their heads and weapons in their hands! Had anyone stirred them up, they would have thrown themselves upon these miscreants and killed every one of them, for they regard their churches as profaned by the presence of pagans. It is thus, by the way, that they call all other peoples of the earth, in the heart-felt conviction that they alone have the right to call themselves Christians, for they are most fanatical about their religion.

The Kremlin exits were guarded by numerous sentries. A single gate was opened, but only the Poles, the great lords, the nobles, and the foreign merchants could go in. The common people, small and great, were sent outside, and this stirred up great indignation. They saw that the tsar himself had ordered things so. This is quite possible, as he feared an invasion of the Kremlin.[144]

Returning from the church after the marriage ceremony, the procession of lords marched off. Bogdan Sutupov, the chancellor Afanasy Vlasiev, and Shuisky scattered handfuls of gold pieces several times under the feet of the tsar and his wife, who were holding hands. The tsarina also now wore a great imperial crown on her head. The couple were conducted to their apartments by the whole procession of lords and ladies, both Polish and Muscovite.

The gold scattered was of the most refined quality. The pieces were of various denominations, ranging from reichsthalers down to small pfennigs.

As soon as the procession had entered, a deafening thunder of kettledrums, trumpets, and flutes was heard. Then the tsar and his wife were led to the imperial throne, all inlaid in silver, which is mounted by steps. The tsarina placed herself on an identical throne beside him. Before them stood a table. At the foot of the throne were several other tables. The lords and ladies came to sit there and they were served a splendid feast. A richly ornamented stage had been set up, where an orchestra of musicians played all manner of instruments. These musicians had been brought from Poland by the palatine of Sandomierz. They were Polish, Italian, German, and Brabançon. Their sweet harmonies added joy to the feast.

That day did not pass, however, without many mishaps which seemed of evil omen to some. The tsar lost a diamond worth 30,000 reichsthalers that he wore on his finger, and the palatine of Sandomierz was taken ill at table, and had to be taken back to his palace by carriage. Finally, in the Kremlin itself, a Pole was wounded by musketeers. These auguries occasioned much foreboding, but no one said anything.

The next day, a Friday, was the great feast of the Muscovites, that of St Nicholas. They would not hold a wedding feast on that day for all the gold in the world. Imagine the indignation of the people when they saw the tsar flaunt his contempt for a usage as sacred as a law in going so far as to profane this solemn day. This conduct was bitterly censured.[145] There was yet one more reason for discontent. Several burghers, and even some people of quality, had been rudely abused and pushed back for trying to get into the Kremlin and catch a glimpse of the interior. They were greatly angered that the tsar should have more regard for a crowd of worthless Poles than he had for them, natives of Moscow. All this was a factor in favour of the conspirators' achieving their aims without great peril, and they seized their opportunity.

More than three thousand men had come to Moscow from Novgorod and elsewhere with concealed weapons. They desired to avenge the fatherland, and they had agreed on a signal to begin the attack.

The third day after the wedding, all the lords, bishops, chancellors, officers, and merchants from every nation were admitted to present their homage to the tsarina, kiss her hand, and offer her presents, which were accepted. She invited them on her and her husband's behalf to a feast that day. At this meal, all the foreigners were seated at their tables so that their faces were towards the tsar, while most of the Muscovites were seated facing the other way.[146] Moreover the former were served on golden dishes, the latter on silver. Neither the tsar nor the tsarina ate in the presence of their guests. They dined in their apartments in the company of a number of lords, and they were very joyous.

On the Sunday, the Polish king's ambassador hinted to the tsar that he wished to receive the same honours that had been rendered the Muscovite envoy in Poland. He was told that he would be given precedence after the palatine of Sandomierz, but he would not accept this. He claimed the right to sit at the tsar's table. He was invited to the feast and placed beside the tsar, but particular care had been taken so that he sat at a small table, though he believed that he was sitting at the imperial table. He was so satisfied that he came with even more costly presents than he had brought before.[147]

On the Monday and Tuesday, all kinds of instruments and drums and trumpets were played incessantly. The program for these days had also included a hunt in the Kremlin and a mock attack on a fortress prepared for the occasion, but because of various ill omens seen in the heavens and other inexplicable things, these diversions did not take place. The marriage did not proceed as it should have. Everything went from then on in so cold and dry a manner as to astound everyone.

Celestial apparitions in Moscow

As to the signs appearing in the heavens, I can say that I saw them myself, as did my employer – with whom I lived amid all his family – and also two or three Muscovites. Prodigious as they were, these signs were seen by many as insignificant. Here is what they were: at about four in the afternoon the sky was blue, without a trace of cloud; all of a sudden, a mass of clouds was seen descending from the Polish side, like unto a mass of mountains and caverns, which no one had seen coming up on the horizon; they appeared to have fallen from the vault of heaven. We first distinguished a lion, perfectly delineated, which disappeared after advancing. We then saw a camel which also disappeared, and, thirdly, a giant, who disappeared striding into a cavern. After this we distinctly perceived, afloat in the sky, a town with walls and towers from which smoke was billowing, and then this vision dissipated like the rest; but they had offered images of such perfection that the most skilled painter could not have depicted them better in his art. Some people who had witnessed them were filled with fear, but others mocked openly.

On the Thursday, new rumours reached Dmitry's ears through either warnings from his adherents or reports from halberdiers, who were by no means certain of what was going on, but had noticed something nevertheless. On this advice, strong guards were mounted and the Poles ordered to keep watch all night.[148] Aiming to intimidate the people of Moscow, these Poles were continually discharging their weapons.

Several thousand of the conspirators also stood armed watch that night, ready to strike their blow. Seeing that their plan had come to light and that they were by no means sure of success, they halted for fear of shedding too much blood and remained quiet, hiding their weapons. The next day the guard was reduced again, but all the shops refused to sell powder and lead to the Poles.[149] The merchants pretended not to have any, whereas they could have given the Poles as much as they wanted. A remarkable calm reigned in the city. It seemed even quieter than usual. This alarming symptom should have been a warning to those who were losing themselves in pleasure, voluptuousness, and drunkenness, with no care for the people, but by God's will they had become blind and deaf. They esteemed the Muscovites less than dogs, and abandoned themselves to all their disordered fantasies.

That very evening several Poles had tried to snatch the wife of a great lord from her carriage and do violence to her, despite the servants accompanying her. But the burghers sounded the tocsin and rescued the lady unharmed from the hands of her ravishers, who took flight.[150]

At the sound of the bells ringing at an unusual hour, I imagined that a fire had broken out somewhere, and ran to the roof of the house to see where the mishap had occurred, but I did not see or hear anything. Suddenly, looking towards the moon, I noticed that it was all the colour of blood. At this sight, I was seized with fear, and made haste that very night to hide our furniture and possessions. A number of other people did the same, burying their jewels, money, and precious objects. We shut our doors tightly for fear of misfortune, and set a close watch. Nobody had the slightest inkling of a conspiracy that involved thousands, and even the common people knew absolutely nothing about it.

The same night, joy reigned in the chambers of the tsar. The Polish lords were busy dancing with great ladies. The tsarina, with her maids of honour, was preparing disguises for a masquerade that she was planning to offer the tsar as an entertainment on the Sunday following.[151] In the midst of the feast, no one was thinking of misfortune. However, the proverb is still true: 'Extremes of joy are jostled by grief.'

Dmitry is killed in Moscow with about seven hundred Poles

On Saturday morning, 17 May, towards the second hour of the day, a fearful pealing of bells resounded, first in the Kremlin and then through all the town. At the same time there was a tumult of horsemen riding armed and at a gallop towards the castle, and the cry the heralds of the conspiracy sounded in all the streets: 'Brothers, the Poles want to assassinate the tsar! Do not let them into the Kremlin!' By this ruse, the Poles, seized with terror and armed in their houses, were pinned down by the multitude outside, eager to pillage and murder all of them. Even those found on the street in Polish garments were massacred relentlessly. When a patrol of Polish cavalry appeared in a street, they were barricaded at once by the closing of the barriers, where there were such, so that the horses could not get out. In streets without barriers, they made barricades of beams, the same that are used in this town to pave all the roads. Thus, there was a terrible massacre of all the Poles who could be found. The crowd also broke into a great number of Polish houses. Anyone trying to defend himself was run through with the sword. As for those who surrendered, almost all were spared, but they were so thoroughly plundered that they were not even left with shirts. The riot spread through the town; the entire population, including young boys and children, began running through the streets with bows, muskets, axes, sabres, pikes, and clubs, crying out and howling: 'Death to the Poles! Let us take all they have!'

It was then that the conspirators killed the tsar in his apartments. Here is how this event took place. They had bribed a chancellor who was a saint in their eyes. He was very zealous in their religion, drank no strong liquor, and ate very sparingly; he was called Timofei Osipov. On that day – it was the day of the solemn oath with the kissing of the cross, which was sworn to the tsarina as sovereign lady of Moscow – this person was to present himself to the people and speak against this inauguration. The conspirators were to profit from this incident to attack the person of Dmitry. This Timofei had taken the sacrament twice, and receiving absolution from the priest or confessor, he had also been blessed in a great ceremony as a hero going to his death for his country and the well-being of his fellow citizens. In the morning, he had said his last farewell to his wife and children, who understood nothing about it, though his wife believed that he wanted to enter a monastery.

After he had done all this, Timofei went resolutely to the palace and entered the hall where the oath was to be administered. There, he cried that he recognized Dmitry, not as the tsar's son, but as an unfrocked monk named Grishka Otrepiev who had won the throne of Moscow only through the agency of the Devil; he held this throne unjustly. As for the tsarina, he refused to swear her allegiance. She was a lady Jesuit, a pagan whose presence had profaned the sanctuaries of Moscow, and it was she who was the cause of the country's ruin. He would have said more had he not been struck dead on the spot and thrown through a window. Thereupon, the conspirators began sounding the tocsin and mounted hurriedly, their muskets loaded, by all the staircases at the same time.[152] These conspirators were for the most part Muscovite lords and merchants. A great number came from Novgorod, Pskov, and other towns. For a long time, they had been coming secretly to Moscow to forward their design. The first thing they did was attack the halberdiers guarding the entrance hall of the palace. They disarmed them and took them prisoner. They were all shut in a room on the ground floor and threatened with death if they dared utter a single sound. At that moment, precisely half the guard were absent from their posts. Half the men had gone one way, half the other. In the end, God let all this happen to them through their own fault, for they could have kept a close watch. The conspirators spread out everywhere, killing anyone who resisted, and moved on the tsar's apartments firing musket shots.

Meanwhile, Dmitry had come out of his apartments, demanding to know what was happening and what was the cause of the tocsin and uproar. Those he questioned were seized with such terror that they did not know what to reply. Then he called for his sword, but he who was responsible for presenting it to him had already managed to escape, taking the sword with him. Sensing danger, the tsar seized a halberd and rushed into his apartments, closing and barring the doors. Hearing shots being fired through the windows and axe blows striking the door, he fled from room to room by secret passages, and finally leapt into a small room which was on a lower floor than the other apartments. While jumping, he was caught in the arms of a Livonian gentleman called Fürstenberger who was trying to save him, for he was already spitting blood, but this gentleman was killed.[153] Dmitry succeeded in reaching a bath-house through an alley. He hoped from there to gain the outside by a hidden door and lose himself in the crowd, which was already rushing in hundreds up the back stairs. If he had been able to get himself into the crowd he would doubtless have escaped, and the townspeople would have massacred the lords and conspirators; but, knowing nothing of the affair, the people believed that the tsar was being attacked by the Poles, and that the conspirators were trying to save him. That was what they had been told so that they would pin the Poles down in the city. The conspirators pursued Dmitry into the secret passage, where he was trapped. They laid hold of him and quickly dragged him out, firing on him and striking him with their sabres and axes, for fear that he might escape again.

It is said that the lords who held him still questioned him on certain matters; but that was impossible, because they did not have time to pause. As soon as Dmitry saw the people, he cried: 'Bring me on to the square, and listen to me! I will tell you who I am!' Then the conspirators, for fear of the people pressing about them, killed him in haste, shouting: 'It is a renegade monk, and not Dmitry! He has admitted it himself!' They tied a strap to the corpse's feet, dragged it naked as a dog out of the Kremlin, and threw it on the square. Some conspirators went behind and ahead of this sorry procession, carrying masks, and calling to the people: 'Here are the gods whom he adored!' Now these masks had been taken from the apartments of the tsarina, where they had been prepared for the masquerade that was to have been held for the tsar's entertainment. Not knowing what these objects were, the Muscovites believed, and still believe today, that these masks were really Dmitry's gods.

Various opinions concerning his death

Some claim that he was still in bed, and that he was killed fleeing in his night-shirt; but this version cannot be believed, for why would they have slit that chancellor's throat? They would have said that the chancellor was killed during the evening, but that is false, because I have the facts as I have reported them from eyewitnesses who were with the conspirators.

Meanwhile, the tsarina was half dead of fright. A crowd of people surrounded her apartments, breaking and pillaging everything they could find. A gentleman, one of the conspirators, came to her and conducted her to a vaulted chamber built of solid walls, where he placed a strong guard around her and some of her companions. As for the maids of honour, they underwent the most extreme outrages. They were all stripped naked, each of the conspirators taking from them his part of the booty, and having one of them as his share. They were led through the streets of the city like lambs by wolves, suffering all manner of humiliation. Some were even sold by their enraged ravishers, many of whom killed one another over the spoils.

It was amazing to see the mob carrying off what they had pillaged from the Poles – beds, bedding, mattresses, clothing, horses, harness, saddles, and furniture. It looked like the salvage from a conflagration.

At the beginning of the uprising, Basmanov was still in his bath. It is said that he had spent the night with two women, and, according to the Russian custom, was purifying himself in the bath-house.

As soon as he heard the tocsin, he hastily dressed only in his undergarments, jumped on his horse, and, telling ten or twelve armed servants with loaded muskets to follow him, went off at the gallop towards the Kremlin. He believed that conflict had erupted between the Poles and the Muscovite lords, and had no suspicion of what was really going on. Reaching the palace, he came to the apartments, where a gentleman from Novgorod began to abuse him, calling him a traitor and the tsar a renegade monk. He made ready to reply, but was not given the chance. Ten swords struck him at once, and he fell. His body was thrown outside next to a wall, and dragged on the square. There, he was laid on a bench at the feet of the body of the Renegade Monk, or Dmitry, which lay on a table, and they were left there exposed to the view of the entire populace.[154]

The house of the palatine of Sandomierz was guarded all round by soldiers and safeguarded along with those within. The same was done with the palace of the king's ambassador. The palatine of Sandomierz had sent a messenger to the ambassador, warning him to remain calm, and gave the same advice to his own son, who was in his lodgings surrounded by three hundred armed cavalrymen.[155]

After Dmitry's death, the principal lords went about the town on horseback, urging the people to cease their murdering and looting. It was by their efforts that the three aforesaid dwellings were saved. They exhorted the Poles, who in some houses were under arms, to lay them down so that they would not be massacred. The majority followed this advice. In the street called the Pokrovka there was one house with a great number of armed Poles putting up a vigorous defence. The chief of the conspirators, Vasily Shuisky, went and begged them to cease fighting so that the people's fury and bloodletting could abate; but before obeying, they insisted that he guarantee their lives by oath, and he did so. They were still not reassured, so they sent one of their number through the door to parley with him. Shuisky threw himself around his neck, embraced him, and swore that nobody would do him any harm. Then peace was made, and the populace went elsewhere.

All houses offering resistance were sacked and their defenders massacred. Those who surrendered saved their lives, but they were completely despoiled. Nearly all the musicians were killed; a Polish lord who had been present at the wedding feast given in Poland by the Muscovite ambassador perished with all his family; many other lords and gentlemen lost their lives.

In the palace where the lord Wisniowiecki resided, they fought valiantly to the end. It was there that this lord and his people had assembled after the invasion of the Kremlin by the conspirators. This palace was situated in a vast meadow close to the Neglinnaia river. It was quickly surrounded by thousands of besiegers, who began to fire, pillage, and loot the kitchens, the stables, and the apartments on the ground floor. The Poles, who occupied the upper stories, put up a stiff resistance, and fired on the Muscovites from the upper windows, killing a great number of them. From time to time, they threw precious garments and fistfuls of gold from the windows. The besiegers would fall in masses upon these spoils, and then the Poles would let fly with terrible volleys into the middle of these crowds, slaughtering them like flocks of birds or wild beasts. Three times, they pretended to be on the verge of surrender. Deceived by this feint, the Russians rushed in hundreds on to the staircases to begin the pillage, and crowded together in the vestibule of the upper storey, which the Poles had opened. As soon as the room was filled, forty or fifty muskets were discharged all at once into the crowd of besiegers, who fell and rushed down the stairs like rats being chased from a granary. Such was the ardour of the assailants, inspired by hope of pillage, that they went to fetch artillery from the ramparts. They trained cannon on the building and fired at their own people, who were still blocking the staircase. The fight lasted a long time.

At length the lords arrived, and by their entreaties and supplications persuaded both sides to lay down their arms. More than three hundred Muscovites had lost their lives there, and a great number had been wounded. The Poles suffered no more than two or three fatalities. Thus, after this great frenzy in Moscow, the killing and pillaging ceased.[156] Several persons became wealthy by buying up articles looted by the rioters, who were for the most part the scum of the earth, scoundrels and thieves, a class quite numerous in this country. Orders were given at once that all the objects were to be brought to the treasury in the Kremlin so that they could be divided up, but very few paid any attention to that order. The horses were nearly all returned, however, probably because nobody knew how to conceal them and they would have been recognized straight away. Some carriages were also returned. As for jewels, money, clothing, or furniture, the looters had hidden all these safely away, and they did not reappear.

Towards the afternoon, the people's frenzy abated, thanks to the lords' intervention. The people were satisfied; they had wreaked their vengeance on the Poles, whom they regarded as their enemies. They were in great ecstasy at the revolution, and considered its authors to be the saviours of the country and the sanctuaries of Moscow. Strong guards were set everywhere, the tranquillity reigned in the capital once again. The corpses were gathered up; there were about eight hundred on the Muscovite side and fifteen hundred on the Polish side. Among the latter were a number of lords and young gentlemen; their bodies, pierced by blows and despoiled, were left in the streets three days, along with those of Dmitry and Basmanov. The Russians milled around these cadavers and flung insults and anathemas at them as if they could have heard. Among the Poles, the most prominent to lose their lives were Sklinski, Wonsowicz, Pomecki, Lipnicki, Iwanicki, Bal Jan Pologowski, and many other noblemen, several of whom had jumped from the Kremlin walls into the river, where they were pierced by arrows. Buczynski had hidden under the plants and trees of a garden behind the tsar's palace. He was discovered there and saved, along with several others in the ambassador's house.

Innocent people killed in the massacre

Most to be pitied were those who had come to Moscow for the sole purpose of selling their merchandise, several of whom were taken for Poles simply because they were dressed in the Polish style. Thus were Nemiecki [Neueskij], Volsky, Andreas Nathan, Nicholas Demist, of whom I have already spoken, and who had brought with them such precious treasures, despoiled of everything, and lost thousands of florins. When they went to the Shuisky regime to claim payment for objects they had sold to the tsar, they were told that they should claim their money from the Renegade Monk with whom they had been dealing. They added that the treasury was empty; Dmitry had drained it completely to send to Poland. This was the only answer they were prepared to give. A number of merchants from other countries suffered similar misfortunes. The people of Philip Holbein of Augsburg were mortally wounded, having first been plundered of everything they had. A Milanese,

Ambrogio Cellari, utterly looted by these scoundrels, still gave them all the gold, silver, and effects he possessed. He was left with only a shirt to cover his nakedness, but the brigands insisted that he take off this last garment, and when he refused, they stuck a knife in his belly. He fell dead to the ground, but was not found among the dead, however diligently they sought him.

A Brabançon named Jacques Marot was also murdered, but his body was found. He could then be buried, with a number of others, by permission of the new court, after the riot ended.[157]

Dmitry's appearance

Dmitry was a strong and well-built man. He was clean-shaven, with solid shoulders and a large nose, beside which a small blue mole was noticeable. His face was broad, his tint brownish, and his mouth large. He was endowed with extraordinary strength in his hands. Brave and hardy, he loved to see blood flow, but did not let this tendency show very much. There was not a lord or chancellor in Moscow who had not seen proof of the violence of his character. He had strange caprices. Thus, he wanted to launch an attack on Narva in midwinter. And he would have done so had the lords not restrained him, arguing the unseasonableness of the venture. We have seen that in his life he sent great quantities of munitions and provisions to a town named Elets, allegedly to prepare a campaign against Tatary; but his secret design was really to attack Poland, conquer it, and drive out its king, or else capture him by treachery, and make Poland subject to Muscovy.

His undertakings and great designs: his plan to change the religion of Muscovy and destroy all the noble families

In this, he was following the advice of a number of Poles – Sandomierski, Wisniowiecki, and others. He also contemplated some ambitious and extraordinary enterprises. He had at first resolved to kill all the Muscovite lords and great families. Having fixed a day for the execution of this plan, he secretly brought a large quantity of artillery to a place outside the town, with the aim, he said, of staging a mock battle after the marriage celebrations in the presence of all the lords, in the guise of a military parade; but he had given secret instructions to the Polish lords, his army commanders, Basmanov, and his other adherents. Each of them knew where he was to be, either in the town or in the Kremlin, and exactly whom he was responsible for killing. He himself was to be outside the city with all the artillery, Polish troops, and his supporters. If this attempt had gone according to plan, who would have been able to offer him any resistance in Moscow, since all the means for defending the town were in his possession? But God would not permit it, and gave the Muscovites the strength to destroy him who had conceived it.[158]

Only Buczynski had the courage to dissuade Dmitry from his project, pointing out to him how contrary to God's will it would be, and advising him to draw the magnates to him by tokens of favour, giving them functions in which they could not become too powerful. With the aid of time, he would thus be reconciled with all hearts; but he, who knew the Muscovite character better, replied that these people could not be governed by gentle methods; rather, the most rigorous means had to be used with them. This is true, for a Muscovite must be held by fear and led by force. As soon as he is allowed his own will a little, he does no good. Dmitry thought it best to dispose of the magnates first so that he could then reign uncontrolled over a wicked and ignorant people, doing anything he desired with them.

This proved to be ample justification for the Muscovites' actions as far as all the foreign rulers were concerned, for after Dmitry's death, written evidence of his plans was found – lists of those who were to be killed and the names of the Poles who would replace them in their offices. These documents were read out to the people, who thereby felt all the more joy and security in what they had just accomplished. Copies were sent to Poland and other foreign powers in order to make these facts known to all.

There is no doubt that if these plans of Dmitry and the Jesuits had succeeded, much harm would have befallen the country. Much harm would also have been done to the whole world through the machinations of the court of Rome, of which Dmitry had been the mere instrument. But God, who rules all, overturned their designs, for which all true believers should render him thanks.

Although he was a hero and a warrior, Dmitry was a very dissolute man. He abused innocent young girls every day, and got a number of young nuns with child. He also had a shameful passion for a young gentleman of the powerful family of Khvorostinin [Guorostinin].[159] He conferred great honours on this conceited young man, who was full of arrogance because he was allowed to do anything he pleased.

Some persons flee; others are arrested

After the tsar's assassination, when the tidings of it spread, Mikhail Molchanov, one of his secret counsellors in both his acts of tyranny and his debauches, took flight and went to Poland. After his departure the disappearance of a sceptre and a golden crown was noticed, and there was no doubt that he had taken these objects with him.

Another of these intimate counsellors, named Yury Mikulin, fled on one of the tsar's horses but was captured at Viazma,[160] about six miles from Moscow on the road to Poland. Several Polish servants, appropriating their masters' horses, took flight as the rioting began. They had only their bare sabres to defend them, and as they did not know the roads, they were lost in the countryside. Some of the nobles set out in pursuit and attacked them vigorously. Nearly all these unfortunates were left on the road, because the nobles, being armed with pistols, killed them from a distance. The latter still lost 11 men, even though they were very numerous.

The English merchants, and we also, were not without anxiety in the midst of a riot in which the tsar's very doctors were despoiled; but God surrounded us with his protection, and we emerged safe and sound.

When the fury had died down, I ventured out to see the corpses, on which the conspirators were still testing their sabres. The bodies of Dmitry and Basmanov, his favourite, were stretched out on a table where the crowd came to rain insults for three days. However, some people wept on seeing these examples of the inconstancy of human affairs. As for myself, I looked at him with great interest and was able to convince myself that what I saw before me was the same tsar whom I had seen many times, the same who had reigned for a year. It was indeed he, despite the assertions of those who, in this new war, claimed that the true tsar was not assassinated, but another in his place.

Dmitry's corpse is cast into a ditch

I counted his wounds. They were to the number of 21. His skull had been stove in from above, and his brain lay beside him. The following Thursday, the body was thrown into a ditch. As for Basmanov, he was buried by his brother with the permission of the court.[161]

We have said enough about the character of this tsar; but there are those who claim that he was none other than Satan himself – who later, using the same mask and the same name, caused yet further evil, and continues to cause evils that are ten times more terrible than those of the past. Is it not extraordinary, in fact, that they are always occasioned by the same name – Dmitry's? God's justice appears in such diverse and astonishing ways to punish nations and cities. Did not the divine Homer rightly say: 'God looks upon mortal things and punishes justice, and the just deeds of men. Jupiter sees all the actions of men, and punishes the wicked. The immortal gods detest crimes; they love justice and the men who practice it.'[162]

DMITRY THE UNFROCKED MONK

> Tell me your name, hero of this tragedy
> Which covered Muscovy with blood and ruin.
> You did not expect that cruel treatment
> That you made so many others suffer unjustly.
> But once more your name will serve as a banner
> In a struggle, alas! even more murderous.
> And as your name is raised, it seems
> That of your country is daily abased.
> But God, whose puissant eye
> O'ersees men, space and earth,
> Will never permit against his will
> A land to be diminished or o'erthrown.

Dmitry's body is burned

There was a great prodigy the same night Dmitry's body was thrown out. Within a radius of twenty miles from Moscow, all the plants, from blades of grass to trees, were dried up at their tops, as if a fire had passed by. The pine trees, which are always green, winter and summer, had their crowns and sprouts burnt. It was a sad spectacle, and on seeing this prodigy the Muscovites commented that the late tsar had yet again, with Satan's help, sent his spirit on the earth to do evil. To put an end to this, they saw fit to burn his body. They went to dig him up, and at the same time seized the wooden castle he had built on the ice during the winter, called the 'Monster of Hell' by the Russians. They carried it out of the city to the small stream of Kotly, and enclosing the body inside it, burned it completely, and the wind dispersed its ashes.[163]

Vasily Ivanovich Shuisky becomes emperor in Moscow

After that, the Muscovites believed they had done everything possible and won a complete victory, and could live thereafter without fear or care. The magnates elected a tsar from their own number; their choice fell upon Shuisky. They led him on to the square before the assembled people, and their orator cried out that they had just chosen Vasily Ivanovich Shuisky as tsar; that they had not been able to find a better or more worthy man among them. He was a man who many times risked his life for the public good and the country's well-being. Then the orator, addressing the community, asked if they approved the choice they had just made, seeing that the land could not long remain without a sovereign. With one voice, the community shouted that they were completely satisfied, that nobody was more worthy of the throne. Everybody submitted to the newly-elected, and they prostrated themselves at his feet, saying: 'Health and prosperity to Vasily Ivanovich, tsar and Grand Prince of all the Russias!' Then the magnates led him to the church, where thanksgiving was offered to God for the deliverance of the empire.

A great frost came to grip all the country, and destroyed the greater part of the crops. All the Muscovites were full of consternation. Having burned Dmitry's body, they did not know whom to blame for this scourge, and stared at each other, seized with the greatest astonishment.

Tsar Vasily Ivanovich was crowned as his predecessors had been, according to the Muscovite usages, and gold was also strewn under his feet.

On 30 May, the entire community was summoned on to the square. Most of the magnates came, and there ordered the reading of the motives which they thought justified depriving a crowned tsar, the previous sovereign, of his life. These were their arguments.[164]

Accusations against Dmitry

First, he was accused of not having been born of the imperial blood, of being, not the son of Tsar Ivan Vasilievich of blessed memory, but merely a scoundrel and an impostor inspired by Satan. His real name was Grigory Otrepiev, and he had been born at Galich, where his father and mother still lived. His parents were poor people. They had been ordered to appear and had admitted that he was truly their son. They had said, moreover, that after gaining control of the country he had sent emissaries to Galich to seize all the members of his family and throw them in prison, where they were narrowly guarded so that they might not divulge the secret of his identity. These unfortunates were about sixty in number.[165] They added also that after his arrival in Russia he had bribed a worthless person, who then claimed to be Grigory Otrepiev and feigned insanity, wandering around in a monk's cowl. After Dmitry's death, this false monk also confessed that he had been paid to play this role. Dmitry had truly been in a monastery in Moscow, and the lords repeated in their proclamation everything I have already reported about his flight into Poland with stolen papers and documents, and the manner in which he said he was the true Dmitry.

Furthermore, some said he was Satan himself, while others said that he was a Pole sent by the machinations of the Jesuits into Muscovy, whose language he had learned, and that he had travelled throughout the land to gather information about the state of the country, learning at the same time, through reading, the peculiarities of its history. After this journey he had returned to Poland, where the Jesuits and their supporters, backed by the pope, had him play the part of the person whose adventures we have recounted. This opinion is very plausible, and a number of people hold it to be the truth.

They also accused him of having been a sorcerer in communication with the Devil. His tutor, a Pole, came to affirm that he was devoted to magic and other occult sciences, and the Muscovites supported this opinion with various conjectures, such as the 'Monster of Hell' he had built, and other fables of the same sort.

Thirdly, they accused him of having been a heretic, because he had not observed their days of rest or their feasts, and did not go to church.[166]

For the fourth charge, they showed the letters addressed by the pope to Dmitry during his reign, letters in which he was warned that it was time to begin work on the reform of the country, building schools for children similar to those in Poland and purging the churches of altars and images of the Greek religion in order to sanctify them by Roman Catholic images with the help of people sent for that purpose, and other such abominations.[167]

For the fifth charge, they brought forward the agreement made in Poland between Dmitry and the palatine of Sandomierz, whereby the latter was to obtain the principality of Pskov with all its dependencies, and also the land of Novgorod; and his son, the tsarina's brother, the whole land of Siberia[168] and the Samoyed, with all the adjacent territory. Dmitry had also promised to cede the principality of Smolensk to some Polish lords who would have governed it jointly with the Jesuits, but to do this he had to begin by ridding himself of the magnates of the country, as we have related.[169]

Sixthly, they accused him of not having had the least regard for them, and allowing them to be the butt of the injuries and insults of the Poles without being able to obtain justice. On the contrary, he himself had added to these slights, raining blows on the magnates of the country and sending them to die in exile.[170]

Their seventh complaint was directed against his extravagances and excessive expenditures, made without taking the slightest account of the country's resources. He had had a throne erected that was far greater than those of any of the preceding tsars, and had a sceptre, crown, and orb borne before him, and also a great sword. He rewarded his halberdiers, life guards, and captains as richly as lords, without at all considering that he might drain the treasury dry.

They accused him under the eighth heading of having been the most corrupt and debauched of men. He did not even respect the sacred character of virgins consecrated to God, and dishonoured a great number of them in the convents. He also indulged in unnatural vice. He celebrated his wedding on one of the feasts of St Nicholas in the springtime; that was a great crime in their eyes, for they hold this saint to be almost as important as Christ, and honour him ten times as much. He often borrowed thousands of crowns from the treasuries of the holy monasteries without giving any of them back. Many times, he had caused priests, monks, and other holy persons to be beaten with rods. Now this was a treatment to which they had never been subjected. He had dismissed and sent into exile the venerable patriarch of Moscow, replacing him with a wicked and impious man, and this with no regard for the rights of election of the bishops and clergy.[171]

Under the ninth heading, they accused him of having provoked the appearance of an impostor who was to come and lend him assistance in case of danger. This impostor, with a large party of Cossacks, had descended on to the banks of the Volga, where he wrought great depredations, plundering loaded boats which came from Astrakhan and causing millions in losses. He claimed to be Peter Fyodorovich, a natural son of Tsar Fyodor Ivanovich, even though it was quite certain that this tsar, who had lived like a saint, as we have already said, would never have strayed away from his wife to get bastards by other women.[172]

The tenth heading of the accusation was the invasion of the Poles, and the insolence of these strangers whom he had summoned. They took objects from all the shops without payment, did not tolerate one word from the Russians, and answered them with their swords. If a Russian lodged a complaint he could be certain that he would not obtain justice, but would instead be treated and repulsed like a dog by the wicked judges appointed by Dmitry's will. These Poles pushed their audacity beyond all bounds. In the evenings, in the open streets, they dared attack carriages, and, despite the escorts of footmen, seize the ladies in them, even if they were princesses or boyars' wives. Intolerable affrays often arose from these incidents.

To conclude this catalogue of crimes, the lords affirmed that no matter what person he had been in reality, Dmitry would still have been their tsar had he wished to reign in peace, marry a Muscovite princess, and observe their religion and their laws; but, alas, they did not see that it was all a punishment inflicted on them by heaven for their manifold sins and their wilful hardness of heart, which increased daily.[173]

Civil war

They sent this bill of accusations throughout the country, and in it announced the proclamation of Tsar Vasily Ivanovich Shuisky. All the towns greeted this news with joy, except those where Dmitry had been. These towns headed the opposition, and killed the lords' messengers. Putivl and Elets broke out in open rebellion and began a new civil war.

I will give here a list of the sums Dmitry sent to Poland at the beginning of his reign. This list does not include those used to pay the debts he had incurred there, and which, according to the accusation of the lords, had drained the treasury completely dry. These are the sums of which there is a firm record.

An image of the Holy Trinity, embellished with jewels, which he sent on behalf of his mother to the princess of Sandomierz	fl 14,000
A portable globe	fl 16,000
A necklace	fl 48,000
A large ornament, on which a beast with wings of heliotrope was depicted	fl 12,000
A cup in hyacinth, with a gold handle	fl 32,000
A cup of gold, filled with jewels	fl 26,000
A pelican in vermilion, weighing 50 marks	fl 1,600
A peasant seated on a stag, a piece of gold sold ten years previously to Philip Holbein for	fl 7,000
An ebony clock, from the same	fl 10,000
A ship in vermilion, from the same	fl 5,600

Two birds	fl 2,240
Forty strings of pearls, at 30 crowns an ounce	fl 48,128
Three precious sables	fl 60,000
Twelve lengths of velvet and rich satin	fl 4,000

The ambassador Afanasy Vlasiev, who had been sent into Poland, gave the following presents at Krakow on behalf of his sovereign:

To the town of Krakow, a Persian tapestry, very artistically woven with battle scenes	fl 16,000
Several sables, approximately valued at	fl 14,000
A necklace with a great pendant	fl 38,000
Several sables, on behalf of the dowager tsarina	fl 10,000
Finally, in cash	fl 400,000
Total	fl 754,868
or, in Russian money	130,761 rubles

This figure includes only those gifts we are certain of, and not the many precious things he sent secretly to Poland so that the bride and her suite might make their triumphal entry into Moscow, as we have related earlier.

Later, it was learned that he had sent the crucifix in fine gold commissioned by Tsar Boris to Poland, along with a quantity of goblets, cups, and other rare objects formerly given to the tsars by the shahs of Persia. Beyond these, he did not, of course, forget the pope.[174]

The old tsarina, whom he had called his mother, was able to remain unmolested in her residence. However, they railed against her cruelly for her falsehoods about her putative son; but she said that she had merely acted out of fear, and in her joy at her deliverance from her sad prison she had not known what she was doing. Thus, she was allowed to remain in her former state.

All such Poles as the haiduks, musketeers, and others of inferior rank, since there was no point in keeping them under guard, were disarmed and taken under heavy escort to the frontier, where they were set free. All along the way, there were those who killed or wounded soldiers of the escort, but the culprits paid with their lives for this act of rebellion.

All the lords, nobles, and rich merchants were taken to various towns and narrowly guarded, whether under surveillance or in prison, and they were kept on short rations.

The palatine and his daughter, the former tsarina, with some of their gentlemen to the number of about four hundred, had to report to Yaroslavl on the Volga, where they gave them a residence, setting a strict guard around it. The citizenry were required to reinforce the guard themselves.

His son, the brother of the former tsarina, was conducted with three hundred of his gentlemen to Kostroma, a town also situated on the Volga, where they were closely guarded.[175]

The Moscow palace where the ambassador resided with three hundred men, both of his suite and those who had taken refuge there during the uprising – these had thus fared better than the others – was guarded from view and surrounded by barriers and a rampart of beams, near which sentinels stood watch day and night.

The lord Wisniowiecki of Kiev and his troop of about three hundred men, who had defended themselves so valiantly, as I have reported, were interned in the same fashion.

Food was provided for all these prisoners, but not in sufficient quantities. To buy food, they were frequently obliged to sell some of their effects to the Muscovites at half price.

Severia and the Komaritsk district rise up against Moscow

We have seen earlier that all the towns were happy about the events that had taken place in Moscow with the exception of those bordering on Poland and Tatary. Thus it was that in the lands of Severia and Komaritsk, in the towns of Putivl, Elets, Tula, Kromy, Rylsk, and others of the same order, the emissaries of the lords were put to death. The manifestos of the tsar of Moscow were burned, and he was denounced as a scoundrel and a traitor. The inhabitants of these lands and towns swore an oath to fight to their last drop of blood. They demanded to know why the Muscovites had dared, without consulting them at all, assassinate a crowned tsar for no reason. They drew into their rebellion several other towns, all the region of the Volga, and Astrakhan with its surrounding countryside, and formed a league sworn to avenge Dmitry.

To lead them, they called one Peter Fyodorovich from the Volga, who claimed to be the bastard of Fyodor Ivanovich, as we have seen in the act of accusation against Dmitry. This league possessed munitions and provisions for at least three years and it had powerful artillery, for, as we have related, Dmitry had gathered all this material at Elets in preparation for his war against Tatary. Thus, supplies enough for an army of more than three hundred thousand men fell into their hands, and they were ready to wage war.[176]

New rebellions in Muscovy

Before the outbreak of the revolt, a great army commanded by one of the magnates of the empire, Peter Sheremetev by name, had already been dispatched from Moscow for the Volga and the neighbourhood of Astrakhan. When Sheremetev came near this town, he found the inhabitants in rebellion, and there was disagreement among them, so that he was compelled to withdraw with his troops to an island in the Volga where he was besieged. This island, called Balchik, or Boesan, is three miles from Astrakhan. Almost fifteen hundred merchants from Astrakhan and other towns on the Caspian Sea went there with all they had to take refuge, placing themselves under the protection of Sheremetev's army. They remained for about two years under the most unfortunate conditions, unable to leave as they were under siege by the enemy. They perished in great numbers from sicknesses caused by cold, hunger, and poverty.

The merchants in Saratov, Samara, and several other localities resolved to flee across the country, where they wandered desolately, though some managed to reach Moscow. Seeing Moscow in the grip of internecine warfare, the Nogai defected once again, banded together to the number of thirty 'ulus,' or tribes, each of which could muster thirty thousand men, and began to ravage all the areas they could reach. As for the town of Astrakhan, it was plunged into complete confusion, and people slew each other there.

When news of these events reached Moscow, the people were cast into utter perplexity. The fear was such that everyone longed for death. The tsar desired with all his heart to become a monk and enter a monastery, but the magnates prevented him. Feeling that if the sovereign took the cowl the throne would pass to the female line, they made vigorous preparation to resist the rebel towns, and put the tsar's own brothers, Dmitry and Ivan Shuisky, in command of the army, along with young Skopin and a number of other lords and captains. They soon had troops in the field; they told all the towns to furnish their contingents, but from all sides they received the answer that the towns, reduced to the last extremity by previous disasters, no longer had the resources necessary to raise levies of men. However in the long run they amassed a large, but powerless army.

There were a number of foreign officers in Moscow – Germans, Frenchmen, and Scots. Seeing the entire country racked by civil war and apprehensive of disaster, these officers requested leave to return to their respective countries. Through the influence of their friends they obtained their leave, and went by sea.[177] Everybody was surprised to see them go, obtaining leave at a time when their services were so much needed, especially since those who take service in Muscovy are hired only on condition that they stay there all their lives. However, a few remained active. There were even some who defected to the other side, among them a captain called Skotnicki.

Tsar Vasily Ivanovich sent his army, commanded by his two brothers, the young Skopin, and others, against the traitorous rebels, as they were called; but they achieved nothing of importance; instead, they were so badly beaten by the rebels in all encounters that fewer than half returned. Despite these defeats, the tsar succeeded by constraint or friendship in gathering even greater forces, and put a fresh army one hundred and eighty thousand strong in the field under the same generals' leadership.

Fresh wars; the tsar sends his army on campaign against the rebels

In addition, he sent Prince Ivan Mikhailovich Vorotynsky to Elets with a special army that was to seize that town, one of the strongholds of the rebellion, but he was beaten and put to flight and his army was dispersed. Vorotynsky himself escaped with great difficulty, and returned to Moscow.[178]

There were many other encounters, with the rebels always obtaining victory and remaining the masters of the field. They were valiant soldiers, free and independent men, living in a fertile country.[179] During these two years of war, abundant harvests had brought them great wealth, so that they were better provided than their adversaries from the north. Thus, they were always victorious.

Embassy to Poland

The Muscovites sent an embassy to Poland to inform the king of the reasons why Dmitry had been put to death and justify themselves in the only way possible, by saying that in all this blood-letting not one of his subjects, or anyone dear to him, had perished, except a chamberlain and his suite on their way to the wedding at the invitation of the Muscovite ambassador, who were slain in the people's frenzy. They expressed their regrets over this incident. Then they gave the king a list of the prisoners detained in Muscovy.

At the same time, they sought to discover whether the king was sending aid to the rebels and find out about various other matters of concern to their country. But before they could be heard, or obtain an audience, they were turned away at least three times. Finally, the council of Poland saw fit to hear them. The envoys were the boyar Yury Konstantinovich Volkonsky and the secretary Andrei Ivanov.

The Poles complain of the great slaughter of their countrymen in Moscow

The council replied that no help had been given to the rebels, that they did not even know about the troubles, and that the king of Poland had never come to Dmitry's aid. This, moreover, had been amply explained to the ambassadors who had come to Poland previously on Boris's behalf. At that time, the king had had no reason to declare himself against Muscovy or to break the oath he had sworn, but he was repudiating that oath now.

Furthermore, the Muscovites had broken the oath, massacring a great number of innocent Poles, subjects of the king, among these one of the king's chamberlains who had been treacherously invited to a wedding feast only to be assassinated with all his followers. Beyond this, against all the dictates of the law of nations, they were keeping his ambassador prisoner in Moscow. The Poles had sufficient motive, not only to furnish aid to the rebels, but also to march against Muscovy themselves, seeking vengeance for the many injuries they had sustained, now as before.

The envoys made ready to reply to these accusations and offer excuses, but they were ordered out and made prisoner, and were not freed until the next year.

The Muscovites also sent an ambassador to the Crimea to renew the peace treaty and convey the news that Dmitry, the enemy of the Crimeans, had been put to death. This envoy was to recount Dmitry's deeds and crimes and justify to the best of his ability the change that had taken place.

A third embassy was sent to Sweden, carrying letters of friendship and details of Dmitry's death to King Karl. This death gave much joy to King Karl, who, for reasons extraneous to our story and pointless to repeat, had been in great fear of Dmitry. Karl promised, therefore, to come to the aid of the Muscovites in the event of pressing danger. This promise was extremely pleasing to the Muscovites.

The rebels continued masters of the field meanwhile, defeating all sent against them, and luck attended them in more or less the same fashion as it had Dmitry on his entry into Muscovy. All the towns in the land of Severia opened their gates to them and joined their side. A great number of soldiers in the Muscovite army went over to the other camp. These were Germans, Livonians, and Russians. The Germans, all valiant and determined men, were appointed commanders of cavalry, captains, or governors of captured towns, so that they climbed from inferior ranks to the most exalted positions, and even common soldiers almost became kings.

Bolotnikov assumes command of the rebel army

In the rebel army, there was a certain Ivan Isaevich Bolotnikov.[180] In Moscow he had been the serf of the boyar Andrei Teliatevsky, then, fleeing his master's service, had taken refuge with the Cossacks on the steppe. He went on campaign in Hungary and Turkey, and, finally, joined the rebels with a party of ten thousand Cossacks. He was a big, strong, and very courageous man, who distinguished himself in the wars of the Cossacks by his bravery and boldness. Although he was a Muscovite by birth, they appointed him hetman, or chief general, of their army while Peter Fyodorovich was besieged by the Muscovite forces in the town of Tula. Bolotnikov advanced with all his troops as far as Serpukhov, eighteen miles from Moscow, seizing the surrounding countryside, and also Kolomna, a fortress on the Moskva close to the Oka. Taking this town, he camped twelve miles from the capital, facing the Muscovite army.

News of these events struck terror into Moscow. The ramparts were strengthened hastily with artillery to prepare for resistance. They built a barricade of wagons outside the wall. They called up men aged sixteen and over to bear arms against the enemy, and asked for help from all the other towns, which made haste to dispatch daily reinforcements. Once more, the inhabitants took an oath of allegiance to the tsar, swearing to defend him and fight for him as they would for themselves, their wives, and their children. They were well aware that the rebels had resolved not to spare a living soul in Moscow, intent on holding them all responsible for Dmitry's death. Therefore they had to resist to the end.

A new Dmitry appears in the land

Suddenly, a strange rumour ran through the land; God only knows whence it sprang. Dmitry, who was believed to have been assassinated in Moscow, was still alive. A great many people attested to this, even in the capital. The rebels taken prisoner were being brought into the town every day, and thrown by the hundreds, whether innocent or guilty, into the waters of the river. They held to their last breath that Dmitry was not dead, and that he was once again in the field. In short, a new miracle seemed to be occurring. This double resurrection of Dmitry sowed confusion in all minds; no one knew what to say or think; it seemed that everyone was going mad.

Thus, two parties emerged. One affirmed that Dmitry was alive, that he had taken flight two or three days before the revolt, and the conspirators had killed someone in his place without knowing it. The opposing party asserted that the tsar was indeed dead. They had seen for certain that the person killed in Moscow was the same who had given himself out to be Dmitry and reigned under this name for about a year. I am of the latter persuasion. I had often seen him in life, and observed him too carefully after his death to doubt for an instant that they had struck down him whom they wished to kill.

Arguments of those who asserted that Dmitry was still alive, and refutation of these arguments

Those of the rebels and the inhabitants of Moscow who believed in Dmitry's existence alleged the following as proof.

1. The naked body, which had been stretched out on the square for three days, and was held to be Dmitry's, was so covered with wounds and soiled with mud that it was impossible to recognize.
2. The person who had been assassinated had long hair, while the tsar had had his hair cropped since his wedding.
3. Nobody had been able to distinguish on this body the well-known mole at the side of Dmitry's nose, or the birthmark on his left breast, a mark his own secretary, Buczynski, affirmed that he had seen while in the bath-house with the tsar.
4. The corpse had very misshapen toes, with very long nails. They looked more like a peasant's than an emperor's.

5. On the day of the assassination, he who had been struck down cried out that he was not Dmitry. In fact, he was, they say, a damask weaver the tsarina had brought from Sandomierz in Poland, who completely resembled her husband. He had been chosen to lie on the morning of the murder in the imperial bed, wearing the tsar's clothes, or at least to move about thus in the tsar's apartments. Dmitry, they claimed, had already taken flight. The weaver, not knowing all this, believed he was playing this role for a diversion, a wager or masquerade. Thus, when he saw the armed murderers arriving, he cried, 'Ya ne Dmitry! Ya ne Dmitry!' which means, 'I am not Dmitry!' Hearing these words, the conspirators and the lords began striking the harder, saying: 'He now admits he is not Dmitry, the true heir to the throne, but a renegade monk!' Afterwards, they killed him so that he would not escape. But all these details, and others with them, are not credible.

6. They burned the body because there were many reasons why he should not be seen. They should have embalmed him, so that they could show him off as an unimpeachable piece of evidence. Now some people swear that he is alive. They let themselves be put to torture to confess him and die in this belief. A number say that they have seen him with the same sceptre and crown as he had worn in Moscow. Now we have seen that as the riot began, the sceptre and crown, and also three or four of the tsar's horses, had been removed. It was on this fact that they wished with all their hearts to base their belief in his survival.

Against all these assertions, I oppose those which my good sense and humble mind suggest to me, and I think that they will be accepted by those who, like me, believe him to be truly dead. Here they are:

1. When I saw him stretched out on the ground, I recognized him readily, even though he was battered and covered with dust and blood dried by the heat. I recognized him readily from his physiognomy, broad shoulders, and slender build. Thus, I was certain that he was the same person who was called Tsar Dmitry in Moscow in the years 1605 and 1606, and reigned in these two years.

2. As regards his hair, nobody was able to find out for certain whether Dmitry had had it cut or not, for he always had his head covered, and did not take off his hat for anyone, even though everybody uncovered in front of him, as was customary.

3. As for the mole on his face, I noticed it quite distinctly on the body, and a crowd of other people besides myself also noticed it. As for the circumstance of the birthmark on the left breast, I do not know whether its existence was asserted by his secretary. In any case, I did not look for it. But I do not

believe a word of this. The secretary could very well have said it in his own interest rather than in the interest of truth.

4. The story of the deformed toes and the nails being too long is completely childish. It is quite possible that he had not always bothered to have his feet manicured, even though he frequently used the bath. But when he was at the bath-house, he was undoubtedly too busy with the young nuns and girls, who were probably quite unconcerned if his feet were dirty, or his nails long or short.

5. The tale of the weaver is a ridiculous fable, for if Dmitry had known what was going to happen he would have taken flight well beforehand and in quite a different manner, and he would not have failed to warn his friends of it. With all the power in his own hands until his last hour, he would have been perfectly capable of seizing all the conspirators and thus preventing the catastrophe. Also, would his Poles have been sound asleep? Would they not have been on their guard? It is quite true that the sceptre, the crown, and the tsar's four horses were removed, but is this at all surprising? The palace was open to everyone, and in the fury of the uprising everything was taken that could be removed, from the imperial palace as from the lodgings of the Poles, and some of the objects of which we speak are nothing in comparison with what was pillaged elsewhere in jewels, clothes, and precious furniture. There was enough for a figure a thousand times greater.

6. They burned the body; they say it would have been better to have embalmed it. But how? Would they have embalmed one whom they regarded as an impostor and a scoundrel? Why should they render him this honour? Besides, who was expecting this catastrophe? If they burned him, it was in accordance with the wishes of the people who cried that they wanted to see him reduced to ashes because his spirit was still casting spells, as witnessed by the drying up of the crops around Moscow, a scourge of which they accused him as the cause.

Now it is true that the rebel prisoners maintained to their deaths that they had seen him in person, carrying the same sceptre and wearing the same crown that they had formerly seen him wear at Moscow, and it is quite true that neither punishment nor torture succeeded in extracting any testimony to the contrary from these wretches. But what proof can we draw from that? It would be easy to find any number of men whose faces resemble Dmitry's. For my part, I saw at least ten after his death. Several of the tsar's intimate circle succeeded in escaping from Moscow during the uprising; they were quite capable of creating a new Dmitry, for in these kinds of affairs people have recourse to all manner of fraud; however, we must accept the role of Satan in all this. It is he, very likely, who must have obtained permission from God almighty to punish this land for the many and enormous sins it is constantly committing, and in this he is much aided by the rabble of Jesuits, who are the Demon's acolytes.

Resolution in Moscow on how to destroy the false belief in Dmitry

The tsar and his council discussed at length by what means the false and insane belief in Dmitry's existence was to be driven from the people's mind. After long deliberation, they resolved to send somebody to Uglich with the responsibility of burying there a young boy resembling in every respect the true Dmitry whom Boris had put to death. The corpse would by then have decomposed completely, for it can be seen from my narrative that many long years had passed since the prince's murder, which had taken place in the reign of Fyodor Ivanovich. The young boy's body, newly buried, was then to be exhumed; the people would be led to believe they had found the body of the prince in a state of perfect preservation, and therefore it was wrong to believe that this prince had ever escaped from the sword of his assassins. Finally, they were to bring the coffin to Moscow, spreading the rumour that the body was working miracles, and lay it to rest in the presence of the entire people in the church of the Archangel, the ancient burial place of the tsars.

The murdered child Dmitry is exhumed fraudulently and exhibited in Moscow as a miracle

All this was done according to plan. Secretly, by night, they slipped another coffin containing a young boy into the murdered prince's tomb, and carefully sealed it up again.

Then they sent Prince Ivan Mikhailovich Vorotynsky from Moscow to Uglich, there to exhume the true Dmitry's body. When he had accomplished his mission and come back to the neighbourhood of Moscow, he gave warning of the body's approach. It was then received with a great procession. The tsar and the lords went on foot; the bishops, monks, and priests carried images, crosses, and banners; the old tsarina, mother of the true Dmitry, did the same. This whole procession went out of the town to escort the body in, and all the community followed. I did the same myself, as I was curious to see how this would end.

When they came out of the city, the body was there on a bier set upon a carriage. The tsar, the lords, and the bishops came and gazed at it. The tsarina did the same, and cried out: 'Oh, I see him now, the true Dmitry, murdered at Uglich! And by the grace of God, his body is as fresh as if they had just put him in the coffin!' Hearing these words, all the people began to praise and thank God, and they covered the bier. I would have liked to look at it too if they had let me, and many monks and priests were as anxious to see it as I was, but no doubt they were afraid that we would be too curious and profane this sacred corpse. It was borne into the city like a saint and holy man [sanct en heiligen], and laid to rest on its catafalque in the church of the Archangel, but nobody could approach it except the principal lords and bishops, who were party to the affair.

I do not think there was a single bell in Moscow that did not toll at that moment, and the sound of bells was deafening to the ear. Scarcely had the corpse entered the church when it began to work miracles. The blind saw clearly, the lame began to walk, the dumb recovered their speech, the deaf heard. As soon as one of these miracles took place, all the bells began to peal, and the onlookers intoned the *Gaudeamus*.

There were some who spoke only a little before entering the church, and then on coming out were struck dumb, or at least answered with grunts the questions put to them. People were allowed in only if they were specially admitted. If I had been allowed to enter, I am sure that I would have gone out blinded, at least by the smoke of the incense being burned, or else deafened, by the wailing of the priests. All this foolery came close to being unmasked. They came with a sick man, or one who passed for such; the moment he was brought in, presumably to be restored to health, he died in the church, and they had to carry him out lifeless. The charlatans were masters of their trade, however, and despite this setback they still claimed that all the miracles wrought there were consistent. If the sick man was not healed, they said, it was because his faith faltered, and thus he deserved to die. The people, rich as well as poor, were so blinded by this that they believed all the fables and nonsense they were told. My zeal sometimes prompted me to tell them to take the blind beggars sitting at the threshhold of our house by the hand, along with the lame and paralysed asking for alms at every crossroads, and get them into the church to bring them back sighted and healed. But I was told that all these unfortunates still lacked sufficient faith. 'And how,' I would reply, 'do you know that only those you take there have sufficient faith in the eyes of the saint?' 'It is the angel of God,' they replied, 'who reveals to our bishops and priests those the saint wishes to favour, and shows them where they are to be found.' In short, they had a ready reply to all my objections, and firmly believed themselves in the reality of these miracles themselves, even though this was in fact nothing but trickery, and trickery of the grossest kind. For all these so-called healed were merely worthless people paid to lie. They rubbed their eyes with some substance, and carried their legs in such a fashion as to have people think they had been struck by paralysis. All their impostures were of the same order, and they had also taken good care to get fellows for these roles who had come from afar, and were little known or unknown in Moscow.

Thus did the Muscovites, sightless already, become even blinder. May God deign to enlighten them by his Holy Spirit, as also all those who walk in darkness.

It was in this manner, then, that faith in Dmitry's existence was expunged from the minds of the people. These miracles did not last long, and they did not end any too soon.

Lawlessness of the people

The people of Moscow demanded death for all the lords on whom honours had been conferred under Dmitry, or the Renegade Monk, even if these people had all been innocent of crime. Among them was Afanasy Vlasiev, who had gone to Poland to fetch the tsar's bride. For all the arguments of the magnates, the people, who were in control, would not modify their demands. To satisfy them, the lords had to exile the ones they singled out. Afanasy and Nikita Godunov were sent to Kazan on the Kama river; Mikhail Tatishchev was sent to Novgorod; others were sent away to different towns.

Victory of the rebels; they approach Moscow; aided by treachery, the Muscovites put them to flight; many are captured and executed

Meanwhile, the imperial troops were defeated once again, and Bolotnikov gained the upper hand. He dispatched a corps of ten thousand men in haste for Moscow, and he himself was to follow at once with the bulk of his army. This body of troops was soon a mile from the capital, near a small stream called the Danilovka, and seized the village of Zagoria, where they dug in.

For this purpose, Bolotnikov had furnished them with several hundred sleds, which the soldiers bound together by ropes of straw and woven hay, and stacked two or three high. Then, sprinkling them copiously with water and letting them freeze, they made an improvised rampart as strong as stone. Well provided with cattle, horses, and munitions for several days, they shut themselves up in this camp and waited for Bolotnikov with all his army.[181]

For its part, the Muscovite army under the command of the tsar's brothers set up camp behind the barricade of wagons outside the city gates. They attacked the enemy's encampment several times with strong artillery support, but achieved nothing. The Muscovites also launched bombs into the village, but the besieged extinguished them instantly with wet briar. The rebels had their eye on Krasnoe Selo, a rich village near by, as large as a city. It was an important position from which they would dominate the entire capital. The imperial army, which greatly feared the loss of this village, set a large body of troops under the young Skopin's orders along the river Yauza, which the enemy had to cross, in order to prevent their passage. Then, for two whole days, they attacked with all their forces, amounting to about two hundred thousand men, but once again with no result but heavy losses for themselves.

In the meantime, Bolotnikov dispatched reinforcements of thirty thousand men under Istoma Pashkov for his supporters. This Pashkov came three days later and had his troops pass to the other side of the entrenchment where his besieged companions were, pretending they wanted to attack the Muscovites; but he and his senior officers had been bribed by the tsar, and he had agreed by secret treaty to hand all his troops over to the Muscovites.[182]

The Muscovites, who knew about this, attacked the entrenched rebels in great numbers, and sent a detachment to meet Pashkov, who passed over at the first impact to the ranks of the imperial army with five hundred of his men. Taken aback at this, his army began to retreat, and the Muscovites made prisoners of a large number of them.[183] The besiegers, who witnessed all this, took flight, and lost half their number passing through a copse where the Muscovites lay in ambush. Hideous carnage took place, and six thousand of them were taken prisoner. The jails of Moscow were full, and in addition, a number of citizens were obliged to keep two or three in their houses. They were also cast in large numbers into the dungeons under the great halls and chancelleries, where they presented a fearful spectacle. They were nearly all Cossacks, Muscovites by birth; no foreigners, or very few, were to be seen among them.[184]

They did not stay in their prisons very long. They were brought out by the hundreds at night and led off to their deaths like lambs to the slaughter. They were lined up and butchered like cattle with cudgel blows to the forehead, then thrust under the ice of the river Yauza. Among these prisoners was a hetman called Anichkin, who had carried letters from Dmitry all over to sow rebellion in the people. He was condemned to impalement, and while he was undergoing his torture, though still alive, the tsar sent him a gentleman named Istoma Bezobrazov, who begged him, while he still had a few moments left, to tell the assembled people the identity of the impostor who was once more claiming to be Dmitry. To which the condemned answered resolutely that this person was the tsar's own brother, also named Dmitry, and that for all his presence in the ranks of the imperial army, it was he who had been fomenting the troubles. He said this in the hope that his words would stir up fresh unrest in the populace. Accompanied by the magnates, the tsar had come before the crowd to swear that it was all preposterous, and that he knew his brother's mind full well; but the hetman's words remained – a fire hidden beneath the ashes.

Two monks were sent to the rebel camp from Moscow to unearth secrets about the person who called himself Dmitry. When they came near Kolomna and Serpukhov, and the place where the Muscovite army had recently been defeated, they met two men who said that they were defectors surrendering to Moscow; these swore that Dmitry was still alive, and that they had seen him. Hearing this, the two monks dared go no farther, and the people who had met them went away.

Bolotnikov was confident that the capital would fall to the large force he had sent, and in fact he could reasonably have counted on this, given the panic that reigned in the city and the wavering of its inhabitants, if he had not had to take Pashkov's treachery into account. On hearing the quite unexpected reports of the escapers, he retired with all his army to Kaluga on the Oka, a town which appeared to him suitable for his winter quarters, and which he furnished at once with all he needed. It is a very populous city, carrying on much trade in salt[185] with the inhabitants of Severia, Komaritsk, and other districts in the same region, who bring honey, wax, linen, hides, etc. to the city. This town thus lacked nothing. During the retreat, however, the Muscovites killed many of his men close to Kolomna, and it was with but the remainder that he entered Kaluga, where he entrenched himself.

Peter Fyodorovich, who, as we know, claimed to be a bastard of Tsar Fyodor, was at Tula, where he was besieged by the Muscovites. Sometimes victorious, sometimes defeated, he held his position with vigour even though he was down to his last resources.

Their hetman Bolotnikov

As soon as Bolotnikov had fortified himself in the town of Kaluga, the Muscovite army came to invest it – a greater army than the one that had besieged Kromy at the beginning of the Dmitry affair, as we have previously related. Bolotnikov in Kaluga was in the same position Korela had been in at Kromy. Like him, he made numerous sorties, inflicting heavy losses on the Muscovites. Not a day went by, so to speak, when he did not kill forty or fifty of their men, whereas he lost hardly a man on his own side. The besiegers wasted their time in useless salvos, and abandoned themselves to revelry, drinking, and gambling; they did no great damage to Kaluga's defenders, and thus wasted an entire winter. As for the tsar, he could think whatever he wanted about it!

The Muscovite army forced the peasants of the surrounding districts to cut wood from the forests every day, bundle it up into faggots, and take it in front of the army on hundreds of sleds at a time. Thus, they built up mountains of wood around the besieged town, and laboured to bring this rampart of combustible matter closer and closer, hoping to set it alight one day when the wind was blowing towards the place, and in this way suffocate the defenders. But the latter, learning of this strategem through the reports of defectors, dug tunnels under these wooden mountains, which, collapsing suddenly, crushed some of the Muscovites. They gathered combustible matter also, and putting it on top of these heaps of wood, set fire to it when the wind was blowing in the direction of the besiegers. Making a strong sortie at the same moment, they killed many of their people. In short, they still had the advantage, as formerly the besieged in Kromy had.[186]

At this time, a plague broke out in Novgorod that killed a great number of people in the city and the surrounding countryside, and also many priests.[187]

The Tatars of the kingdom of Kazan were still very quiet, maintaining their neutrality, but they were waiting for a chance to throw themselves into the struggle on one side or the other. On the Volga, these towns were still most devoted to the tsar's cause: Kostroma, Yaroslavl, Uglich, Nizhny Novgorod, Samara, Saratov, and some others, except for Astrakhan, which was in full rebellion, and the banks of the river, that were made unsafe by the depredations of the Cossacks.

Peter Sheremetev was still encamped with his troops on the island of Balchik, three miles from Astrakhan; they had built a fort that held the town in check. Between these two sides there were frequent encounters in which they killed one another.

The Nogai Tatars, as I have said, had also opened their campaign, defecting from the Muscovites, and become involved in a struggle with the Cheremissians and their kings. They also killed one another, and this went on incessantly.

Some traitors apprehended in Yaroslavl

The soldiers appointed to stand guard in Yaroslavl over the palatine of Sandomierz and his daughter, the former tsarina, had tried to set fire to the town and put it to the sack. Those at Kostroma carrying out the same mission for the palatine's son had attempted the same thing. Their aim was to join the Polish prisoners with the palatine and his son and rush over to the ranks of the tsar's enemies, but their plot was discovered. Most of these traitors were captured and some delivered to the executioner; and custody of the town and the prisoners was entrusted to the community itself, which took charge.

The Poles and gentlemen interned at Rostov also tried to force an escape and join the rebels, who were not far from there, but their plan too was discovered. They were separated and sent a hundred miles from there, to Vologda and Beloozero. Among them were the two Buczynski brothers, who were taken to Pustozersk, and Domaradzki, who was thrown into prison at Totma. Kosonowski, a young Polish lord and a relative of the tsarina, was sent to Kotsinga on the Vaga. But most of them, and these included some ladies, left for Beloozero, where they were treated very harshly.

The rumour spread in Moscow that the palatine's wife was at the frontier with an army of about thirty thousand men, ready to come to the aid of the rebels. This army was commanded by the Mikhail Molchanov who had fled the palace after Dmitry's assassination. The rumour caused fresh consternation, but it was soon discredited.

False tidings sent from Moscow to all the towns

Every day, dispatches left Moscow for all the towns to announce victories by the tsar's troops, even when they had been sustaining defeat all the time. When these tidings came, all the bells were rung and everybody celebrated. This was an expedient to prevent the people from defecting and hold their allegiance. It was the same expedient that Dmitry had used to attract them to his cause from the time of his arrival in Moscow. The example was turned to profit.

1607

In January, a priest from Moscow was beheaded for distributing satirical letters, announcing that Dmitry was still alive.

At the same time, letters came from the Muscovite army saying that the enemy were daily increasing their forces and supplies by reason of their great courage, despite all the efforts of the Muscovites to prevent them. Therefore Fyodor Ivanovich Mstislavsky was dispatched from Moscow in a higher command than that of the tsar's brothers or anyone else, together with the young lord Skopin and many other young lords and nobles, and also a large army with orders that wherever it went, it should destroy the enemy. When they came before Kaluga, they were to join up with those already in the encampment; but they were no more successful than the others.

At this time, the dwelling or apartment of the tsar was completed. It was our duty on this occasion to come according to Muscovite custom and present our greetings to the sovereign. He had given this residence the name of Novoselie [Nova Zelia].[188] He had not wished to live in Dmitry's sumptuous palace for fear of a nocturnal visit from the Demon, for he still held Dmitry to have been a sorcerer, and all the places he had inhabited were thought impure. Everyone came to bring the tsar presents, and offered bread and salt along with their congratulations according to the Muscovite usage. The tsar accepted the salt and the bread, but gave us back our presents. In addition, to thank us, he had morsels on silver platters and refreshments in gilded cups served to us and to everyone.

Towards the end of January, serious dissension was seen to break out among the Muscovite commanders, but it was suppressed and hidden carefully from the troops. The next day, the besieged in Kaluga were informed of this, and made it the object of their mockery.

At the same time, a detachment of prisoners was brought to Moscow from the small town of Venev, where the Muscovites had suffered a setback. Simultaneously, there were reports that Mosalsky and Teliatevsky, two great lords who had gone over to the other camp, were coming to Dmitry's aid with thirty thousand men – Poles, Cossacks, and Russians. This news caused such panic in the capital that they had to send for the old patriarch, Job by name, whom Dmitry had deposed and exiled to Staritsa, to ask his advice.

Now blind of old age, the patriarch begged to be left in peace. Despite his protests, he was dragged to Moscow; but his advice did not help improve the situation any more than the others'.[189]

Mosalsky was advancing towards Tula meanwhile with a body of troops to relieve Peter Fyodorovich, who was called Petrushka in Moscow, but he was beaten by the imperial forces and brought captive to the capital, where he died from his wounds. Those taken along with him were thrown into the river.[190]

The Muscovite army camped beneath Kaluga announced the defeat of Mosalsky and his troops to the town's besieged from the top of a hill by the Oka, and urged them to think on this and surrender soon; but Bolotnikov made mock of this counsel, and on the same day hanged some of his servants, including his own cook, who had been suspected of treason, in view of the besiegers. In addition, he and his followers swore once again that they were fighting for the true Dmitry.

When news of the battle below Tula and Mosalsky's defeat reached Moscow, there was a complete about-face, and they all celebrated. No one dared believe in Dmitry now, and they sent Vorotynsky to Tula with a party of troops to press the siege and seize Peter's person.

Names of towns taking part in the uprising

In the month of March, the tsar ordered the leader of the Kasimov Tatars to report for duty with his troops and ravage the surrounding countryside, so that the rebels would be prevented from getting any supplies or munitions. But the country was already completely despoiled, and did not need to be laid waste any further. All the towns in the rebels' sway had good garrisons. On the side of Tatary, they held the towns of Riazan, Karachev, Livny [Nalifna], Orel, Venev, Mikhailov, Bolkhov [Bolgou], Serebriannye Prudy, and Novosil [Noua Zeel]; in the land of Severia, they had Putivl, the first and chiefest of the rebel cities, where they held counsel. Besides Putivl, they held Chernigov, Briansk, Elets, Kozelsk, Rylsk, Pochep, Sosnitsa [Satzca], Roslavl [Roscoula], Monasterishche, Novgorod Seversky, and many others; they also held Kolomna, Kashira, Aleksin, Epifan, Peremyshl, Lgov [Liguin], and Dedilov, as well as Kaluga and Tula, where Peter was holding out. Beyond this, they were masters of the whole course of the Volga, and this area had been ravaged completely. In short, they had a powerful army and occupied fine provinces. Several other towns were wavering.

Alarmed at the situation, the tsar in Moscow resolved at his magnates' entreaty to lead his troops when summer was near. Thus, he sent letters to every town commanding that all the boyar sons, or gentry, be summoned, together with all the able-bodied men who were still in the fields, not having left for the army, and threatening recalcitrants with forced recruitment and confiscation of their goods.[191] This severe ordinance brought forward a great number of soldiers who were sent out to the army at once. Matters so remained until springtime. Then, they brought prisoners to Moscow some of whom declared that they had seen Dmitry and others that they did not know why they were fighting. At all events, guilty or not, they were all cast into the river.

Eight Poles flee Moscow

In the month of March, eight Poles succeeded in escaping disguised as peasants from the lodgings of the Polish ambassador. They reached their own country, where they no doubt told of the true state of affairs in Moscow. Several of those charged with guarding the prisoners were put to torture and severely punished. A great many bodies of guards were set on watch, and some of the city gates were even closed.

Finally, to get some money and pay his mercenaries, the tsar ordered old objects, such as clothing, brought out of the treasury and sold; he also borrowed large sums from monasteries and Muscovite merchants. They could scarcely refuse to render him this service, as they knew they were partly to blame for these internecine wars.

Hearing that there was about to be a seditious outbreak in Yaroslavl, and that the palatine would not have enough men about him, the Muscovites tried to detach seventy gentlemen from his suite, promising solemnly to conduct them to Poland. But this was a ruse, employed as a way of reducing the numbers of the defenders about the Palatine of Sandomierz. Moreover, the Poles turned a deaf ear to these proposals, and gave no credence to them. All the people then came together and surrounded the place where they were quartered. Thinking they had designs on their lives, the Poles resolutely took up arms and made ready to resist to the death. Fearing great misfortune from this imminent struggle, the Muscovites held, with the most solemn oaths, that their offer was genuine. At last, the Poles allowed themselves to be convinced. Seventy of them surrendered in the hope of returning to their own country. Without being brought into the town, they were led straight to the wharf, where it is very probable that they were killed.[192]

Meanwhile, Peter Fyodorovich, with all the Tula garrison, launched a vigorous attack on the Muscovite army besieging him and put it to rout. Vorotynsky, Simon Romanovich, and Istoma Pashkov, who were the commanders, fled with all their troops.[193] Peter took advantage of the situation to relieve several neighbouring towns, and then hastily re-entered Tula, fortifying himself there once again.

Towards the end of the same month, the clapper of the great Moscow bell fell down in the night; this was thought a bad omen.

The river Oka breaks up below Kaluga

The great river Oka broke up, and ice-floes began descending in great numbers towards the Volga. At this sight, the Muscovite army busied itself, and on both sides of the river built solid rafts which were then laden with troops and artillery, their purpose being to stop Bolotnikov from leaving Kaluga and fleeing on the Volga, which would have been a great setback for the Muscovites. Bolotnikov could quite easily have done this, for he had enough sailboats and barges at Kaluga to carry all his troops, but he was prevented.

In the first days of April, when all the rivers began to clear, the Crimean ambassador asked permission to return to his country, but this request was refused. He was given lodging and food, and was closely guarded and spied upon.

The tsar takes a Polish nobleman into his service

There was a Polish gentleman in Moscow who had been chamberlain to the late Dmitry. Having sworn to the tsar that he would serve him faithfully, he was accepted as a cavalry captain and formed a corps of two hundred men, Livonians as well as Poles, who had done long service in Moscow. He always showed courage, but had done nothing of note. Having entered into contact with some of the rebels who held the town of Aleksin, he hoped to make himself master of that town, but his plan failed. The bulk of the army that had been sent towards Kaluga, beyond the Oka, to attempt a campaign against a number of towns in that quarter, had no success and was everywhere defeated.

New treason among the Muscovite forces

The force sent from Kaluga along the river Oka with the aim of attacking various towns also suffered reverses, and was defeated everywhere. The army besieging Kaluga was in complete mutiny, and when the besieged in Kaluga threw all their forces against the Muscovites, they defeated them utterly and put them to flight, setting fire to their camp from all sides. This misfortune fell on the imperial side because of the treason of their leaders and the division prevailing among them. This reverse was similar to the one that had taken place two years previously below Kromy, for the commanders scarcely had time to emerge from their tents, and the besieged also captured all the artillery. The fugitives who passed through Moscow could not say why they were fleeing, but they said with effrontery: 'Go on campaign with the tsar and see for yourselves!' As for Mstislavsky, he did not dare come to Moscow, but halted with a body of troops on the banks of a small stream about six miles from the capital,[194] and they began to uncover the source of the treachery. It emanated chiefly from a Muscovite lord, Prince Boris Tatev,[195] and the Zaporozhian Cossacks. The latter, learning of the double defeat of the imperial side, began first to wonder about the true Dmitry's existence and then to believe in him. Turning to Bolotnikov, they asked the favour of admittance into his forces, and this was granted them. Their defection made them the cause of the whole army's defeat.

Bolotnikov then went to the pretended Dmitry in Putivl, who heaped honours and presents on him to reward his faithful service. He had held out in Kaluga for about half a year, and when he left that town, he put two generals, Dolgoruky and Bezzubtsov, in command.

Mstislavsky then proceeded with his troops to Borovsk, a small town not far from there which he seized, putting all its inhabitants to the sword. Vorotynsky arrived at Serpukhov, but Ivan Ivanovich Shuisky, the tsar's brother, re-entered Moscow unobtrusively without anyone's knowing of his return.

It is certain that if the rebels had had an army with which to march on the capital at this moment, they would have taken it without resistance; but they proceeded slowly, and during this time the inhabitants regained courage, and set themselves on a footing for defence. They knew, or at least they had been led to believe, that the rebels would kill them to the last man, together with their wives and children. They swore that they would defend the city and the tsar to the last drop of blood; once again, they assembled a large army, and the tsar left the city.

Ivan Fyodorovich, who was also called Kriuk-Kolychev, was put at the head of this army. He was a man well esteemed by the people. He left in the month of May to take up his post.

The Muscovites once again assemble their forces after their defeat, but are unable to achieve anything significant, and so the tsar goes on campaign in person

Kriuk-Kolychev opened his campaign. He established himself near Serpukhov, joining up with the troops camped in that neighbourhood. With each day, new groups came to reinforce him, and so there assembled a great army.

The tsar prepared to go and rejoin his soldiers, and ordered offerings made and prayers said in all the churches. He also went to visit the infernal prophetess, Elena, of whom I have already spoken, but she wished neither to see nor to hear him, and shut her door in his face. Again he tried to see her. She let him enter then with several lords. He came out an hour later; but nobody knew what she had told him, and they made a great secret of it.

Before his departure, a courier dressed in the Polish fashion was seen coming into Moscow accompanied by two servants. He brought letters from Poland, but the rumour spread among the people that he had come from Sweden. Nobody learned any more about the matter. After a secret audience, this courier was spirited away to Novgorod by night, and held in prison there.

They also took to Moscow two other couriers who had been seized near Tsaritsyn on the Volga, with manifestos from Dmitry that were calculated to attract the surrounding towns to the rebel side. Then they sent strong reinforcements to Peter Sheremetev, who was still holding out on the island of Balchik. The main force, with the chief generals, was at Serpukhov, about eighteen miles from Moscow. A smaller force was camped at Borovsk, not far from the capital. There they awaited the coming of the tsar, counting greatly on his presence to strike fear into the enemy.

Praying in a number of Moscow churches, the tsar mounted his horse before the church of St Mary, took his quiver and bow, and departed with all his court at noon on 21 May,[196] leaving his brother Dmitry to govern Moscow in his stead.

As soon as the tsar was on his way, crowds of soldiers rushed up from all directions to follow him. They were moved by fear of great punishment if they failed to report for duty and the tsar returned in triumph. The monasteries were forced to pay a contribution in proportion to their wealth, and also provide a certain number of men. In this manner they gathered great forces; but little by little, the country was being drained, and losing the flower of its inhabitants.

Many merchants leave Moscow

According to custom, it was now the time for the merchants to turn to plying their trade and loading and unloading their ships. Each left in his own direction, the English and the Dutch going to Archangel on the White Sea. The Poles, Armenians, and Tatars also wished to set off, but they were forbidden to leave Moscow. Since they would be going into enemy territory, it was felt that they should be prevented from uttering indiscretions.

As soon as the tsar went on campaign, he was continually afraid of advancing with all his army. Forever apprehensive lest he be betrayed, he did not wish to go far from the environs of Moscow, and sent troops off in all directions. These were all surprised, alas, and defeated when they least expected it, and the rebels were victorious in all encounters.

But on the other hand, the rebels did not know how to profit from their victories. Just when their campaign was going the best, they halted, following I know not what counsels, and did not follow up their success. It must have been that the time fixed by the Almighty had not yet come.

It was discovered later that they had held a great assembly at Putivl, but it is not known what resolutions were adopted there. In any case, Dmitry's name was hardly mentioned. In Poland, they believed that their chance had come to throw themselves on Russia and wreak their vengeance. They sent back the embassy that had been detained for such a long time, and any lord who so wished could open hostilities. Many of them took advantage of this permission. This was the first act of hostility Poland had committed. A great many bodies of troops commanded by various captains or generals were seen leaving that country and invading the territory of the empire on all fronts, proclaiming Dmitry, who, they assured everybody, was still alive.

Several of these new aggressors dedicated themselves to the war with great passion. These were the ones who had a relative or friend, massacred during the marriage celebrations, to be avenged. They were also stung to the quick by the taunts of their enemies in Poland, who told them to go to the wedding in Moscow.

Poland declared herself even more openly when the Grand Chancellor, Lew Sapieha, was ordered by the king to prepare for war.

The Muscovites capture Tula, and also seize Peter Fyodorovich, the rebel leader

The Muscovites, for their part, won great success with their captures of Tula, which occurred through treason, and of Peter Fyodorovich, the supposed bastard of Tsar Fyodor.[197] Peter was hanged at Moscow. They also captured several little towns, but nearly always by using traitors. The brave hero Bolotnikov was sent at once with troops to meet the imperial army and put a stop to their successes. While the rebels were holding counsel with the Poles and Cossacks, the Muscovites seized the intrepid Bolotnikov and killed him. Some said that he had surrendered voluntarily, others that he was captured through treachery.[198] However it was, the rebellion had just lost its two most valiant leaders. Seeing that his people had regained some little ground, and that war would not be resumed before the spring, the tsar was content with these small successes and returned to Moscow, leaving his generals and troops in the field. In Moscow and in all the imperial party, victory was believed complete; but they were mistaken.

The two sides fought all winter. The Polish invasion simply intensified, and the land was reduced to the final extremity, even as it had been at the time of Dmitry's last appearance. This similar situation, on which I therefore refrain from elaborating, lasted until the summer of the year 1608.

1608

Meanwhile, the magnates of Muscovy were strongly advising the tsar to take a wife. They were persuaded that from the moment their sovereign had a wife and heirs, the land would accord him more respect and devotion. Heeding their pleas, he married the daughter of a great Muscovite lord named Peter Buinosov, who was of an exalted family, and crowned her tsarina. But things went badly there also.

The wedding was celebrated on 27 January 1608,[199] in the midst of misfortune and sadness that were only made worse by the daily executions of unfortunates thrown into the waters of the river.

These drownings were so frightful that I shudder to recall them. They had already been going on for two years, and nobody could see an end to them. In springtime, with the breakup and the river's flooding, the bodies were carried by ice-floes to the middle of the fields, the flesh half gnawed by pike and other fish, and remained there to rot in their thousands as food for crabs and worms, which left nothing behind but the bones. I have seen this spectacle in Moscow with my own eyes.

Every day, there were announcements in Moscow that great enemy forces were coming from Poland, and that the Muscovites had been defeated on many fronts. They then brought the palatine of Sandomierz back to the capital with his daughter, the wife of Tsar Dmitry, as well as the principal Polish lords and nobles, fearing that they might be freed, since the enemy was everywhere. So they kept these prisoners under close guard in Moscow, hoping to get a rich ransom for them.

One day, an ambassador from Poland was seen entering the city proudly and resolutely with his suite to the sound of trumpets, to which the trumpeters of the Polish ambassador, who had been kept under guard since Dmitry's time, were heard to reply. This envoy's arrival spread joy among all his countrymen who were being kept prisoner.[200]

The ambassador brought the tsar a threatening message, upbraiding him for the outrage done the king's ambassador and the murder of a number of his subjects, and warning him that the king would see himself forced by his people and his estates to avenge these acts of violence. The Muscovite court answered this communication as best it could, and detained the ambassador.

At the same time, reports came to Moscow that the Muscovites had suffered great defeats and were everywhere put to flight;[201] terror ran through the capital once again. The tsar contrived to steady the people by his many exhortations, for he swore to them that the enemy would kill all the inhabitants, including women and children, if they surrendered. Since they had all been to some degree accomplices in Dmitry's murder, they once more resolved to stand firm.

Thus, the enemy came close to Moscow, and on 2 June[202] appeared beneath the city walls with Tsar Dmitry, as he was called, a crowd of Lithuanian and Polish lords, the Wisniowiecki, the Tyszkiewicz [Kithivitz], with other relatives of the palatine of Sandomierz, and the Grand Chancellor, Lew Sapieha.[203] The city was at once invested and besieged; the enemy occupied all the monasteries and hamlets of the neighbourhood as far as the Simonov monastery. Sapieha led his troops to the Trinity monastery, a large fortified cloister 12 miles from Moscow on the Yaroslavl road. This monastery was a very useful stronghold.

Prior to the enemy's arrival before Moscow, the Muscovites had sent the young Skopin with troops to Novgorod, to protect that city and to keep the road to Sweden open, as they expected the Swedish troops King Karl had promised them. A contingent of Swedes and Germans were to join Skopin's force at Novgorod. Peter Sheremetev had also received the order to leave the island of Balchik, close to Astrakhan, and join Skopin to deliver the capital with their combined forces, but they moved so slowly that the junction almost failed to take place. Belying the general opinion, the city held out for more than a year, and those who were to raise the siege had still not got under way or come together. During this time, the enemy ravaged all the surrounding countryside and seized most of the fortresses.

Hardly had the siege begun when scarcity was felt in Moscow; but the great stores of the monasteries were able to allay this scourge somewhat. A great number of merchants and other people had had the foresight to leave the town before the siege. The tsar threatened to kill the palatine of Sandomierz along with all his companions, reproaching him for being the cause of all these happenings. This reproach was well founded. Through fear of death, the palatine promised to devote all his efforts to ending the war with a good treaty if only they would set him and all his followers at liberty, as well as the ambassadors. He further promised to negotiate a peace treaty between Poland and Muscovy, provided that Poland would be restored to some of the privileges she had formerly enjoyed. Despite the oaths exacted from him and his followers, nothing came of all this except that the palatine and his companions were released, and freely left Moscow.

The state of affairs being thus, Peter Sheremetev left the island of Balchik in the Volga and went with his troops to Saratov, a town on the Volga. He left there to proceed to Nizhny Novgorod, where he spent the winter season.

Skopin was camped with his army at Novgorod, where he was strongly established and keeping the road open. Then he sent for aid to the king of Sweden, who raised a corps composed of Scotsmen, Frenchmen, and Swedes, and sent them by way of Livonia to Novgorod, there to join with Skopin's army.

Camped below the walls of Moscow with all the rebel army, Dmitry had great quantities of timber assembled in the surrounding villages, and with this built huts and houses which added up to a vast suburb. Sapieha had established himself in the same manner close to the Trinity monastery. A number of Polish lords attacked Yaroslavl, took it through treachery, and, burning and completely pillaging the city and its magnificent monastery, and killing many people, added this conquest to the others their side had made.

The traitors who surrendered the town were the governor himself, Prince Fyodor Bariatinsky, and a monastery servant, who came to terms with the enemy. As soon as the inhabitants had sworn allegiance to Dmitry, they were given another governor, with the same Bariatinsky as his subordinate.

Six miles from Yaroslavl on the Vologda road, there is a village called Romanovskoe, where troops from Vologda who adhered to the Moscow party had their camp. A Polish lord was sent with a detachment from the great rebel army to defeat them and capture Vologda, which they wished to attach to Dmitry's party. This lord, whose name was Tyszkiewicz, was so soundly beaten by the Vologda army that he was scarcely able to make good his escape, and returned to Yaroslavl sadly on foot. A little later, three messengers were dispatched to Vologda, summoning the city to surrender to Dmitry on pain of being razed to its foundations and seeing its inhabitants, men, women, and children, put to the sword if it refused. At this threat, the town swore allegiance to Dmitry. The rebels would have succeeded in taking all the country in this way, had the citizens of Vologda not rallied to the tsar's party again towards winter of the following year.

The town of Pskov had also been entirely destroyed by fire, its surrounding countryside abandoned to pillage and left a wasteland. A great number of rich inhabitants were massacred. The town of Ivangorod, or Russian Narva, underwent the same fate and did not recover.

Severia and the Komaritsk district prosper

The territories of Severia and Komaritsk, adjacent to Poland, enjoyed peace and tranquillity. The people there worked and sowed their fields undisturbed, leaving the Muscovites to fend for themselves. In all the empire, moreover, bread was cheap except in the besieged towns. In Moscow, a 'chetvert,' a measure slightly smaller than a bushel, cost 28 florins, sometimes more, and also sometimes less. At Vologda, the same measure cost only one florin. Such was the difference in price between the two towns.

1609. Rebellion in Yaroslavl and Vologda

During the siege of Moscow in the year 1609, the town of Vologda was the first to fall to the opposing party, as I have reported. At that time, they had

Nikita Mikhailovich Pushkin as their governor, and Roman Makarovich Voronov as chancellor. These two had been dismissed from their posts, shamefully treated, and although they were completely innocent, even thrown in jail by the city's inhabitants, who are cruel, stupid, blown with every wind, mindless of their past, present, and future oaths, and live like wild beasts. They were given as governor a certain Fyodor Ilich Nashchokin,[204] a scoundrel of base descent who left the great army of the rebels to take up his post. Three days later, they appointed Ivan Verigin Koverniv [Cofrasin] to replace the chancellor; he saw fit to seek to place his seal on the traders' merchandise, but they refused to let him do this, and removed him when he would not confess that he had sealed their merchandise intending to confiscate it.

The new governor summoned the inhabitants to have them acknowledge Dmitry as tsar and administer the oath of allegiance to them. He also had his predecessor brought before him, and threatened to load him down with chains and send him thus to the army and, at the same time, subject him to ill treatment and injury. He behaved similarly towards several rich merchants, who offered presents to buy his favour.

Vologda rallies to Moscow

That same night, some Poles who had been prisoners in the town of Vologda for a long time and had now regained their freedom attacked the peasants of the surrounding countryside, subjecting them to the cruellest of insults and despoiling them of everything, even their clothes. They came back into the city after this expedition with their sleds heaped with booty, intending to rejoin the army the next day. That same night, the peasants came to Vologda to lodge their complaints about these acts of brutality. The community, seeing the truth of their account, bitterly regretted rallying to Dmitry and swearing him allegiance. So to make up for the results of their vacillation, they recalled Chancellor Voronov, an honourable old man whom they had removed some time previously, and reinstated him in his duties. Then they took counsel on the matter of returning to their own duty and ridding themselves of all supporters of Dmitry and all the Poles. The commune also delivered the governor, Pushkin, from jail, and put him back in his post, disclosing to him a plan they had conceived, and which he approved. On that occasion, Pushkin gave the inhabitants a fine speech, as much in his own favour as in the Muscovites'. He reproached them for their frivolousness, the prime cause of the miseries with which God was punishing them, and warned them that God would continue to punish them for as long as they refused to go back to the right path. These words made them repent. In their frenzy, they left the fortress, ran with all haste to the house of the Bulgakovs where the new governor was residing, besieged it, broke in, seized Nashchokin, Verigin, and all the Poles and prisoners in the town, and cut off their heads with axes. Then they rolled the heads and the bodies to the foot of the hill, into the stream called the Zolotitsa, where these human remains were frightful food for dogs and pigs. Having thus rallied openly to the Muscovite party, they swore to be forever faithful to the tsar and spill the last drop of their blood for him.

The news of this spread gladness in Moscow, and proved to the people of that city that not everyone had abandoned the tsar's cause. Straight away, then, the tsar sent a letter filled with affection thanking the people of Vologda for what they had done, and he addressed a similar letter to Governor Pushkin in particular.[205] These letters were inserted in a loaf of bread and entrusted to messengers disguised as marauders or beggars. Thus, even if these bearers had been apprehended, letters would not have been found in their possession. In his letter to the governor, the tsar ordered him to choose some of the Dutch and English merchants at Vologda to be sent to General Skopin in Novgorod, where they would be helpful to him as much by their counsel as by their energies, and furthermore ordered that they should obey him as they would obey the lords and boyars. The Muscovites have such a high opinion of the wisdom of the Dutch and the English that the tsar was convinced our advice would be of great assistance to him. But we thought otherwise, and had no wish to undertake this mission. Thus did we address the governor, and so persuaded him with our gifts that he kept the letters on his person, and did not admit that he had received them.

All the merchants who regularly do business with this country had gathered in Vologda, taking refuge in the house of the English – their factory, which is very large, and like a castle. There, with a good guard around them, they passed the winter in perpetual fear and anxiety. The town could expect to see the rebels come any day to wreak vengeance for the defection of its people. But they kept watch valiantly, and one day even set an ambush; they put the enemy to flight, and came back into the town laden with booty.

Then they urged the English and Dutch merchants to withdraw into the fortress, where they were assigned quarters as vast as the hall of a castle and defended by doors and windows with double bars, and they gladly accepted. Though they had to mount close guard there day and night, they were much safer none the less. However, their anxiety revived to the point that they expected death from one day to the next when they were told that the Poles had sworn to exterminate all the people of Vologda in punishment for their shameful defection from Dmitry's party, accusing the English and the Dutch merchants of prompting this by their counsel, and boasting that they knew where to find them. In this extremity, we wrote memoranda to exonerate ourselves from this accusation. One of these memoranda was in Latin, another in German, and the third in the Muscovite language. At the approach of the Poles, or Dmitry's soldiers, they were to be given to some brave young men, who would go to the enemy and deliver them; we hoped by this to prove our innocence and save our lives.

Fortunately, this turned out to be unnecessary, for about Eastertide, when the town of Yaroslavl too had forsaken Dmitry's cause, the whole route from this town to the White Sea was free once more, so that right after the breakup, the merchants went gladly downriver to the sea at Archangel. There they found their ships from England and Holland, which they had despaired of ever seeing again. But since there was no trade, and they had suffered great losses, the vessels left almost empty after they had waited for some merchants who had still not arrived from the interior of the country. Everybody gave thanks to heaven that they had come through all these adventures safe and sound. Thus has it been possible for me to give this true account of all these events. As we embarked for our homeland, we left the empire prey to the misfortunes of civil war. Moscow was besieged, and Yaroslavl, in rallying to the tsar's cause, had been given Prince Sila Ivanovich Gagarin and Nikita Vasilievich Buslaev as its governors.

1610. Skopin, fighting for the Muscovites, is still in Novgorod

The young Skopin was still camped at Novgorod awaiting the Swedish reinforcements, which came towards spring, and the troops of Peter Sheremetev, who, leaving Balchik during the winter, had fought the Cheremissian Tatars and reached Nizhny Novgorod. All these forces joined Skopin's in the summer, and they marched together to relieve Moscow.

Kazan and its Tatars remained completely neutral. Astrakhan on the Caspian Sea, obliged to defend itself against the roving Cossacks who were plundering the surrounding countryside, likewise remained neutral.

The Nogai Tatars and the Cheremissians, together with the Mordvinians [Mordirisk], made their appearance during the winter in the neighbourhood of Cheboksary and Svyiazhsk on the Volga, and encountered Sheremetev. When the latter had moved on, they fought among themselves.

Dmitry occupied all the country from Poland and the frontiers of Tatary up to Moscow. He also held the towns of Pskov and Ivangorod. Smolensk and its territory were of the tsar's party.

From Moscow to the White Sea, all the country had remained loyal, fought for the tsar's cause, and sent aid in men and money every day. Such was the situation of the country as we were about to leave, but at the moment we were embarking we received news that Moscow had been relieved by Skopin and Sheremetev, supported by the contingent from Sweden. From what we heard, the Swedes had pursued the rebels with vigour. In this pursuit, the Muscovites under Skopin, enticed by the prospect of booty, had fallen on Dmitry's camp and looted it completely. Seeing this, the returning Swedes had fallen treacherously on the Muscovite soldiers loaded with booty and made a great carnage of them. We still thought that all had happened for the best, and Moscow had been delivered. God grant that this news was true! There are a number of reasons, appreciated easily by intelligent minds, why it would be a misfortune if the Poles ever succeeded in conquering this country. Even if they captured Moscow and established a new Dmitry there, they could not hold out a year; for the Muscovites and Russians, who are very independent and more obstinate than the Jews, would massacre them a second time, unless all Muscovy was widowed of its people and no more than a ruin, which may the Almighty prevent!

Later, we had fresh tidings that the rebels had approached the town and besieged it once again. Time will tell what will become of all this. According to letters received from Danzig, the king of Poland besieged Smolensk, promising the inhabitants forty years' exemption from taxes if they embraced his cause. In a word, this war could last for some time yet.

May almighty God, whose eternal will rules the things of this world, and punishes in diverse manners peoples and kings, permit that all this end for the best. I would very much have wished that this account could end with peace, and yet it seems that God's wrath will not be turned from this country, but intends to overturn and undermine it even more, thus to punish its crimes and the contempt both sides there show his church, as the Lord said himself by the mouth of his prophet Ezekiel, chapter 38, verse 21: 'I will call for a sword against him throughout all my mountains, saith the Lord God; every man's sword shall be against his brother.'

I earnestly pray that you will cherish this account, which contains only facts I have witnessed during my stay in this country, for the purpose that has prompted it, and that you will not regard it as a useless and insignificant gift. Consider it also as a warning. It will in fact show you how Antichrist, with the aid of Satan, has long sought by insidious snares to oppress God's holy church, and being unable to assail it from one side, is trying to surprise it on another. But I hope that we will soon see the end of his rage, and hear the triumphal song: 'It has fallen, it has fallen, the great Babylon! It has become the habitation of devils.'[205] May heaven grant that the time of the elect be nigh. And I pray God almighty that, by the blood of his son, Jesus Christ, he will deign to pardon our faults and receive us in his eternal kingdom, where all who believe must come. Amen!

Appendix A

Letter of Isaac Massa to the States-General

Archangel, 2 August 1614

... I know of no empire in our time that is in so much danger as this one. The tsar, it is true, has been chosen by the army, and is of the stock of former sovereigns, that is to say related to Ivan Vasilievich, and about twenty years old. But what does this matter? He is like to a sun partially obscured by stormy clouds, so that the soil of Muscovy has not yet received the least of his rays. The princes of the blood have little authority, he himself cannot write, and I am not sure whether he can read. His mother is a nun, and his father, after the Tsar Shuisky's surrender into the hands of the Poles, was sent as an ambassador to Poland, where, contrary to the law of nations, he has been kept prisoner to this very day. The tsar cannot get any help from him and, furthermore, his kingdom is assailed from all sides, given over to plunder, murder, and incendiarism by the Poles, the Swedes, the rebels in Astrakhan, the Crimean Tatars, and also that licentious soldiery, corrupt and wild, called the Cossacks, which is entrusted with the defence of the country. Last Easter, the Crimean Tatars, arriving like a lightning-bolt before the walls of Moscow, carried off twenty-five thousand people from all over the country, and throughout the spring, the aforesaid Cossacks, instead of going to attack the Swedes around Novgorod, have been roving continually in those territories, wherever there was a prospect of plunder. They do not do all these things out of lack of subsistence. In the Polish quarter, the Cossacks won another great victory in the springtime, and good tidings have come recently from Astrakhan to announce that Zarutsky, formerly a general in Polish service and then the service of Russia, who had revolted again with a body of mutinous troops, was blockaded at that moment in the citadel of Astrakhan under siege by the inhabitants of that town. This Zarutsky had with him the former tsarina and her son, the child of the late Dmitry the monk. This tsarina was the daughter of the palatine of Sandomierz in Poland, as Their High Mightinesses of the States-General can read in my work on the troubles in Muscovy, which I have dedicated to His Excellency the prince. At the time of the regency of the prince and Dmitry Pozharsky, seeing that the people were demanding to be given a tsar, and that Pozharsky was marching on Moscow to recapture it from the Poles, Zarutsky began to oppose him, and withdrew with a part of his troops, traversing the country like an enemy, devastating everything in his path, and arrived in the vicinity of Astrakhan on the Caspian Sea, where he concluded an alliance against Muscovy with the Nogai Tatars. He said that he had with him the tsar, the son of Dmitry, and his mother, and succeeded in influencing the people of Astrakhan against the Muscovites. Taking possession of this realm, and wishing to make himself more secure there, he sent to the shah of Persia, demanding that he come and aid him in his designs. But the shah had no confidence in him, and refused. Zarutsky was driven by fear to appeal to the Cossacks, who were at the walls of Smolensk and Novgorod that winter. They seemed to welcome his proposals, and promised to join him in springtime even if they had to fight their way across the country, coming down the Volga or else over land. To make even more certain, Zarutsky proposed to cede the realm of Astrakhan to the sultan if he would order the Crimean Tatars to come to the aid of the young Tsar Ivan Dmitrievich, help him conquer the kingdom of Kazan, and, after that, the empire of Muscovy.

Meanwhile, the tsar of the true imperial tree, being established in Moscow and aided by the magnates of the empire, set about the task of defending himself against this menacing storm and extinguishing this conflagration that was sowing far more terror than all his other foes. Gathering all their troops in the most favourable locations, they formed an army that moved on Kazan; proceeding down the Volga on more than a thousand boats, they placed garrisons in all the towns as far as Samara, a small town bordering on the wildernesses of Tatary. Beyond this, they held off all their enemies with other armies. Needless to say, these supreme efforts have exhausted the country completely.

So as I have related, with these fresh tidings the people of Astrakhan abandoned Zarutsky's cause, for he had sought to betray the realm of Astrakhan to the Turks. They laid such siege to the citadel that it was obliged to surrender. I think this affair will be completely over within a couple of months. Apart from this, all the Nogai Tatars in the vicinity have submitted to the Muscovites, and the rebel Cossacks, seeing that their cause is hopeless, have withdrawn once again, pillaging all the country and retreating past Novgorod. All the army sent against them will now be able to return, and be deployed against Smolensk and Novgorod.

In conclusion, this is one of the first and greatest successes of the tsar, and if everything continues in this vein, it will be a great blessing for Russia. All he needs is good counsellors, for all now closest to the tsar are young and ignorant men. Even the most honest officials are ravening wolves, who pluck and pillage the common people most of all. No one obtains justice from the tsar. Nobody can even petition him without paying a great deal of money, and even then one cannot be sure that his petition, even if it is considered, will have a fortunate outcome.

If things so remain, this situation will not last a year. But I hope that God will open the eyes of the young prince as he opened the eyes of the old tsar, Ivanovich. That is the kind of sovereign Russia must have; otherwise, she is lost. For this people does not prosper unless it is oppressed by the mighty, and it is in slavery that it becomes rich and happy. That is why the situation will not improve so long as the people cannot be persuaded that the tsar should sit in blood up to his elbows.

I am convinced that, as a result of this great victory, the present tsar will later become a very fortunate sovereign, if God wishes to open his eyes, and inspire in him the idea of eradicating the noxious weed that is growing at his court, and punishing the injustices of his officers. But this will take time. Already, the tsar has shown promise. Just after his election, when he was told of the case of a lord who should have been punished for some misdeed, he replied: 'Do you not know that the Muscovite bears do not devour the stag in their first year, but only begin to hunt step by step with advancing age?' If he is as good as his word, the country will soon enjoy rest and tranquillity.

(*VdL, vol. 1, pp. 226-36*)

Appendix B

1 / Letter of Isaac Massa to the States-General, written at Archangel on 4 September and received on 17 November 1618

To the Gracious and High Mighty Lords of the States-General of the United Netherlands:

My Lords! Our arrival here occurred without mishap on 22 August. We were very contented on the journey, and, given the circumstances, we have been received honourably. The report which the ambassador transmitted about us describes such actions, with all hearts along the Dvina so well disposed towards our nation, that if the same report should be delivered in a similar manner before the tsar and Grand Prince in Moscow, we could wish for nothing better.

The English ambassador came to Archangel before us and was greeted rapturously by a salvo of musketry. They were unusually hospitable to him, and attempted to entertain him lavishly at the expense of the impoverished citizenry. Two or three weeks passed before he decided to proceed towards Moscow. At last, he went upriver, but halted at Kholmogory. His entertainment cost in excess of three hundred guilders a day. He did not wish to go any farther than Kholmogory, despite the pleas of the governors. Hearing of our arrival in Archangel, he departed from Kholmogory stealthily four days later, taking with him his retinue and money, and deceiving the bailiffs and commissioners whom he had taken along for protection two or three days previously. Reaching the fortress of Archangel in the morning, he turned aside and came hither across country with reinforcement from the crews of two English ships. The next day, just before dinner-time, it was learned in Kholmogory that he had fled on two Russian boats. The bailiff sent people in pursuit through all the towns, but it was too late. The bailiff himself was put under arrest and sent in chains to the governor at Archangel, there to be held until instructions come from Moscow, where messengers are sent repeatedly to report to His Imperial Majesty on all these matters. The musketeers who had been assigned to escort and guard the ambassador were put to interrogation. They confessed to everything, and so it now appears that the bailiff was at fault, not having carried out his duties conscientiously. The commanders of the city are very fearful. Since they are responsible to the tsar in this matter, this is their concern, but they hope to be able to exculpate themselves. Some nobles and the English agent tried to dissuade the ambassador, but he did not wish to heed them, and on 2 September, he departed on two ships that fired broadsides. One shot went right through one of the houses. The Russians were astounded and greatly perturbed. They sent the Englishman's compatriot and his secretary to Moscow in disgrace. I cannot rightly guess the cause of this commotion. Some say it was caused by ill tidings from upriver, others that it was caused by my arrival, for there is a rumour current that we had come with a huge subsidy, together with many other things the English did not have. It is also said that the ambassador found this country very unpleasant, and that the East India Company in England had deceived the Muscovy Company. In short, everyone has his own version, and it is hard to distinguish the truth. This at least is true; the English are embarrassed, and our credit is good. Finally, the princes in Moscow will realize the truth about trade with England, from which the tsar has derived no benefit in the course of fifty years, whereas a significant sum has accrued annually from the customs duty paid by the Dutch. Now they will realize who has better served Russia's interests throughout the world. The Russians will take note that nobody has offered the Muscovite state an insult such as the English have offered, not even the Turks in the course of all their wars against the Russians. Never have they been so insulted. As highly as the English were regarded before, so now are they despised. As much as they exalted themselves, so now they hang their heads and are notably ingratiating to us. Henceforth, they cannot do otherwise, and unless something unforeseen occurs, their company will dissolve within the year; for only three of their ships have come this year, whereas we have had more than thirty, selling every kind of merchandise. These return to the Netherlands with full cargoes of Russian goods. The governors also gave me a bailiff and a guard of honour, and asked my intentions. I replied that I was ready to proceed to His Imperial Highness with gifts sent to the tsar by Your High Mightinesses. They asked me what I was bringing, to which I answered that I would expound on all these matters in Moscow, and that I was requesting an armed escort and convoy for the goods in question. This was granted me. We intend to set out tomorrow. We will do our utmost in everything, and take advantage of the present favourable circumstances.

Incidentally, there is a burnt-out monastery here in Archangel, and the Russians say in jest that they will transfer the English counter to that monastery, because there is no other building suitable, and the English have done hardly any business during the current year. Their purpose was to expel the Dutch with the subsidy they were bringing, and keep all the trade for themselves. But things have turned out quite differently. Even if their ambassador does proceed to Moscow he will be turned back, since the council knows about his beggarly circumstances, of which I am ashamed to write. Furthermore, although I do not know all the details, I will report in full on these matters to Your High Mightinesses on my return from Moscow.

The Danes have attacked our ships near the coast of Lapland and driven them off by force. They have also sent ships with merchants who have complained against the Dutch in the name of their king. But as we had bribed the Russians a little, and since in any case these officials are friendly to our own merchants, they dismissed the Danes.

The Russians have behaved particularly graciously towards our merchants this year. They have not levied more than two per cent on our purchases or sales, even though some are discontented at this and grumble. But we cannot omit one complaint. From the time of our arrival, the Russians have given our people such freedom in trade that many of our merchants have concealed half their goods, and thus paid only half the duty. I cannot applaud this action on their part. It is, however, more a matter of honour.

I had no funds for powder or lead, though the Russians have provided a skipper and ballast free of charge. I had to hire an additional cooper. I am not presently in a position to give any further information. I will carry out conscientiously all the instructions given me, so that Your High Mightinesses will be satisfied. I will be silent and act, commending Your High Mightinesses to the merciful protection of the Almighty, who I pray will grant Your High Mightinesses a happy and tranquil rule, and to me a constant desire to serve the fatherland.

Archangel, 4 September 1618

P.S. Today I received information that the 'Great Ostrich,' i.e. the Grand Chancellor, has died. He was always a great friend of the English and an enemy of ours. It is rumoured that he was poisoned. May God grant a similar end to all the enemies of our country, or at least a more amicable frame of mind.

Isaac Massa

2 / Report of Isaac Massa concerning his adventures during his journey to the Grand Prince of Moscow, delivered on 2 March 1620

High and Mighty Lords! Your High Mightinesses will have seen from the letters I wrote you on 4 September, 1618, that I had reached Archangel with gifts, and with the ambassador of His Majesty the emperor of all Russia, who was returning from the Netherlands. Your High Mightinesses also learned of the English ambassador's flight by the sea with all he had brought to assist His Majesty of Russia, as well as other events that occurred about this time.

Our journey upriver towards Moscow prospered until 12 September, on which day we reached the neighbourhood of Korobitsa, where the boat on which I happened to be travelling with my companions, my wardrobe, and silk furnishings, sank on account of her poor construction. To the amazement of many, we managed to escape from the boat. We were obliged to hire couriers, whom we sent to the governor of Archangel for another boat with supplies. All this was immediately sent to us. Our bailiffs were arrested because they had given us the first boat, which was not sound, and they were compelled to reimburse us for all our losses, except for two trunks of clothing which we had lost.

On the 16th, we proceeded once again almost to Ustiug and Totma on other boats, with the supplies sent at the bailiffs' expense. On 11 October, we came to Vologda. Here, the governor sent his own horse to fetch me, and I entered the city with the town garrison as escort. They lodged me in one of the most prominent houses. We had to stay in the aforementioned town until 18 November, not only to await the onset of winter, but more especially because the road between Vologda and Yaroslavl was perilous, for the enemy was appearing with some seven or eight thousand Cherkassians every day. They came so close to the city that we even considered ourselves besieged.

Meanwhile, the governors had received letters from the uncle of the Grand Prince, who was stationed with his retinue below Yaroslavl to prevent the enemy from crossing the Volga, with instructions to send a detachment to Moscow, which was being besieged by the Polish prince, Wladyslaw. At that time, Wladyslaw had attacked Moscow by night with sixteen thousand men – French, English, German, Irish, Scottish, Polish, and Cherkassian troops. But he was repelled, and retreated to the outermost confines of the city, whence he did not make a second attempt. The Poles even began to sue for peace, since from all parts of the country there came a rumour that the English and Dutch emissaries were arriving with military supplies, money, and four thousand Dutch troops. These tidings sowed panic among the

Poles, but the Germans were pleased, for they were not at all contented with the Polish prince, and were looking for an opportunity to defect. Added to this was the news of the Bohemian war, which forced the Poles to conclude peace. There also came orders to dispatch us with a large convoy to Yaroslavl, with all we were bringing. But first they brought the English ambassador there, and then they assigned me a captain with five hundred troops, and in addition, a few persons of noble rank. The powder and shot were brought overland on sleds. The carriage charges for taking the military supplies from Vologda to Yaroslavl were, in my estimation, three times the actual cost. From the shape of the load, the people thought we were bringing silver, not lead; but the lords commander wished it so for the sake of glory. Prayers were said for our good health in all the churches, and so we arrived in Yaroslavl on 24 November. On the way, we were twice surrounded at night by the enemy, numbering four thousand men, whom we saw in various hamlets not more than a full mile distant. But the captain kept me at his side for my protection, saying: 'Let everything be lost, only let me bring you through unharmed; otherwise I shall answer for it with my life.' In this manner, we twice survived misfortune, I and ten members of my suite. I gave my captain a substantial gift, which I could not honourably fail to do. Then the entire cargo arrived at Yaroslavl. There, I was honourably received, and the goods deposited in the treasury vault while I was assigned my quarters. Here, the Russian ambassador made his report in terms that were favourable to us, in which I bore witness to his conversations with me, and the respect he had shown me. For example, he conducted me across the Volga to my lodgings on a horse belonging to the Grand Prince's own kinsman, an honour which had hitherto been accorded to no one, and certainly did not please the English.

In the town of Yaroslavl, which has never been conquered, we remained for twelve weeks, awaiting the conclusion of peace between the Russians and the king of Poland and the Grand Principality of Lithuania. This peace was concluded near the great monastery of the Trinity, which lies between Moscow and Yaroslavl, with the king's son and Lew Sapieha and all their army ten miles away. They had been unable to capture that monastery by any means, since it was well fortified and plentifully supplied with arms. Meanwhile, in Yaroslavl there was a great conflagration that caused much damage. It started in the English ambassador's house, and was caused by tobacco smoking and drunkenness. Three Englishmen perished in this fire, as well as two Russians. Much wheat was destroyed also, and much grain. The emissary, the nobles, and other people in his suite barely managed to save their lives, but all their belongings were consumed by the flames. However, the remainder of the money sent to His Majesty was in safe-keeping in the fortress.

On 4 January, I set out for Moscow with three hundred gentry who were equipped to form my convoy. They were commanded by Daniel Yaroslavsky. We were commanded to leave the powder and lead in Yaroslavl, because there were not enough horses on the route to transport it all. We went by way of Rostov, Pereiaslavl, and the Trinity monastery, and came to Moscow on 1 February. Outside the city, we were met by people especially appointed for this task, who conducted us to the quarters assigned to us. I was lodged in the house of Bishop Bosdalsky. According to the Russian custom, food and drink was allotted to me in greater quantities than in the previous year. But they did not provide me with a cook, cooking utensils, a bed, or other like necessities, and so I was obliged to obtain these for myself.

They also gave me a guard in Moscow, as they had in other towns, but no one of our company was to leave the house as we had done before. I asked permission for some of my acquaintances to come and visit me. This permission was granted, but on condition that these visits should be kept secret. But the English in Moscow and other towns were guarded very closely.

Both the English emissary and I frequently requested an audience, but we were both informed courteously that we would have to be patient, as first, peace had to be concluded and confirmed by the embassies that had been exchanged by the two sovereigns, which required much time and expense. But in the meantime, I was admitted to the chancellery to visit the secretary Savva Romanchukov, who at that time was carrying out the responsibilities of the late chancellor. He greeted me in the name of His Sovereign Majesty with the utmost courtesy and kindness. He inquired about my journey, and asked me about the adventures I had had along the way, and then he accompanied me back to my lodgings. Instead of the regular meal, as they call it, he sent me special food and drink on that day. So matters stood until the end of March.

My friends and acquaintances, and also His Imperial Majesty's kinsman, Ivan Nikitich, who is now Grand Constable, advised me against demanding an audience with His Majesty. The English agent who remained at Moscow had been trying by all means, and at very great expense, to secure an audience for me at the earliest opportunity. There were good reasons for this, since nearly all the officials in the chancellery were devoted to the English, and very avaricious. They would have frustrated our plans, for it was well known to all that His Imperial Majesty has not only callously tolerated the goings-on in all the provinces of the realm, but also, with great meekness, turned a blind eye to the activities of his courtiers and other servants – this was because he had so many enemies, not only outside but also within the country – awaiting the return of his father, to whom he intended to entrust the administration of the country, as the man who alone could uphold the dignity of the Great Principality. It would therefore be to my advantage to await this change, which some were anticipating in hope, others in fear, and which in fact came to pass with the arrival of the tsar's father and other statesmen who had spent eight years in Polish captivity. For this and no other reason, Russia had ceded to Poland 14 Lithuanian towns that had belonged to the Russians for more than a hundred years. These towns lie on the river formerly called the Boristhenes, but which is now called the Dnieper.

Meanwhile, the English agent was trying everything to find out why I had been sent here. He guessed the purpose of my mission quite mistakenly, since I was living quietly and peacefully. At this time, there were quite a number of rumours about. Some said that I had come to settle Russia with Dutch subjects, that the Swedes had been attacked by the Russians, etc. They painted us in the blackest colours. The English demanded an audience, which was granted them at the worst possible time, namely Ash Wednesday.

When the English envoy appeared before the tsar, he had no gifts for His Majesty, since the English ambassador who had fled had taken all of them with him. He did, however, bring some gifts provided at his own expense and out of contributions from the gentlemen of his suite, but these were returned to them on their departure from Moscow, to their shame and that of the English company. Moreover, gifts from His Imperial Majesty that far exceeded their own in value were delivered to their lodgings. When the credentials issued by His Majesty the king of England were examined, it was discovered that they related exclusively to the ambassador, Sir Dudley Digges, and when it was realized that the uncle of the aforesaid Digges had been sent in his stead, he was told that he could not request an audience on that basis, since he was not the king's ambassador, but merely the king's servant, with no mandate from His Majesty. They were also informed curtly that they did not wish to have any dealings with them, adding that they were truly amazed that the servants of the king of England, the gracious brother of His Imperial Majesty, did not show him greater respect, and that they should have the temerity so to abandon their responsibility as to send such a base person to the throne of so great a sovereign as the tsar; that they had not thought such a thing possible, but if indeed they did have with them a portion of what had been promised the tsar, then they should deliver it. This they refused to do. For this reason, they had to remain for three months under guard. At length, they requested an audience with the members of the assembly, and, having obtained it, explained then and there that they would not hand over the money unless the Dutch were altogether prohibited from trading in Russia. They replied that they did not wish to consider this proposal, even if the king were to make such a demand in person. Since the sum of money they had was so insignificant, and consisted of Spanish reals needed for the purchase of certain church ornaments, they sent them some merchants entrusted with the task of exchanging these reals. The English wanted six per cent more than the customary rate of exchange for this money. Finally, they were told that the Russians did not wish to have any more dealings with them. It is said that they had 100,000 reals with them. From that time on, the English, purely to undermine the position we enjoyed, tried in every possible way to stir up hatred against Your High Mightinesses the States-General. They even went so far as to deliver a letter in which they stated that Your High Mightinesses the States-General represented a people that desired to meddle in the affairs of all governments and sow discord among them; that Your High Mightinesses were also to blame for the Swedish war, which was carried on with your power and supplies; that you had proposed an alliance with Poland against Russia, and many other false tales, which I would be ashamed to repeat. The Russians replied that His Imperial Majesty thanked them for their solicitude, and then laughed behind their backs, since by their slanders they had injured only themselves. I have not even wished to bother refuting them, but I am prepared to prove anything if by chance anyone should come to grief thereby. When the English envoy was leaving Moscow, the gates were shut in his face three times as he tried to leave his lodgings on horseback. They did this to him no fewer than three days in succession. When they escorted him from the city, he was accompanied only by the basest court officials and scribes, who are reckoned the least of the nobility in Moscow. Thus, he left extremely dissatisfied, angry not only with the Russians but also with the English agent, whom he holds responsible for all that happened.

Before he left Moscow, we were granted an audience. I and my suite were given horses from the stables of the Grand Prince, with outriders and pages. It was ordered that our route should pass the English lodgings; to their great humiliation, they all saw my servants on the tsar's horses, while they themselves had been compelled to hire horses on a similar occasion.

Appearing before His Imperial Majesty, I greeted him respectfully in the name of Your High Mightinesses, delivered the gifts I had brought with me, and also some personal gifts, as emissaries who had been in Russia before me had done. Then I was permitted to approach the throne, I handed him the documents from Your High Mightinesses and asked that deputies be appointed to speak with me. The tsar indicated a wish to speak with me personally, and I had to answer his questions without an interpreter. He asked whether Your High Mightinesses the States-General, as well as the prince of Orange, were all in good health. I replied that when I had left, Your High Mightinesses were all in excellent health, and were wishing His Imperial Majesty a long life and a peaceful reign. The tsar nodded his head, and inquired about my own health, asking also whether I had not had some unpleasant experiences on my journey through his dominions. I thanked His Imperial Majesty for the honour he had shown me as the representative of Your High Mightinesses. Even though I had cause for complaint, I would have endangered the lives of those responsible, and, besides, I did not want to stir up hatred against myself, and so preferred to remain silent, and avoided the subject at this meeting. The tsar then dismissed me, and, instead of the customary dinner, sent me special food and drink. This interview occurred on 1 June.

I had several audiences thereafter, following the return of the tsar's father to Moscow; this furthered my cause, which was the subject of 22 meetings in the patriarch's cell with His Majesty and all the lords of the land present. It was decided that in no manner should we be barred from the Russian trade, but rather admitted on an equal footing with the English. As soon as this decision was made, Ivan Nikitich sent me a trustworthy and discreet friend to assure me that the matter had definitely been resolved, and to advise that Your High Mightinesses not delay in sending emissaries to conclude a treaty about the aforesaid matter. I rewarded Ivan Nikitich's messenger with a gilded cup.

Your High Mightinesses can verify my account of this matter from the letters of His Imperial Majesty. When these letters were handed to me, I was urged by the chief advisers and the chancellor himself to beg Your High Mightinesses not to delay in sending emissaries if we desire conditions favourable to our country. The Russians themselves are extremely satisfied and pleased, since they know that they will get much profit and advantage from these transactions.

The newly appointed chancellor, Ivan Tarasievich Kurbatov, who had been ambassador to the Holy Roman emperor, is like a native-born German, astute and judicious in all things, for he had learned much as a captive of the Poles and Prussians. He questioned me closely on all the details. Where did we propose to establish our counters? What goods would we export or import? – and other similar matters. We answered these questions. I named the products that were desirable and necessary to us, and stated that whatever we agreed to, we would fulfil our part of the bargain. The goods are as follows: raw silk, dyestuffs, chandlery goods, striped woollen cloth, brocades, damask, etc. From our country, we would send all kinds of cloth, without exception; canvas, because of its special whiteness – in which it excels silk or parchment material – and which on that account the Russians particularly value and like. Several of our cities can produce canvas that is extremely well suited for trade with Russia. Thereafter, I listed special goods, and products from Nuremberg.

On 14 June there was the triumphal entry of the tsar's father, Filaret Nikitich, with all the others who had been with him in captivity. His Imperial Majesty met him an entire mile outside the city, with the people of all nations. More people gathered than had been seen since before the recent troubles. They were greeted with palms and branches, and brought in on sleds pulled by four horses, according to the custom of the local clergy. They rang all the bells, and prayed in all the churches. All the inhabitants of Moscow prayed for several days, spending half of each day in the churches and the other half feasting.

The Polish captives were also freed, given clothing, and then escorted to the frontier. In all jurisdictions, the officials were changed, and all their subordinates replaced, but this change was not always for the better. All this was done at the personal command of the tsar's father, but had actually been arranged and ordered beforehand.

On 4 August, I received a reply from the state chancellor and an immediate exhortation to urge Their High Mightinesses the States-General of the United Netherlands not to put off the dispatch of a full-scale embassy any later than the English. They assured me that they knew full well that what was planned would be to the advantage of our country, more advantageous by far than the terms in the documents sent to His Majesty the king of England. I was also ordered to prepare for my farewell audience with His Imperial Majesty on 6 August.

On 6 August, they brought me and my suite to the palace on the horses of the Grand Prince. I presented myself to His Imperial Majesty and received documents, and was then permitted to approach His Imperial Majesty's throne. He commanded me to convey his greetings to Your High Mightinesses, and wish you health and a fortunate rule. He then instructed me specifically to invite you to send ambassadors with plenipotentiary powers. He also ordered me to convey the same greeting to Prince Maurice, his gracious friend. Then, after the customary ceremonies, I turned and bowed to all the princes who sat on the tsar's left. They rose and returned my bow.

The next day, they sent teams of horses and guides to my house. I was given three bales of sables, to the value of nearly nine hundred guilders, that is, half the value of the gifts I had brought; even though the tsar always orders that all ambassadors and emissaries be given presents to half the value of those they had brought, this order is not always carried out, and the emissary may not complain or demand anything, nor would it be proper for him to do so.

On the 7th, we left Moscow, and I was given up to twenty mounted escorts who accompanied me to Yaroslavl, where I was also joined by troops and guides. On the 14th, I came to Vologda, which is about one hundred German miles from Moscow. There, we were met by a courier who informed us of a conflagration that had occurred in Archangel.

We proceeded from Vologda on 16 August in a large vessel with oarsmen and soldiers. We drifted past Suska and Totma to Ustiug by way of the Sukhona, and on the 21st, we reached the Great Dvina River.

On 26 August, I reached Archangel. I was met by troops and provided with supplies. I was witness to the destruction caused by the fire, in which the Amsterdam merchants had lost one and a half million guilders. They did, however, manage to save about half of their possessions – with the exception of myself, being absent at the time, and so I lost nearly all my belongings. The fire was attributed to the English. The Muscovy Company in England has collapsed, and its commissioners in Archangel could thus more conveniently close their accounts. But God only knows! Furthermore, it is known here that the greater part of the English goods had already been loaded on their ships, and a few days before the fire, some of them had even transferred their personal belongings on board. The autumn was coming on, and so I could not stay and wait for news from Moscow. Since I could not find a suitable naval vessel, I had to take passage for myself. The voyage on that ship took about nine weeks in storms and foul weather. We were twice forced to put into port in Norway, which cost us much time and money.

Such is a brief description of what happened to me in the course of this journey. I thought it might be useful to Your High Mightinesses for me to set down everything, assuring Your High Mightinesses that I have carried out all the tasks entrusted to me. Now, nobody will have reason to complain that our trade throughout that country is being hampered. We now enjoy freedom equal to that of the English. As will be apparent from the missive of His Imperial Majesty, he intended to dispatch his second letter by special courier, but to prevent delay, I took the second letter from him, and have forwarded it to Your High Mightinesses.

In all conscience, I must say that in every circumstance I have upheld the dignity of Your High Mightinesses and the best interests of our country. I do not doubt that we will obtain the Persian trade, so long as you see fit to send a high-ranking embassy to the Grand Prince of Muscovy as His Imperial Majesty's letter demands. Your subjects will enjoy great advantages, and recoup all the losses we have incurred in the Muscovite state.

Commending myself to your graciousness, I pray God that he will grant Your High Mightinesses all good fortune and long-lasting rule.

Concluded 3 December 1619
Your High Mightinesses' most humble servant,
Isaac Massa

P.S. It must be pointed out that the war supplies sent by Your High Mightinesses, and delivered by me, were valued at 40,000 guilders, and that they were received and accounted for at that evaluation by His Imperial Majesty and the princes of the realm, despite the fact that their value in Holland would not have exceeded 20,000 guilders.

(Vestnik Evropy, *August 1868, 800-14*)

Abbreviations

AAE	*Akty sobrannye i izdannye v bibliotekakh i arkhivakh Rossiiskoi Imperii Arkheograficheskoiu Kommissieiu*, vol. 2 (St Petersburg, 1836)
AK	Archeographic Commission edition of Massa's text, *Rerum Rossicarum Scriptores Exteri*, vol. 2 (St Petersburg, 1868)
Beschryvinghe	*Warachtige ende Eygentlijcke Beschryvinghe vande wonderbare ende seer gedenckenweerdighe geschiednissen, die in Moscovia zyn voorgevallen ende in dem naestvoorleden ende in den teghenwoordighen jare 1606* (Amsterdam, 1606)
Kordt	B.A. Kordt, 'Ocherk Snoshenii moskovskogo gosudarstva s Republikoi Niderlandov do 1631 god,' *Sbornik Imperatorskogo Russkogo Istoricheskogo Obshchestva*, 116 (St Petersburg, 1902)
Légende	*La légende de la vie et de la mort de Démétrius, dernier Grand-Duc de Moscovie, traduicte nouvellement l'an 1606* (Amsterdam, 1606)
MERSH	*Modern Encyclopedia of Russian and Soviet History* (Gulf Breeze, Fla., 1976+)
Morozov	Alexander Morozov's translation and edition of Massa's text, *Kratkoe izvestie o Moskovii v nachale XVII veka* (Moscow, 1937)
Popov, *Izbornik*	A.N. Popov, *Izbornik slavianskikh i russkikh sochinenii i statei vnesennykh v khronografy russkoi redaktsii* (Moscow, 1869)
PSRL	*Polnoe sobranie russkikh letopisei*, vol. 14 (St Petersburg, 1910)
Reporte	*The Reporte of a bloudie and terrible massacre in the Citty of Mosco, with the fearfull and tragicall end of Demetrius, the last Duke, before him raigning at this present* (London, 1607)

RIB	*Russkaia istoricheskaia biblioteka*, vol. 1 (St Petersburg, 1872), and vol. 13 (St Petersburg, 1909)
SGGD	*Sobranie gosudarstvennykh gramot i dogovorov*, vol. 2 (St Petersburg, 1819)
VdL	The van der Linde edition of Massa's text, *Histoire des guerres de la Moscovie, 1601-1610*, 2 vols (Brussels, 1866)

Notes

INTRODUCTION

1 A. van der Linde, *Isaac Massa van Haarlem: een historische Studie* (Amsterdam, 1864). A French version of the same was incorporated into the 1866 Brussels edition of Massa's *History* (see p. xxii).
2 Johannes Keuning, 'Isaac Massa, 1586-1643,' *Imago Mundi: a review of early cartography*, 10 (1953), 65-80.
3 The patent is reprinted in Kordt, 116 (St Petersburg, 1902), ccxxxi-ccxxxiii.
4 Page 5, below.
5 Haarlem: Gemeynte Archief, *Doepboek*, 7 October 1586.
6 Keuning, 67.
7 *Beschryvinghe vander Samoyeden Landt in Tatarien Nieulijks onder 't Ghebiet der Moscoviten gebracht. Uyt de russche tale overgheset Anno 1609* (Amsterdam, 1612). English translation in *The Arctic North-east and West Passage* (Amsterdam, 1878).
8 Keuning, 67-70; J.A. Leerink, 'Een nederlandsche cartograaph in Rusland,' *Phoenix*, 1 (1946), 4.
9 The text of this letter is contained in J. Scheltema, *Rusland en de Nederlanden*, 1 (Amsterdam, 1817), 371-85.
10 Resolution of the States-General, 12 March 1614.
11 The text of this letter is to be found in VdL, 1, xxxix-xl.
12 VdL, 1, 228-30.
13 VdL, 1, 233-6.
14 VdL, 1, 237-40.
15 Resolution of the States-General, 23 October 1615.
16 Resolution of the States-General, 31 October 1615.
17 Massa's letter to the States-General, dated 31 October 1617, is reprinted in VdL, 2, xc-cxii.

18 Massa's report, VdL, 2, cviii-cix.
19 Massa's *Remonstrance* to the States-General is reprinted in Kordt, 116, cccxxvi-cccxxx.
20 Ibid., clxi-clxvi.
21 Geraldine M. Phipps, 'Britons in Seventeenth-century Russia,' PHD dissertation, University of Pennsylvania, 1971, 109-15.
22 Haarlem: Gemeynte Archief, *Doedboek*, 11-18 April 1621; *Trouwboek*, 25 April 1622.
23 E. de Jongh and P.J. Vincken, 'Frans Hals als voortzetter van een emblematische Traditie: bij het huwelijksportret van Isaac Massa en Beatrix van der Laen,' *Oud-Holland*, 76, pt. 3-4 (1961), 117-52.
24 Kordt, 116, cxxxii-cxxxv.
25 Ibid., cxxi-cxxxiii.
26 Massa's *Propositie* is to be found in VdL, 1, 263-7.
27 Kordt, 116, cxci.
28 'Vervolcht van Haet en nijt, vooruluchte hij tot d'eer bij Keyser, Koning, Heer / Er won er gonst met dienst, Slants Staaten hem betrouden, wiens liefd' eens weer verkoude / Als hem die nijt belaagd, omstutten sijnen loop gesterct van Godt in hoop, / Erlangd hij meerder gonst, bij 't grootste Hooft der Gotten, dies hij de nijt bespotten, / Gadelt en verrijct, nu sijn gemoet na d'eeuwich goet.' The 'commander of the Goths' apparently refers to the king of Sweden.
29 Haarlem: Gemeynte Archief, *Doedboek*, 10 April 1639; *Trouwboek*, 22 April 1640; *Doepboek*, 10 November 1641 and 15 February 1643.
30 N.S. Trivas, *The Paintings of Frans Hals* (London, 1941), 9.
31 Haarlem: Gemeynte Archief, *Doedboek*, 14-21 June 1643.
32 The Hague, Koninklijke Bibliotheek, ms 128.A.33.
33 '26. Remarques touchant la guerre de Moscovie en 1610. Parch,' *Catalogue des livres de la bibliothèque de S.A.S. Frédéric-Henri, Prince d'Orange* (The Hague, 1749), 232.
34 See appendix A.
35 Friedrich von Adelung, *Kritisch-literärische Übersicht der Reisenden in Russland bis 1700 deren Berichte bekannt sind* (St Petersburg, 1846), 2, 217-21.
36 Frederic Muller, *Essai d'une bibliographie néerlando-russe* (Amsterdam, 1859), 105-16.
37 A. van der Linde, *Isaac Massa van Haarlem*.
38 Adelung, 2, 198-204.
39 Oxford: Bodleian Library, Pamphlet 4.L.70.Art. Also, London: British Museum, C.32.g.40 and 9455.b.19. The copy supposed to be at the Royal Library in The Hague (344.H.20) has apparently been mislaid.

40 Utrecht: Rijksuniversiteit, Pamflet UB 58.
41 For a discussion of the three texts, see Muller, 107-8.
42 See note 70, below.
43 My deciphering of the manuscript was considerably facilitated by consulting W. Bogtman, *Het Nederlandsche Handschrift in 1600* (Haarlem, n.d.).

MASSA'S TEXT

1 Maurice of Nassau (1567-1625), stadholder of Holland, Zeeland, and West Frisia (1585) in succession to his father, William the Silent. In 1589, he was stadholder of several other provinces and supreme commander of the military and naval forces of the United Provinces.
2 William the Silent (1533-84), Prince of Orange and Count of Nassau, one of the principal leaders of the Netherlands Revolt. He was assassinated by a Spanish agent.
3 Massa: *Risomes*; Morozov, tr. *Rizom*. This reference is probably to Rustam, the eponymous hero of Ferdowsi's *Book of Kings*.
4 Jacob van Heemskerk, Dutch navigator and admiral. He took part in the quest for the North-east Passage in 1594-5, in the Dutch expedition to India in 1598-1600, and was admiral of the east Indian expedition of 1601. He was killed in an action off Gibraltar against the Spanish fleet in 1607. See Morozov, n. 2.
5 Massa is referring here to the virtual cessation of commerce in the turbulence of the Time of Troubles.
6 Doubtless a pun on Ivan's patronymic, Vasil'evich.
7 Ivan was born 25 August 1530. Vasily III died 3 December 1533, Elena Glinskaia 3 April 1538. Vasily and Elena also had a second son, Yury, born shortly before his father's death. He was a deaf-mute, was made prince of Uglich, and died without issue on 24 October 1563.
8 The coronation took place on 16 January and the marriage on 3 February 1547.
9 A similar account is to be found in the chronicle of Ivan Timofeev: O.A. Derzhavina and V.P. Adrianova-Peretts eds, *Vremennik Ivana Timofeeva* (Moscow and Leningrad, 1951), 20.
10 VdL: 20; AK: 23. The original manuscript quite clearly reads '23.' Actually, Ivan Ivanovich was 27 at the time. Similar accounts are contained in the narrations of Jerome Horsey and Giles Fletcher, *Rude and Barbarous Kingdom: Russia in the accounts of sixteenth-century English voyagers* (Madison, 1968), 128, 300. Antonio Possevino, in his *Moscovia*, also states that the tsarevich was only 20 years old, and that the fatal quarrel was caused by the tsar's

mistreatment of his daughter-in-law, which resulted in a miscarriage. *The Moscovia of Antonio Possevino*, S.J., tr. Hugh F. Graham (Pittsburgh, 1977), 12-13.

11 Morozov (n. 11) suggests that this reference is to the walls built around the Kitai-Gorod in 1535. However, this work was done during Ivan's minority. It is more likely that Massa is referring to Ivan's later building of concentric fortifications around Moscow, such as the 'White City' and the 'Earthen City.' These were extensively rebuilt after the Tatar invasion and conflagration of 1571.

12 Massa uses the term *coningen*, Morozov *s tsariami*. Perhaps the more correct term would be 'khans,' though the term 'tsar' was frequently applied to Tatar rulers.

13 The truce with Poland was actually concluded in 1554, *after* the capture of Kazan.

14 Ivan's only living son at that time was Dmitry, not Fyodor.

15 Massa, '*die op staende voet van rouwe stirff.*' The Kazan ruler captured by the Russians was in fact Ediger, not Safa Girei. Ediger died in 1565.

16 This Semeon (Bekbulatovich) was not originally from Kazan, but from Kasimov, a Tatar principality which had long been tributary to Moscow.

17 *Motrogan* probably means Tmutorokan, with which Massa evidently confused Astrakhan. Tmutorokan was situated on the Taman Peninsula, and was the seat of an ancient Russian principality and eparchy until in the twelfth century it was detached from the Russian land by Polovtsian attacks.

18 Also known as Yanalei or Djan-Ali.

19 Abdul Rahman was expelled from Kazan in 1537, Ediger sought service with Moscow in 1542, while Kaibula came to Moscow from Astrakhan in 1552 (Morozov, n. 18).

20 II Samuel, x, 4. Morozov (n. 19), according to the usage of the Slavonic Bible, cites II Kings. Sebastian was dispatched in 1551 and Astrakhan captured on 2 July 1554 (Morozov, n. 20).

21 Massa incorrectly calls Basmanov 'Alexander' in the original.

22 Once again, Massa is making a pun, perhaps unintentionally, on Ivan's patronymic. Similar stories are related in the accounts of Taube and Kruze, Albert Schlichting, and Giles Fletcher.

23 Evidently by *cancelieren en secretarisen* Massa means 'secretaries and undersecretaries' (*d'iaki i pod'iachie*).

24 Massa may be confusing Ivan's wives with those of his son Ivan, who was compelled to repudiate two successive wives, Evdokiia Saburova and Praskoviia Solovaia, for sterility. Ivan actually divorced only two of his seven wives, Anna Koltovskaia (1575) and Anna Vasil'chikova (1576). The tsar's mar-

riage to Koltovskaia did in fact last approximately three years, but this scarcely established a pattern, since his union with Vasil'chikova lasted less than a year.

25 Reinhold Heidenstein (1551-1620), Polish historian and secretary successively to Stephen Bathory and Sigismund III. His Latin account of the Livonian war was published at Krakow in 1584, and subsequently appeared at Basle (1585) and Cologne (1589), later being translated into German (Morozov, n. 25).

26 Martha was actually her religious name, since she had been forced to take the veil in 1591. Her secular name was Maria.

27 Bogdan Belsky (d. 1611) was Ivan IV's last principal favourite, and afterwards a partisan of Prince Dmitry Ivanovich. He was exiled during the reign of Fyodor, being appointed voevoda of Nizhny Novgorod. In 1598, he led a conspiracy once again, this time against Boris Godunov. In 1600, he built a town on the steppe, which was named Tsarev-Borisov, but because of his injudicious behaviour he was arrested and imprisoned. A supporter of the false Dmitry, he was elevated to the rank of boyar in 1605, but after the fall of the Pretender he was once again sent into administrative exile as voevoda of Kazan, where he was murdered in 1611. See MERSH, 4 (1977), 1-2.

28 Johan Eyloff, a Dutch physician and Anabaptist, who was active against the Catholic interest during the mission of the Jesuit Antonio Possevino to Russia. He was also engaged in commerce while in Muscovy (Morozov, n. 26).

29 Ivan's death actually occurred on 18 or 19 March.

30 Massa is mistaken in this detail. Fyodor's accession took place amid considerable unrest, and the coronation was hastily arranged for 31 May.

31 Despite the often-repeated myth of the Godunov's Tatar origins, they were in fact a cadet branch of the Zernov family, which originated in the Kostroma region.

32 The Golden Horde, or Zolotaia Orda, of course refers to a people rather than a territory.

33 Her name was actually Irina. After the death of her husband, on entering the Novodevichy convent, she took the religious name of Alexandra, by which she was apparently known by the time Massa resided in Moscow.

34 Grigory Lukianovich Belsky, commonly known as Maliuta Skuratov, was one of the leaders of Ivan IV's oprichnina and also his boon companion. He bore the primary responsibility for many of the oprichnina's repressive measures. He was killed by a stray bullet at Weissenstein during the Livonian campaign of 1571.

35 Irina actually gave birth to a daughter, Feodosiia, in 1592, but the child died in January 1594.

36 The aforementioned campaign took place in the winter of 1589-90.
37 Several other sources agree that Muscovy flourished under Boris's regency. See Peter Petreius de Erlesunda (Petreius), *Historien und Bericht von dem Grossfuerstenthumb Muskhow* (Leipzig, 1620), 283; Popov, *Izbornik*, 186, 284; *Vremennik Ivana Timofeeva*, 63.
38 A similar account of this encounter is contained in the *Novyi Letopisets*, PSRL, 14 (St Petersburg, 1910), 42-3.
39 VdL: 28; AK: 18. On *de visu* examination, I am inclined to support the van der Linde reading.
40 Although it was commonly believed at the time that Boris was guilty of Dmitry's murder, and this belief was reinforced by the publicist literature of the day, it now seems probable that the death of the tsarevich was accidental. See G.V. Vernadsky, 'The death of the Tsarevich Dimitry: a reconsideration of the case,' *Oxford Slavonic Papers*, 5 (1954), 1-19.
41 Kleshnin was not actually a boyar, but held the household office of court falconer (Morozov, n. 42).
42 This accusation is repeated in a number of sources: Konrad Bussow, *Moskovskaia khronika, 1584-1613*, tr. and ed. I.I. Smirnov (Moscow and Leningrad, 1961), 204; *Skazanie Avraamiia Palitsyna*, ed. L.V. Cherepnin (Moscow and Leningrad, 1955), 102-3; Jacques Margeret, *Estat de l'Empire de Russie et Grande Duché de Moscovie (1590-1606)* (Paris, 1946), 30.
43 According to the *Novyi Letopisets*: 'Alexander Nikitch, together with Levonty Lodyzhensky, was sent to the White Sea, to Usolie, and there he was cast into prison, and at [Boris's] command he was killed there by Levonty, and was buried at Luda.' PSRL, 14, 53-4.
44 According to the second edition of the *Kronograf*: 'In the year 7094 [1586] the lord tsar and Grand Prince of all Russia, Fyodor Ivanovich, ordered stone fortifications to be erected all around Moscow to enclose the Great Suburb, behind the Earthen City, and this work continued for seven years, and it was called the Imperial City.' Popov, *Izbornik*, 187.
45 The wealth and power of Boris is described by Fletcher, *Rude and Barbarous Kingdom*, 144.
46 See Margeret, 95; PSRL, 14, 36-7; Popov, *Izbornik*, 187; RIB, 13, cols 4, 176.
47 Boris's attachment to Shchelkalov is also mentioned in the *Tale of Grishka Otrepiev*, RIB, 13, col. 715, and is alluded to by Ivan Timofeev, 73.
48 Actually 7 January (Morozov, n. 50).
49 This story, though probably untrue, was widely current at the time, and was to gain momentum as support grew for the Romanov candidature for the throne in 1612-13. The earliest source for the rumour is a letter written *ca.*

1600 by Lew Sapieha to Christopher Radziwill, though there is a rather bizarre variant of it in Bussow, 205.

50 A similar account is contained in PSRL, 14, 49-50. Bussow (205) suggests that Irina, by a combination of bribery and promises, induced the leaders of the streltsy to support Boris's candidacy. This story is repeated in Petreius (264), and in the report of the Imperial ambassador, Michael Schiele, 'Donesenie o poezdke v Moskvu pridvornogo Rimskogo Imperatora Mikhaila Shiliia,' *Chteniia Moskovskogo Obshchestva Istorii i Drevnostei Rossiiskikh*, 1875, 2, 11-18.

51 The story that Irina-Alexandra urged Boris to renounce the throne is contained in the *Inoe skazanie*, RIB, 13, col. 131; Bussow, 206; Petreius, 266-7; and Schiele, 13-14.

52 An account of the Crimean embassy is contained in Schiele's dispatch, 16.

53 1599 in the original Dutch.

54 Actually 7107.

55 One of Boris's major achievements during his regency was to obtain the establishment of the Moscow patriarchate and place his devoted supporter Job on the patriarchal throne.

56 See also Bussow, 208-9; Schiele, 18; and PSRL, 14, 51.

57 Cf. Bussow (208): 'Besides this, he solemnly promised not to execute anyone for the duration of five years, but ordered criminals to be exiled to distant provinces.'

58 Bussow (218) hints that there was in fact some substance to the charges against the Romanovs, who were also possibly linked to the machinations of Bogdan Belsky.

59 Fletcher (142): 'The second, Kniaz Mstislavsky, was thrust into a friary and his only son kept from marriage to decay the house.' Margeret (84): 'One of the sisters of this boyar was married to Tsar Simeon; the other remained a virgin. Boris commanded her against her will to take the veil, and forbade Mstislavsky to marry.'

60 In fact, the office of treasurer was held by I.P. Tatishchev throughout Boris's reign (Morozov, n. 59).

61 Lit. 'to catch a great bird (*eenen grooten vogel te vangen*) who would be his defender, and to whom he would give his daughter.'

62 Similar accounts of Gustav's sojourn are to be found in Bussow, 209-10, and Petreius, 272-5.

63 An account of the Polish embassy is contained in the *Novyi letopisets*, PSRL, 14, 54. According to the Russian records, the second audience took place on 17 November, not the 16th as reported by Massa (Morozov, n. 64).

64 The ambassador mentioned is Richard Leigh. Thanks to the good offices of the conciliar secretary Afanasy Vlasiev, Leigh managed to obtain confirmation of the charter aimed against Dutch competition, but failed to obtain his request for an English monopoly of the White Sea trade.
65 Albert of Staden was a thirteenth-century monastic chronicler, who composed a great chronicle between the years 1240 and 1256 (Morozov, n. 67).
66 Other accounts of the famine are contained in Bussow, 222-3; Petreius, 292-5; PSRL, 14, 55, and Palitsyn, 108-9.
67 Arent Claesen van Stelingswerth, known in Russia as Zakhary Nikolaev, was a Dutch apothecary who entered Muscovite service in 1576 and served successive rulers at least until 1616 (Morozov, n. 70).
68 An edict against speculation was in fact published in 1601. *Sbornik kniazia Khilkova* (St Petersburg, 1879), no. 62.
69 According to Margeret (95), rumours of the existence of the tsarevich Dmitry had begun to spread as early as 1600, shortly after the departure of Sapieha's embassy.
70 Pierling criticized Massa's speculation on this subject severely, wondering how he could possibly have known about the inner workings of the papal court. Pierling himself stated that he had been unable to find any evidence in the papal archives to substantiate Massa's allegations. The mission of the legates Enrique Miranda and Francisco Costa was to solicit from Shah Abbas I an alliance against the Turks and obtain permission to establish a Catholic mission in Persia. P. Pierling, 'Chilli i Massa: sovremenniki Lzhedmitriia I,' *Russkaia starina*, 80 (1893), 482-3; idem, *La Russie et le Saint-Siège*, 3 (Paris, 1901), 378.
71 VdL: *Blasof*; AK: *Wasof*. I am inclined to support the van der Linde reading.
72 Axel Guildenstierne wrote a detailed account of the prince's journey and his death in Moscow. There was also an anonymous account published in German in 1604 and in Danish in 1606. See Adelung, 2, 111-27. The funeral is also described by Bussow, whose son, the Lutheran pastor Martin Beer, officiated.
73 S.N. Godunov's ill will towards Hans is attested by the account of the *Novyi Letopisets*, PSRL, 14, 56-7.
74 VdL: 'Jurgen Buran'; AK: 'Iurgen Buvar.' For some reason, the name is rendered 'Youri Buran' in van der Linde's French translation.
75 Anne of Denmark, wife of King James I.
76 Concerning Boris Godunov's diplomatic and dynastic proposals, see W.E.D. Allen, 'The Georgian marriage proposals of Boris Godunov,' *Oxford Slavonic Papers*, 7 (1965), 69-79; idem, *Russian Embassies to the Georgian Kings*, 2 vols (Cambridge, 1970).

77 The Hanseatic ambassadors arrived on 25 March 1603, were dismissed on 7 June, and departed 11 June (Morozov, n. 89). See also Bussow, 217, and Petreius, 283.
78 Lachin Bek, the Persian ambassador, arrived in Moscow on 23 August, and was received by the tsar on 4 September (Morozov, n. 90).
79 This is the only complete and circumstantial account of the Khlopko rebellion, although it is frequently alluded to elsewhere.
80 Irina-Alexandra actually died on 24 October.
81 The embassy set out in May 1604.
82 Massa is probably referring to the loss of the Dagestan expedition in 1604 (Morozov, n. 94).
83 See above, 33-4.
84 On the various theories regarding the life and wanderings of the false Dmitry, see H. Skribanowitiz, *Pseudo-Demetrius I* (Berlin, 1913), and Philip Barbour, *Dimitry* (Boston, 1966), especially appendices D-E.
85 A Muscovite source states that a courier named Balsar arrived in Moscow on 31 May, in advance of the main embassy (Morozov, n. 98).
86 Heinrich Logau, a native of Prague. His embassy is related in greater detail by Bussow, 224.
87 I.e., Mniszech.
88 According to Morozov (n. 98) the 'otvernitsa' mentioned by Massa is a type of backslang, rather than a particular dialect.
89 The word 'hetman' is apparently a borrowing from the Polish, which is itself a polonization of the German 'Hauptmann.' Massa's attempt at philology, though ingenious, is nevertheless erroneous.
90 'And the thieving curs called Don Cossacks heard about him, and they sent to him from the Don their ataman Korela, and with him they sent Cossacks and gifts. Many swore allegiance to him, so that he would not delay, but invade the Muscovite state. Thus the Cossacks were all very pleased with him.' PSRL, 14, 61.
91 Actually 25 October. See SGGD, 2 (St Petersburg, 1819), no. 80. According to the *Novyi Letopisets*: 'This accursed Grishka, gathering together with the Lithuanian people and the Cherkassians, made an incursion into the Ukraine below the town of Chernigov, and began to attack Chernigov. The voevoda there was Prince Ivan Tatev, who began to resist him, not knowing that there was treason among the military men, who all came upon him and seized him, while they themselves surrendered to the renegade monk and kissed the cross to him.' PSRL, 14, 61-2.
92 Massa erroneously accords Ivan Godunov and Vasily Morozov the title of prince (*Cnees*).

93 See below, 100, and n. 67.
94 'The Grand Prince sent his emissaries to the Holy Roman emperor and the king of Denmark. He complained bitterly of the wrongdoings of the Poles, with their false Dmitry, and his own subjects' infidelity. He asked them, for the sake of friendship, to send a foreign army to his aid. There was much talk of these doings throughout the land.' Petreius, 304-5.
95 A stuyver was an old Dutch coin, equivalent to one twentieth of a guilder.
96 This is the most detailed account of the devastation of the Komaritsk district by the Muscovite army. Similar details are to be found in Bussow, 228, and Ivan Timofeev, 84.
97 This information is inaccurate. After the desertion of most of his Polish troops, Dmitry lifted the siege and withdrew to Sevsk.
98 'om een blancke.' A blancke was an old Dutch coin equivalent to twelve pfennigs (Morozov, n. 111).
99 Massa's account of the battle of Dobrynichi is in general agreement with those of Margeret and Bussow, both of whom were active participants. See Margeret, 99-100, and Bussow, 227-8. The anecdote concerning the drunken Polish prisoner is to be found in the account of Petreius, 301.
100 Mikhail Borisovich Shein, who later distinguished himself at the siege of Smolensk (1609-11), but was executed on the orders of Tsar Michael for his failure to recapture the same city in the war of 1632-4.
101 See Bussow, 229-30; RIB, 13, col. 36; Popov, *Izbornik*, 62.
102 Boris's death from a massive haemorrhage appears to have been entirely natural. It is unlikely, moreover, that the *skhima*, or highest order of monasticism, would have been given on his deathbed to a suicide. Massa, however, is repeating a rumour that was widely current at the time.
103 According to hetman Zolkiewski, Boris suffered from dropsy. Stanislaw Zolkiewski, *Poczatek i progress wojny moskiewskiej*, ed. J. Maciszewski (Warsaw, 1966), 98.
104 Zolkiewski (96): 'He could neither read nor write, but he had intelligence enough for evil.'
105 The refortification of Smolensk (1596-1602) under the direction of Fyodor Savelev Kon' was one of the greatest feats of military engineering of the age. During his reign Boris also commissioned extensive reconstruction in and around the Moscow Kremlin, the most notable feature being the bell-tower of Ivan the Great, completed in 1600.
106 See also Margeret, 104; Bussow, 230-1; and Petreius, 306-7.
107 Bussow (231) states that 'they held to their oath as long as a hungry dog keeps a fast.' See also Margeret, 104; Petreius, 307; PSRL, 14, 64; RIB, 13, cols 40-1; Popov, *Izbornik*, 267-8, 291, 328.

108 Margeret's account (105) differs somewhat: 'He immediately ordered the army on leave to refresh itself for three or four weeks, especially those who had estates around Moscow, and he sent the rest of the army to cut off the food supply for the city of Moscow.' Margeret's account is in general agreement with that of Stanislaw Borsza, a Polish participant in the false Dmitry's campaign: 'We were on the march with the tsarevich and were proceeding to the capital when the tsarevich sent to the army, telling the soldiers to disperse to their homes, since they were weary. He ordered only the advance units of the army to await him below Orel.' RIB, I (St Petersburg, 1872), col. 396.

109 The actual letter transmitted by Pushkin and Pleshcheev is reprinted in AAE, 2 (St Petersburg, 1836), no. 34. The foregoing passage is a rather free rendering of the substance of Dmitry's letter.

110 The rumour was apparently quite widespread, and is repeated in a letter written by the Polish diplomat Gasiewski. Apparently Sigismund III ordered his agents in England to investigate the truth of the matter (Morozov, n. 129).

111 'All of the Godunovs, Saburovs, and Veliaminovs were sent to prisons in the towns of the lower Volga and Siberia. One of these, Semeon Godunov, was sent to Pereiaslavl Zalessky in the custody of Prince Yury Priimkov-Rostovsky, and there he was killed.' PSRL, 14, 66.

112 *Sine caede ac sanguine pauci / Descendunt reges et sicca morte tyranni.* (Juvenal x, 112-13).

113 *Ecclesiastes* i, 2 and xii, 8.

114 *Qui nunc nascuntur, morientur tempore certo, / Quae plantata vides, auferet hora sequens, / Olim planta fuit, quae nunc succiditur arbor, / Quae nunc destruimus, structa fuere prius, / Nunc fletu nimio deducimus anxia vitae / Tempora, nunc risu solvimur immodico, / Omnia deprendi, nihil res esse, nec ulla, / Semper in infracto parte manere gradu.* Eobanus Hessus (1488-1540) was a German humanist poet and friend of Erasmus, highly esteemed in his day for his skill in Latin verse.

115 Similar details concerning the fate of Boris's family are contained in PSRL, 14, 66.

116 *Beschryvinghe*, f. 2; *Légende*, 4-5; *Reporte*, ff. 2v-3.

117 Similar accounts of the ex-tsarina Martha's return to the capital are contained in RIB, 13, col. 54; PSRL, 14, 67; Bussow, 236; Petreius, 318; and Margeret, 106-7.

118 Massa places the coronation after Martha's return. Some other accounts put events in the reverse sequence. There is also much variation in the date given for Dmitry's coronation, ranging from 29 June to 31 July. The most

probable date is 21 July, three days after the arrival of the tsar's 'mother.' Massa's sequence would therefore appear to be correct.

119 Wisniowiecki was the original patron of the false Dmitry. His estates were on the borderlands of Muscovy, in the west Russian territories of the Grand Principality of Lithuania.
120 *Beschryvinghe*, f. 2; *Légende*, 5; *Reporte*, ff. 3-3v.
121 The deposition of Job took place before Dmitry's coronation. Massa has events out of sequence, therefore, in this part of his narrative.
122 VdL: 800; AK: 8000. The latter reading is correct.
123 Some other accounts give the date of the trial and condemnation of Shuisky much earlier, although Bussow relates it *sub anno* 1606. According to Borsza (RIB, 1, cols 398-9) the incident took place before Martha's arrival. The *Inoe skazanie* and the third edition of the *Khronoghraf* specifically mention the date as 25 June (RIB, 13, col. 52, and Popov, *Izbornik*, 235, 240). The *Tale of Grishka Otrep'ev* places the Shuisky incident before the coronation, which took place according to this particular account some time in July (RIB, 13, cols 734-5). Bussow (239), the *Novyi Letopisets* (PSRL, 14, 67), and Palitsyn, 111, place the incident in the same sequence as Massa, without, however, naming the specific date of 25 August.
124 Dmitry's equestrian skill is also attested by Bussow, 237.
125 Cf. Margeret (109): 'He was wise, and had enough understanding to act as a schoolmaster towards all of his council.' Bussow (236): 'Not a day passed when the tsar did not preside over his council, where the senators reported to him on state affairs, and delivered their opinions to him. Sometimes, hearing their fruitless debates, he smiled, and said, "How many hours do you debate without coming to a conclusion; this is what you should decide!" And in an instant, to the amazement of all, he decided matters over which the most exalted boyars had racked their brains for hours.'
126 *Beschryvinghe*, f. 2v.; *Légende*, 6-7; *Reporte*, f. 4.
127 *Beschryvinghe*, f. 2v.; *Légende*, 8; *Reporte*, f. 4.
128 The contraption is also described in the *Inoe skazanie*, RIB, 13, cols 55-6.
129 See pp. 148-50.
130 Cf. Petreius, 317-18; and RIB, 13, cols 577-9.
131 Petreius (276): 'When Grishka Otrepiev took over the governance ... he sent the prince to the town of Yaroslavl, where he was kept prisoner, simply because he was more well-disposed towards Karl IX, king of Sweden, than towards Sigismund III of Poland.'
132 See also PSRL, 14, 68; Bussow, 239; and Petreius, 323-4.
133 Massa is here simply repeating the narrative relating to the reign of Ivan IV.
134 Lvov was actually within Poland proper at that time, although it did contain a considerable West Russian population.

135 Many of these merchants had extended the tsar credit which his successor refused to honour.
136 See above, 181-2.
137 '*Dum paras thalamum, sors tibi fata parat.*'
138 According to the Polish diarist Dyamentowski, Maryna's arrival outside Moscow took place on 9 May (30 April, o.s.).
139 Margeret (112-13): 'She had Nogai horses harnessed to her carriage, all white and dappled with black, like tigers or leopards, so that nobody could distinguish between them. She had four companies of Polish cavalry, very well mounted and richly attired, and also a company of haiduks for her bodyguard. She had several lords in her suite.'
140 *Beschryvinghe*, f. 3; *Légende*, 9; *Reporte*, ff. 5v-6.
141 *Beschryvinghe*, f. 3; *Légende*, 10; *Reporte*, f. 5.
142 Maurice won a victory over the Spaniards at Tournhout in the Netherlands on 22 January, 1597.
143 *Beschryvinghe*, ff. 2v-3; *Légende*, 11; *Reporte*, ff. 5v-6.
144 'The accursed Renegade Monk married the daughter of this palatine of Sandomierz, and having the ceremony performed in the apostolic cathedral of the Virgin, profaned the church of God by unlawfully admitting unbaptized Latins, and there he was married on 8 May.' PSRL, 14, 68.
145 *Beschryvinghe*, f. 3; *Légende*, 12; *Reporte*, f. 6.
146 *Beschryvinghe*, f. 3; *Légende*, 13; *Reporte*, f. 6v.
147 *Beschryvinghe*, ff. 3-3v; *Légende*, 13-14; *Reporte*, ff. 6v-7.
148 According to Bussow (248), Dmitry ignored these warnings.
149 *Beschryvinghe*, f. 3v; *Légende*, 15; *Reporte*, f. 7v.
150 This incident is also reported by Bussow, 244.
151 *Beschryvinghe*, f. 3v; *Légende*, 15; *Reporte*, f. 7v.
152 Massa surely has events out of sequence here. Most other accounts agree that Dmitry's murder took place in the small hours of the morning of 17 May. Timofei's 'Platonic *attentat*' must therefore have occurred on the morning of the 16th. Even allowing for the highly irregular hours kept at this time, it is most unlikely that such a public function as the administering of an oath would take place at four o'clock in the morning!
153 *Beschryvinghe*, ff. 4-4v; *Légende*, 20; *Reporte*, f. 8v.
154 Cf. Petreius, 351; and RIB, 13, cols 59, 866.
155 According to the German observer Georg Peyerle: 'They did not touch the palatine of Sandomierz, because he had many armed men with him.' N.G. Ustrialov, *Skazaniia sovremennikov o Dmitrii Samozvantse*, 2nd ed. (St Petersburg, 1859), 63.
156 *Beschryvinghe*, ff. 4-4v; *Légende*, 20; *Reporte*, f. 9v.
157 *Beschryvinghe*, f. 4v; *Légende*, 20-2; *Reporte*, ff. 9v-10v.

158 This intention of the false Dmitry is alluded to in the *Inoe Skazanie*, RIB, 13, col. 67; Palitsyn, 114-15; and Bussow, 240. See also n. 169 below. Note the scepticism of the author of *La légende* ('*sed haec non credo*'), which Massa apparently does not share.
159 I.A. Khvorostinin (d. 1625) began his career at the court of the Pretender. During the reign of Vasily Shuisky, he was exiled to the monastery of St Joseph of Volomkolamsk, from which he returned to Moscow in 1610 or 1611. During the reign of Michael he was given a series of arduous military assignments, but under constant suspicion of heresy, he was banished for a second period of monastic confinement on charges of heresy, drunkenness, and 'lack of firmness towards treasonable activity.' He was released in 1624, but shortly afterwards voluntarily became a monk, and died at the Trinity monastery the following year. Platonov, probably on the basis of Massa's assertion, alludes to Khvorostinin's position at the court as founded on 'an exceedingly shameful intimacy with the false Dmitry, who had debauched him in his youthful years.' S.F. Platonov, *Drevnerusskie skazaniia i povesti o smutnoi vremeni XVII veka kak istoricheskii istochnik*, 2nd ed. (St Petersburg, 1913), 232. See also MERSH, 16 (1980), 204-6.
160 VdL: *Veesum*; AK: *Ullsum*. The van der Linde reading is correct.
161 Bussow (257): 'With the permission of the boyars, Ivan Golitsyn, the stepbrother of the late Basmanov, took his body from the square, and on 18 May buried him alongside his son in the English forecourt.'
162 I have been unable to locate the source of this citation.
163 *Beschryvinghe*, f. 4v; *Légende*, 24; *Reporte*, ff. 11-11v.
164 *Beschryvinghe*, f. 4v; *Légende*, 24-5; *Reporte*, f. 11v.
165 *Beschryvinghe*, ff. 4v-5; *Légende*, 25-6; *Reporte*, ff. 11v-12.
166 *Beschryvinghe*, f. 5; *Légende*, 26; *Reporte*, f. 12.
167 Ibid.
168 It is uncertain whether Massa means Severia or Siberia, both of which he renders as 'Sibiria.'
169 *Beschryvinghe*, 5; *Légende*, 26-7; *Reporte*, ff. 12-12v.
170 *Beschryvinghe*, f. 5v; *Légende*, 27; *Reporte*, f. 12v.
171 *Beschryvinghe*, f. 5v; *Légende*, 28-9; *Reporte*, f. 13.
172 *Beschryvinghe*, f. 5v; *Légende*, 29; *Reporte*, f. 14.
173 *Beschryvinghe*, ff. 6v-7; *Légende*, 30; *Reporte*, f. 14.
174 Compare the list in the diary of Dyamentowski. Hirschberg, *Polska a Moskwa*, 16-18.
175 Petreius (368-9): 'The palatine and his daughter and son-in-law, together with all their womenfolk, were taken to Yaroslavl, and a strong guard was placed upon them in the great palace, while the servitors and other Poles

were placed in confinement and distributed to Kostroma, Galich, Vologda, and Kazan. There they were given nothing but bread and water. All the Polish courtiers there were forced to sell at half price their garments, accoutrements, and all manner of other valuable objects which they had managed to save at the time of the mutiny, in order to pay for their maintenance and provisions.'

176 VdL: 300,000; AK: 30,000. The former is correct.
177 VdL: *gingen over see na huys*; AK: *gingen over 500 na huys*. I am inclined to support the van der Linde reading.
178 According to the *Novyi Letopisets*: 'Tsar Vasily ordered his commanders to Severia and the Ukrainian towns with a large army, but the traitors defeated them all. The boyars came below the town of Elets and laid siege to it, but could do nothing against the town.' PSRL, 14, 71.
179 VdL: *en soo voort andere sacken die ...*; AK: *en soo voort andere svoecklude ...* I am inclined to support the van der Linde reading.
180 A full account of Bolotnikov's life and wanderings is contained in Bussow, 268-70.
181 Cf. Popov, *Izbornik*, 332; PSRL, 14, 72; and RIB, 13, col. 99.
182 Cf. PSRL, 14, 73; RIB, 13, col. 114; Bussow, 270; and RIB, 1, cols 121-2.
183 Details of the battle are contained in Tsar Vasily's letter to Verkhoturie: SGGD, 2, no. 150. See also PSRL, 14, 73.
184 According to the *Novyi Letopisets*: 'Many of these rebels were killed, and many taken alive, so that there was not room enough for all of them in the prisons and fortresses of Moscow. The brigand Ivashko Bolotnikov retreated with many of his followers, while others occupied the hamlet of Zaborie. These rebels, seeing their impossible situation, all surrendered. Tsar Vasily ordered them all to be brought to Moscow and distributed among the houses. It was ordered that they should be given food, nor was anybody to molest them; but those who had been captured in battle were ordered to be drowned.' PSRL, 14, 73.
185 VdL: *hout handel*; AK: *sout handel*. I am inclined to support the van der Linde reading.
186 Cf. PSRL, 14, 73.
187 'In great Novgorod there was a plague.' PSRL, 14, 71.
188 Apparently Shuisky had a temporary wooden palace built for him in the precincts of the Kremlin. I.E. Zabelin, *Domashnyi byt moskovskikh gosudarei*, 1 (Moscow, 1862), 54.
189 See AAE, 2, no. 67.
190 This account apparently refers to the encounter on the river Vyrka. According to the *Novyi Letopisets* (PSRL, 14, 73-4), Mosalsky was killed in battle

and the remainder of his forces committed suicide by detonating the powder magazine.
191 Documents concerning this levy are reprinted in AAE, 2, nos 70, 72, and 77.
192 Notice of Tsar Vasily's intention of repatriating the seventy Poles is contained in the diary of Dyamentowski (Hirschberg, *Polska a Moskwa*, 96). There is no support in other sources for Massa's speculation that they were massacred.
193 According to the *Novyi Letopisets*: 'The boyar Prince Ivan Mikhailovich Vorotynsky proceeded from Alexin to below Tula. At this time there were many rebels in Tula. The commander of these rebels, Prince Andrei Teliatevsky, made a sortie with all his forces and repelled Prince Ivan Mikhailovich, who barely managed to escape from Alexin.' PSRL, 14, 73.
194 The small stream mentioned is the Pchelna.
195 VdL: 'Tatov'; AK: 'Fatov.' The van der Linde reading is correct.
196 There is also a reference to this in the *Rukopis' Filareta*. See Morozov, n. 203.
197 Tula was actually captured by a stratagem. The river Upa was dammed, and the town flooded. Popov, *Izbornik*, 337-8.
198 According to Bussow (277), Bolotnikov surrendered voluntarily and offered to place his sword at Tsar Vasily's disposal.
199 The date of the wedding varies in the Russian sources, where it is given as 14 or 17 January (Morozov, n. 207).
200 The Polish ambassador actually arrived on 12 October 1607. Massa would appear to have this event out of chronological sequence.
201 Massa is referring to the Muscovite reverse below Bolkhov in April 1608. For a full account see PSRL, 14, 79.
202 Bussow (282-3) states that 'on 1 June, Dmitry, with all his forces, approached Moscow. On the feast of saints Peter and Paul, which was 29 June 1608 ..., he pitched his camp twelve versts from Moscow, in the village of Tushino.' Bussow was living in Kaluga at that time, whereas Massa was actually in Moscow. Massa's date, therefore, is more probably correct.
203 The Sapieha commanding the invading forces which surrounded the Trinity monastery was in fact Jan-Piotr Sapieha, a kinsman of the chancellor.
204 Nashchokin is mentioned in this connection in a letter from Tsar Vasily to the inhabitants of Vologda. See AAE, 2, no. 94.
205 These letters are reprinted in AAE, 2, nos 118-20, and SGGD, 2, nos 181-2.
206 *Revelations* xviii, 2.

Bibliography

MANUSCRIPT SOURCES

The original manuscript of Massa's history is to be found in The Hague: Koninklijke Bibliotheek, ms 128.A.33. Records concerning the Massa family are to be found in the Gemeynte Archief at Haarlem: *Doepboek* (baptismal register), *Trouwboek* (marriage register), and *Doedboek* († register of burials). Resolutions of the States-General are to be found in The Hague at the Algemeen Rijksarchief.

PRINTED TEXTS OF MASSA'S HISTORY

Histoire des guerres de la Moscovie (1601-1610), par Isaac Massa de Haarlem, publiée pour la première fois, d'après le MS. hollandais original de 1610, avec d'autres opuscules sur la Russie, par M. le Prince Michel Obolensky et M. le Dr. A. van der Linde, 2 vols (Brussels, 1866)

'Een cort verhael van beginn oorspronck deser tegenwoordige troeblen in Moscovia, totten jare 1610 int cort overlopen ondert gouvernement van diverse vorsten aldaer,' *Rerum Rossicarum Scriptores Exteri*, vol. 2 (St Petersburg, 1868)

Demetrius l'Imposteur, par Isaac Masse, publié par Jacques Isaakov (St Petersburg, 1868)

Skazaniia Massy i Gerkmana o Smutnom Vremeni v Rossii, izdanie Arkheograficheskoi Kommissii s prilozheniem, portreta Massy, plana Moskvy (1606 g.) i dvortsa Lzhedmitriia I (St Petersburg, 1874)

Isaac Massa, *Kratkoe izvestie o Moskovii v nachale XVII veka*, tr. A. Morozov (Moscow, 1937)

COGNATE TEXTS

Warachtige ende Eygentlijcke Beschryvinghe vande wonderbare ende seer gedenckenweerdighe geschiednissen, die in Moscovia zyn voorgevallen ende in dem naestvoorléden ende in den teghenwoordighen jare 1606 (Amsterdam, 1606). Utrecht: Rijksuniversitet, Pamphlet UB 518

La légende de la vie et de la mort de Démétrius, dernier Grand-Duc de Moscovie, traduicte nouvellement l'an 1606 (Amsterdam, 1606). Reprinted by Prince M. Obolensky (Moscow, 1839), and also reproduced in the van der Linde edition of Massa's *History*.

The Reporte of a bloudie and terrible massacre in the Citty of Mosco, with the fearfull and tragicall end of Demetrius the last Duke, before him raigning at this present (London, 1607). Oxford: Bodleian Library 4.L70.Art

PRINCIPAL CONTEMPORARY SOURCES

Akty sobrannye i izdannye v bibliotekakh i arkhivakh Rossiiskoi Imperii Arkheograficheskoiu Kommissieiu, vol. 2 (St Petersburg, 1836). Collection of official documents and charters.

Bussow, Konrad, *Moskovskaia khronika, 1584-1613*, tr. and ed. I.I. Smirnov (Moscow and Leningrad, 1961). Memoirs of a German soldier of fortune serving in the Muscovite wars.

Hirschberg, Aleksandr, *Polska a Moskwa w pierwszej polowie wieku XVII* (Lwow, 1901). Contains the diaries of Waclaw Dyamentowski (Maryna's chamberlain) and that of the Polish commander Jan-Piotr Sapieha.

Marchocki, M., *Historya wojny moskiewskiy* (Poznan, 1841). Memoirs of a leading Polish participant in the Muscovite wars.

Margeret, Jacques, *Estat de l'Empire de Russie et Grande Duché de Moscovie (1590-1606)* (Paris, 1946). Memoirs of one of the commanders of the false Dmitry's bodyguard.

Palitsyn, Avaraamii, *Skazanie Avraamiia Palitsyna*, ed. L.V. Cherepnin (Moscow and Leningrad, 1955). Account by the cellarer of the Trinity monastery and hero of the resistance to the Poles.

Petreius (Peter Petreius de Erlesunda), *Historien und Bericht von dem Grossfuerstenthumb Muskhow* (Leipzig, 1620). History by a Swedish diplomat active in Russian affairs during the Time of Troubles.

Polnoe sobranie russkikh letopise, vol. 14 (St Petersburg, 1910). Contains the *Novyi letopisets*, the official chronicle compiled ca. 1630.

Popov, A.N., *Izbornik slavianskikh i russkikh sochinenii i statei vnesennykh v khronografy russkoi redaktsii* (Moscow, 1869). Incorporates several contemporary Russian accounts of the Time of Troubles.

Possevino, Antonio, S.J., *Moscovia*, tr. and ed. Hugh F. Graham (Pittsburgh, 1977). Account by the Jesuit emissary to the court of Ivan IV and intermediary in the negotiations leading to the Truce of Deulino (1584).

Rude and Barbarous Kingdom: Russia in the accounts of sixteenth-century English voyagers, ed. Lloyd E. Berry and Robert O. Crummey (Madison, 1968). Contains the *Travels* of Jerome Horsey and *Of the Russe Commonwealth* by Giles Fletcher.

Russkaia istoricheskaia biblioteka, vol. 1 (St Petersburg, 1872), contains accounts by several Polish participants in the troubles; vol. 13, 2nd ed. (St Petersburg, 1909) is a rich compendium of Russian sources relating to the period.

Sobranie gosudarstvennykh gramot i dogovorov, vol. 2 (St Petersburg, 1819). Collection of official documents.

Timofeev, Ivan, *Vremennik Ivana Timofeeva*, ed. O.A. Derzhavina and V.P. Adrianova-Peretts (Moscow and Leningrad, 1951). Written by a prominent Muscovite functionary, this account is considered to be the first example of truly critical historical writing in Russia.

'Tri poslaniia Massy General'nym shtatam iz Arkhangel'ska ot 25 iiuniia 1616 g., 4 sentiabria 1616 g. i 2 marta 1620 g.,' *Vestnik Evropy* Aug. 1868, 797-814.

Ustrialov, N.G., *Skazaniia sovremennikov o Dmitrii Samozvantse*, 2nd ed. (St Petersburg, 1859). Collection of foreign sources, in Russian translation, on the Time of Troubles.

'Zapiski o Rossii XVII i XVIII vekov po doneseniiam gollanskikh rezidentov,' *Vestnik Evropy* Jan. 1868, 233-45.

Żółkiewski, Stanisław, *Początek i progress wojny moskiewskiej*, ed. Jarema Maciszewski (Warsaw, 1966). Account by the Polish field hetman who occupied the Kremlin in 1610. English translation, *Expedition to Moscow* (London, 1966).

LITERATURE

Adelung, F. von, *Kritisch-literärische Übersicht der Reisenden in Russland bis 1700 deren Berichte bekannt sind*, 2 vols (St Petersburg, 1846)

Barbour, Philip, *Dimitry* (Boston, 1966)

De Jongh, E., and Vincken, P.J., 'Frans Hals als voortzetter van een emblematische traditie (bij het huwelijksportret van Isaac Massa en Beatrix van der Laen),' *Oud-Holland*, 1962

Geyl, Pieter, *The Netherlands in the Seventeenth Century: Part One, 1609-1648* (London, 1961)

Keuning, Johannes, 'Isaac Massa, 1586-1643,' *Imago Mundi: a review of early cartography*, 10 (1953)

Kordt, B.A., 'Ocherk snoshenii moskovskogo gosudarstva s Respublikoi Niderlandov do 1631 goda,' *Sbornik Imperatorskogo Russkogo Istoricheskogo Obshchestva*, 116 (St Petersburg, 1902), cxii-ccv

Leerink, J.A., 'Een Nederlandsche cartograaph in Rusland: Amsterdam-Moscou in de zeventiende eeuw,' *Phoenix*, 1 (1946)

Linde, A. van der, *Isaac Massa van Haarlem: een historische studie* (Amsterdam, 1864)

Makovskii, D.P., *Pervaia krest'ianskaia voina v Rossii* (Smolensk, 1967)

Phipps, Geraldine, 'Britons in Seventeenth-century Russia,' PHD dissertation, University of Pennsylvania, 1971

Pierling, P., SJ, 'Chilli i Massa: sovremenniki Lzhedmitriia I,' *Russkaia starina*, 80 (1893)

– *La Russie et le Saint-Siège*, vol. 3 (Paris, 1901)

– *Rome et Démétrius* (Paris, 1871)

Platonov, S.F., *The Time of Troubles*, tr. John A. Alexander (Lawrence, 1970)

Rijckevorsel, M. van, 'Die beide portretten van Isaac Abrahamsz. Massa op de Frans Hals-tentoonstelling,' *Historia*, 3 (1897)

Scheltema, J., *Rusland en de Nederlanden*, vol. 1 (Amsterdam, 1817)

Skrynnikov, R.G., *Boris Godunov* (Moscow, 1978)

– *Ivan Groznyi* (Moscow, 1975)

Slive, Seymour, *Frans Hals*, vol. 1 (London, 1970)

Smirnov, I.I., *Vosstanie Bolotnikova 1606-1607* (Leningrad, 1951)

Szeftel, Marc, 'The legal conditions of the foreign merchants in Muscovy,' *Russian Institutions and Culture up to Peter the Great* (London, 1975)

Trivas, N.S., *The Paintings of Frans Hals* (London, 1941)

Vernadsky, G.V., *The Tsardom of Moscow, 1547-1682* (New Haven, 1969)

Waal, H. van de, 'Frans Hals, het echtpaar,' *Openbaar Kunstbezit*, V, 25 (1961)

Index

Abdul Rahman, ruler of Astrakhan 12-13, 204
Abo xviii
Akubek, Nogai ruler 12
Albert of Staden, chronicler 51, 208
Aleksin 167, 169, 216
Alexander of Macedonia 36, 67
Alexandra, see Irina Fyodorovna
Alexandrovskaia Sloboda 8
Almelo (Overijssel) xix
Amsterdam xviii
Anastasia, first wife of Ivan IV 7-8, 22, 33
Angelaer, Ivan, translator xx, 75
Anichkin, Cossack hetman 163
Anna, sister of King Sigismund III of Poland 124-5
Anne of Austria, wife of King Louis XIII of France xiv
Anne of Denmark, wife of King James I of England 63, 208
Antwerp ix-x
Arabia 11
Archangel xi-xiv, xvii-xviii, 107, 179, 183, 186, 188
Armenia, Armenians 11, 72, 172

Astrakhan 5, 11-14, 17-20, 23, 65-8, 91, 94, 107, 151, 164, 175, 179, 183-4, 204
Azov 17-19, 120

Baklanovsky, I.I., Russian ambassador xvii-xviii
Balchik, island near Astrakhan 152, 164, 171, 175, 179
Balsar, courier 209
Baltic Sea xix
Bariatinsky, Fyodor, governor of Yaroslavl 176
Basmanov, Alexei 14
Basmanov, Ivan Fyodorovich 65
Basmanov, Peter Fyodorovich 74, 78, 80, 86, 91, 96, 98-9, 113-14, 119, 121, 122, 127, 139, 141, 144, 214; appointed to command of Muscovite armies 78; congratulated on relief of Novgorod Seversky 80; rewarded by Boris 86; promised hand of Boris's daughter 91; declares for the Pretender 98-9; praises Dmitry's clemency 113-14; Dmitry's companion in debauch 119; warns Dmitry of

possible conspiracy 121; dies 139; corpse exhibited in Red Square 139, 141; buried 144, 214

Bass, Dutch resident in Hamburg xii

Beloozero 7, 23, 34, 45, 165; monastery of St Cyril 119

Belsky family 35

Belsky, Bogdan, favourite of Ivan IV 21, 205, 207

Bezobrazov, Istoma 163

Bezzubtsov, Mitka, ataman, rebel commander at Kaluga 170

Bitiagovsky, D.M. 30

Bitiagovsky, M.M. 30

Black Sea 17, 63, 67

Bolkhov 167, 216

Bolotnikov, Ivan Isaevich, rebel leader 155, 161-4, 167, 170, 173, 215-16; advances on Moscow 161-2; retreats to Kaluga 163; holds out in Kaluga 164; refuses to surrender 167; hangs those accused of conspiracy 167; admits Zaporozhian Cossacks into his forces 170; visits pseudo-Dmitry II at Putivl 170; is captured and dies 173

Bordeaux xiv

Boriatinsky, Fyodor, courier 55

Boris Godunov, tsar x, 24-7, 30, 32-65, 70-1, 73-8, 81-96, 104-7, 126, 206, 210-11; brother-in-law of Tsar Fyodor 24; acquires great power and wealth 25; seeks to do away with Dmitry 25-6, 30; prepares to defend Muscovy against the Crimean Tatars 27; orders fires set in Moscow 32; refortifies Moscow 35; is elected tsar 40-1; inspects the military camp at Serpukhov 42; is crowned 43; plans marriage for his daughter 46; his relations with Prince Gustav of Sweden 46-9; receives English ambassador 50-1; sends an embassy to England 51; orders the distribution of alms 51-3; proposes a match between his daughter and Danish prince 55; swears to abstain from shedding blood 55-6; receives papal legate 56-7; his relations with Prince Johann of Denmark 58-62; seeks the hand of a Georgian princess for his son 63; his dealings with Hanseatic ambassadors 64-5; his dealings with imperial ambassador 70-1, 210; prepares defences against Dmitry 74; sends his interpreter to Sweden 75; the reverses suffered by his armies 78; visits the infernal prophetess Elena Urodliva 78; orders reprisals in Severia and the Komaritsk district 81; his victory at Dobrynichi 82-5; rallies fresh forces 86; receives a letter from the Pretender 88; falls into despair 90; rewards Basmanov and promises him the hand of his daughter 91; sends for aid to Sweden 93; suicides 93-4, 210; alms are distributed for the repose of his soul 96; is buried 96; his body is exhumed and reinterred in a humbler grave 106; rumours of his escape and survival 106-7, 211; his physical description 94-5; his wealth 206; his generosity 33; his partiality to foreigners 44, 95; his prodigious memory 36, 95; attempts to root out corruption 95; improvements to the city of Moscow 95; good works all in vain 53-4; his guilty conscience

55-6, 73, 77-8; his illiteracy 36, 95; his hypocrisy 39-40, 44-5, 55-6; his repressions 73; spies and informers 56, 95; his revenge on the Romanov family 34, 44-5; receives Massa and listens to his historical accounts x; Massa's poem 37
Boris-gorod 95
Borovsk 170
Bosdalsky, bishop 191
Brabançons 133, 142
Breznin, Fyodor 121
Briansk 78, 167
Buczynski, Jan, the false Dmitry's Polish secretary 114, 141, 143, 165
Buinosov-Rostovsky, Peter Ivanovich, father-in-law of Vasily Shuisky 173
Bulgaria 23
Burgh, Conrad de, Dutch ambassador xxi
Buslaev, Nikita Vasilievich, governor of Yaroslavl 179
Buvar, Jurgen 62, 208

Caron, Dutch ambassador in London xii
Caspian Sea xix, 3, 11, 13, 17, 18, 23, 63, 65, 67, 72, 152, 179
Cathay 5
Caucasus mountains 67
Cellari, Ambrogio, Milanese merchant 124, 141-2
Cheboksary 180
Cheremissians 18-19, 25, 46, 165, 179
Cherkassians 189-90, 209
Chernigov 23, 73, 78, 167, 209
Christian IV, king of Denmark 55, 60
Circassians 17
Claesen, Arent 52-3, 83-4, 208

Clenck, Georg, Dutch merchant xix
Constantinople 11, 17, 20
Cossacks 43, 68, 71-6, 79-80, 87, 89, 103, 107, 110, 112, 120, 148, 155, 162, 164, 166, 173, 184-5, 209; description 71-2; their brigandage 68; their bravery 87; their skilled marksmanship 89; their devotion to the Pretender 71-2, 80; insults against the Muscovites 89
Crimea, Crimean Tatars 7-8, 14, 17, 20, 26-9, 32, 42, 123, 154, 169, 183-4, 207; are defeated by the Muscovites 14; invade Muscovy 26-7; the defence of Moscow against 28-9; their methods of waging war 29; their embassy 207; their ambassador is refused permission to leave Moscow 169

Danilovka, stream near Moscow 161
Danzig 47, 180
David, king of Israel 13
Dedilov 167
Demist, Nicholas, merchant from Lvov 124, 141
Denmark, the Danes 55-7, 62-4, 116, 188; their herald arrives in Moscow 56; the marriage alliance 57; their courier arrives from Denmark 57; their Grand Admiral 62; their return to Denmark 63; some Danes desire to remain in Moscow 64
Derbysh, Cossack hetman 13
Digges, Sir Dudley, English ambassador xvii, 186-7
Dolgoruky, D.I. 170
Dmitriev, Posnik, ambassador 55
Dmitry Ivanovich, first son of Ivan IV 8

Dmitry Ivanovich, tsarevich 8, 20-1, 24-6, 30-2, 38, 55, 69-72, 75-7, 90, 92, 97, 159-61, 206; born 8, 20-1; banished to Uglich 24; Boris seeks to murder him 25-6; murdered 30-1, 38, 206; buried 32; rumours of his survival 55; the alleged corpse is exhumed and brought to Moscow 159-61; supposed miracles 160-1
Dnieper river 71
Dobrynichi, battle of 82-6, 210
Domaradzki, Matthias, Polish troop commander 120, 127-8, 165
Don river 17, 20, 71, 120
Dreyer, Reinhold 63
Durov, Roman 121
Dus Bakhmet, Turkish captain 120
Dutch merchants 50-1, 119, 135, 166, 172, 178-9, 187-8; take additional security precautions 135; present gifts to Tsar Vasily 166; Shuisky tries to enlist their aid 178; besieged in Vologda 178-9; embark for home 179; favourable position in Moscow 187-8
Dvina river 30, 186, 196

East India Company 204
Ediger, Nogai ruler 12, 204
Elena Glinskaia, wife of Vasily III, mother of Ivan IV 6, 203
Elets 123, 142, 151, 153, 167
Elizabeth, queen of England 50
England, the English xx, 50-1, 106, 119, 144, 172, 178-9, 189, 190-3, 196; desire trade monopoly 50-1; rumoured to have taken Boris to England 106; concerned for their safety 144; Shuisky attempts to enlist their aid 178; besieged in Vologda 178-9; mercenaries 189; embark for home 179; perish in fire at ambassador's house at Yaroslavl 190-1; their adverse reception by Tsar Michael 192-3; blamed for fire in Archangel 196
Eobanus Hessus, poet 109, 211
Epifan 167
Erasmus, German engineer 10
Eric XIV, king of Sweden 46
Eyloff, Johann, Dutch physician 21, 205

False Dmitry xi-xii, xxiii, 68-119, 122-8, 131-8, 141-50, 154-7, 166, 211-14; originally a monk in Chudov monastery 68-9; flees to Poland 69; accompanies the Polish ambassador to Moscow 69; appeals to the estates of Poland for help 70; promises to marry Maryna 70; denounced by Boris to the imperial ambassador 70-1; concludes formal agreement with Mniszek 71; promises to strive for conversion of Muscovites 71; first invades Muscovy 72-3; captures and sets up his headquarters at Putivl 73; known as the Unfrocked or Renegade Monk 74-5; his early victories 76; the inhabitants of Komaritsk district rally to him 77; his military successes 78-81; his bravery in battle 80; his victory over the Muscovites 80-1; defeated at Dobrynichi 82-5; gathers contributions from conquered towns 85-6; launches a fresh campaign 86; sends reinforcements to Kromy 87; reinforces his best strongholds 87; his messengers to Moscow are intercepted 87-8; writes to Mstislavsky 88; his letters to Boris 88; writes to the Muscovite commanders 88-9;

Basmanov resolves to capture him 91; intercepts Boris's letters 93; Severia and Astrakhan remain loyal 94; is denounced by Shuisky 97; the Muscovite army swears allegiance to him 99-100; his letter to the Muscovites is brought by Boris Lykov 101; conquers nearly all the country 101-2; his letter to the inhabitants of Moscow 103-4; recognized by the inhabitants of Moscow 105; sends manifestos through all the towns 106; dismisses most of his army at Tula 106; approaches the capital 107; sends Sherefidinov to murder the Godunovs 108; his entry into Moscow 109-10; the changes at the Muscovite court 110-11; crowned 111-12, 211-12; dismisses yet more troops 112; orders executions 113; builds a new palace in the Kremlin 115; sends great sums of money to Poland 115, 149-50; his love of hunting 115-16, 126, 134; his political acumen 116, 212; builds a portable fortress, 'the Monster of Hell' 117-18; his military tactics 117-18, 134; his dissolute ways 119, 143, 148; his passion for beautiful nuns 119, 158; his homosexuality 143, 148, 214; confronts conspirators among the musketeers 122-3; plans to wage war against the Crimean Tatars 123-4; the preparations for his marriage 125-8; assumes additional titles 131; is angry with the Polish ambassador 131; his marriage 131-4, 213; ignores warning of fresh conspiracies 135; murdered 136-8, 213; his corpse is displayed in Red Square 138, 141; plans to attack Poland 142; intends to destroy the Muscovite nobility 142-3, 147, 214; his physical appearance 142; his corpse is cast into a ditch 144; his corpse is burned 145; accusations against him 146-9; rumours of his survival 156; arguments for and against his possible survival 156-9

Finch, Sir Thomas, English emissary xvii, 187

foreign mercenaries 153, 168

foreign merchants 172

France, the French xx, 153, 175, 189

Frederick Henry, stadholder xxi

Fürstenberger, Livonian knight 137

Fyodor Borisovich, son of Boris Godunov x, 40, 60, 94, 99, 102-9; his passion for cartography x; proclaimed along with his father 40; marriage plans for 46; proclaimed tsar 94; seized by Moscow mob 105; murdered 108-9; his alleged suicide 109; buried 109

Fyodor Ivanovich, tsar 8, 10, 22-4, 27-8, 31-8, 148, 151, 163, 205-7; proclaimed tsar 22; crowned 23, 205; his pious disposition 8, 36; his simplicity 24, 27-8, 33, 36; married 24; his titles 23; is distressed by the death of Dmitry 31; reproaches Boris 34; bequeathes the throne to F.N. Romanov 37, 206-7; dies and is buried 37; Massa's poem 37

Gagarin, Sila Ivanovich, governor of Yaroslavl 179

Galich 146, 215

Georgia 17, 63, 66-8, 208

German mercenaries 26, 29, 71, 83-6, 100-1, 116-17, 133, 189; Basmanov

urges them to change sides 100; as Dmitry's bodyguard 116-17.
Gerritz, Hessel, cartographer xi
Glinskaia, Elena, *see* Elena Glinskaia
Glinsky, Mikhail 9-10
Godunov family 23, 31-2, 45, 88, 96-7, 100, 104-8, 122, 205, 211; its origins 23, 205; accused of Dmitry's murder 31; crimes 32; their tyranny 45; fearful of vengeance 100; the family vault at Kostroma 96
Godunov, Boris, *see* Boris Godunov
Godunov, Dmitry Ivanovich 96
Godunov, Ivan Ivanovich 74, 100, 209
Godunov, Ivan Vasilievich 108
Godunov, Nikita 161
Godunov, Semeon Nikitich 59, 61, 91-2, 97-8, 108, 208, 211; the 'right ear of the tsar' 59; his enmity towards Johann of Denmark 61, 208; his conversation with Basmanov 91-2; 98; tries to get rid of Mstislavsky 97; starved to death in prison 108, 211
Godunov, Stefan Vasilievich 42, 108
Godunov, Stepan Stepanovich 68
Golitsyn family 45, 97
Golitsyn, Vasily Vasilievich 74
Goths xx, 62
Gramotin, Ivan Tarasievich, secretary xviii
Guildenstierne, Axel 59, 63, 208
Gustav, prince of Sweden 46-8, 120-1, 212
Gustavus Adolphus, king of Sweden x, xiv

Haarlem ix-x, xxi; Bavokerk x, xxi
Haen, Jakob de, artist 55
The Hague xiii, xvii, xx

Haiduks, Polish musketeers 128, 150
halberdiers 112, 117, 126-7, 131, 135, 148
Hals, Frans, painter ix, xviii, xx-xxi
Hamburg xii
Hanseatic League 64-5, 209
Hanun, king of the Ammonites 13
Heemskerk, Jacob van, Dutch admiral 4, 203
Heidenstein, Reinhold, chronicler 20, 205
Heliogabalus 15
Holbein, Philip, Augsburg merchant 124, 141
Holland 179
Holland and Zeeland, deputies of xvi
Holy Roman emperor 70-1, 194
Homer 145
Hungary 155

Ignatius, patriarch 112, 132
Irina Godunova, sister of Boris (religious name, Alexandra) 24, 31, 38-42, 205, 207; married to Tsar Fyodor 24; desires to enter convent 31, 38-9; proclaimed sovereign 38; becomes a nun 41-2; urges Boris to renounce the throne 41, 203; dies and is buried 66, 209
Irish mercenaries 189
Italians 11, 133
Ivan Dmitrievich, son of Maryna and pseudo-Dmitry II 184
Ivan Ivanovich, tsarevich 7-8, 21, 203-4
Ivan IV Vasilievich, tsar 5, 7, 10-6, 20-3, 40, 67, 69, 72, 88, 104, 111, 146, 183, 203-5; sobriquet 'Basilisk' 5, 15, 203-4; born 6; lives under the regency 6; comes of age

and marries 6; crowned 6-7; makes peace with Poland 10; assumes the title of tsar 11, 23; conquers Astrakhan 13; his tyranny 14-15, 21; his licentiousness 15, 20-1; his cruel amusements 15-16; dies 21, 205; is buried 22; Massa's poem 5
Ivangorod 47, 57-8, 94, 176, 180
Ivanov, Andrei, secretary 66, 154
Iwanicki, Polish lord 141

James I, king of England xii, 192-3
janissaries 17
Jesuits xxiv, 69-71, 137, 143, 147
Jews 119, 180
Job, patriarch 42, 53, 90, 112, 166-7, 207, 212
Johann, prince of Denmark 55, 58-63, 117, 126; betrothed to Xenia 55; arrives in Russia 58-9; enters Moscow 59; dines with Boris 60; falls ill and dies 61-2; is buried 62-3; his description 63

Kachalov, Nikita 30
Kaibula, Nogai ruler 12, 204
Kaluga 102, 166-70
Kama river 161
Karachev 78, 167
Karelians 71
Kargopol 94
Karl IX, king of Sweden 75, 93, 154-5, 175
Kashira 167
Kasimov Tatars 76-7, 167
Kater, Christopher 46-8
Kazan 5, 9-14, 17, 23, 76, 91, 94, 161, 164, 179, 184, 215; rebellion in 9; siege and conquest 10
Kazanowski, Polish lord 120

Kholmogory xvii, 44, 86, 94, 186
Khoroshevo 35
Khvorostinin, Ivan Andreevich 143, 214
Kleshnin, Andrei 32, 206
Knudson, Matthew 64, 117
Kolomenskoe 27
Kolomna 155, 167
Koltsovaia, Anna, wife of Ivan IV 204-5
Komaritsk district 76-7, 81-2, 85, 91, 151, 163, 176, 210
Kondinsk 23, 94
Kondyrev, Ivan, ambassador xiii, xvi
Koporie 25
Korela, Cossack hetman 87, 89, 103, 112, 164, 209
Korobitsa 189
Kosonowski, Polish lord 165
Kostroma 96, 145, 151, 163-5, 215
Kotsinga 165
Koverniv, Ivan Verigin, rebel governor of Vologda 177-8
Kozelsk 167
Krakow 121, 125, 150
Krasnoe Selo 162
Kriuk-Kolychev, I.F. 171
Kromy 86-90, 93, 98-101, 130, 151, 164, 170; evacuated by the Muscovites 86; captured by the Cossacks 87
Kurbatov, Ivan Tarasievich, chancellor xvii, 194-5
Kurlanders 86-7
Kurliatev, I.I. 132

Laen, Beatrix van der, Isaac Massa's first wife xviii, xxi
Lanton, Albert, Scottish mercenary 117

Lapland 55, 94, 188
Las Viugo, mercenary captain 86
Leigh, Richard, English ambassador 208
Lgov 167
Liège, province x
life guards 117, 127, 131, 148
Lipnicki, Polish lord 141
Lisse xviii
Lithuania, Lithuanians 71, 190, 209
Livny 167
Livonia, Livonians 16, 20, 23, 25, 44, 62-7, 86, 117, 137, 169, 175
Logau, Heinrich, imperial ambassador 209
Louis XIII, king of France xiv
Lübeck 64
Lundius, Johannes, chaplain 63
Lvov 124, 212
Lykov, Boris 101
Lysbeth, Haarlem midwife xxi

Makarius, metropolitan 10
Margeret, Jacques, mercenary captain 83-4, 117
Maria Fyodorovna Nagaia, wife of Ivan IV (religious name, Martha) 20, 25, 32, 88-9, 92-3, 96-7, 111, 118-19, 129, 150, 160, 205, 211; married 20; exiled with her son to Uglich 25; cast into a convent 32; summoned to Moscow and interrogated 92-3; her return demanded by Moscow populace 96-7; returns to Moscow 111, 211; Dmitry's gifts to 150; abused by the Muscovites for her falsehoods 150; recognizes the corpse brought from Uglich 160
Maria Grigorievna, wife of Boris Godunov 24, 36-7, 60, 92-7, 102-5, 108-9; daughter of Maliuta Skuratov 24; her cruelty 36, 92, 95; Massa's poem to 37; tries to blind the dowager tsarina 92-3; proclaimed ruler after Boris's death 94; refuses to allow Martha's return 97; seized by the Moscow populace 105; murdered 108-9; her alleged suicide 109; buried in a small monastery beside Boris 109
Marot, Jacques, Brabançon merchant 142
Maryna Mniszchówna, daughter of the palatine of Sandomierz, wife of false Dmitry xxii, 70, 119, 124-39, 151, 174, 184, 213-15; the Pretender promises marriage 70; receives gifts from Martha 119; conducted from Poland by Vlasiev 125; her proxy marriage to the false Dmitry 125; her entry into Moscow 127-9; marries the Pretender 131-3, 213; receives homage from notables 134; prepares masquerade 136; insurgents burst into her apartments 138-9; interned at Yaroslavl 151, 214-15; brought to Moscow and closely guarded 174; accompanies Zarutsky 184
Massa family, origins ix
Massa, Abraham, father of Isaac ix, xi
Massa, Abraham, brother of Isaac ix-x
Massa, Abraham, son of Isaac xviii, xxi
Massa, Christiaan, brother of Isaac x, xviii
Massa, Isaac Abrahamszoon ix-xxiv, 4, 52, 54, 107, 127-31, 135, 138, 144-5, 157-61, 174, 183-97; his family's origins ix; his childhood ix-x; baptized x; first sent to Russia

x; the eight-year stay in Moscow 4; his interest in voyages of discovery x-xi; witnesses famine in Moscow 52; sees corruption in distribution of charity 54; travels from Moscow to Archangel 107; sees Maryna's entry into Moscow 127-9; his friendship with a Muscovite war veteran 130; obtains a sketch of Moscow xi, 130-1; hears alarm in Moscow 135; hears first-hand reports of Dmitry's death 138; views the corpses of Dmitry and Basmanov 144; discounts rumours of Dmitry's survival 157-8; witnesses the translation of Dmitry's alleged remains 159-61; argues with Muscovites about miracles 160-1; sees victims of noyades 174; leaves Muscovy xi, 179; his subsequent visits to Muscovy xii-xiii, xiv-xv, xvii-xviii, xix-xx; awarded gold medal for his services in Russia xiv; proposes a permanent consulate xiv; the dispute over his expense claims xv-xvi; shipwrecked 189; besieged by marauding Poles 190; his audiences with Tsar Michael 194-6; his Swedish patent of nobility xviii; his letters to the States-General 183-97; accused of treason xix; retires to his country estate xix; his final retirement xx; work as a cartographer xxi; his second marriage xxi; his death and burial xxi; his manuscript is rediscovered and published xxii; his anti-Catholic bias xxiv; his poems: Ivan IV 5; Fyodor Ivanovich, Boris Godunov, Maria Grigorievna 37; Dmitry the Unfrocked Monk 145

Massa, Jakob, brother of Isaac x
Massa, Jakob, son of Isaac xxi
Massa, Lambert, brother of Isaac x, xviii
Massa, Magdalena, daughter of Isaac xviii
Massa, Sara (née Texor), mother of Isaac ix, xi, xviii
Massa, Susanna, sister of Isaac ix-x, xxi
Massa, Willem, son of Isaac xxi
Massaert, Pieter xxi
Masse, Pierre ix
Matham, Adriaen, engraver xx
Maurice of Nassau, stadholder xi-xiii, xviii-xxi, 3-5, 51, 184, 195, 203, 213; Massa's dedicatory epistle to 3-5
Medea 11
Merrick, John, English agent xii-xv
Michael Romanov, tsar xi-xii, xv, xix, 45, 183-7, 191, 193-4; Massa's description of 183; receives Massa 193-4
Mikhailov 167
Mikulin, Grigory, ambassador 51
Mikulin, Yury 144
Mniszek, Jerzy, palatine of Sandomierz xxii, 68-73, 118, 125-6, 133, 139, 142, 147, 151, 168, 174-5, 184, 213-15; agreement with the Pretender 71; enters Moscow 81; musicians brought from Poland 133; his house guarded during riots 139, 213; interned at Yaroslavl 151, 214-15; brought to Moscow under close guard 174; released with companions 175
Molchanov, Mikhail 119, 144, 165
Molin, Karl de, Dutch merchant xix

Monasterishche 167
Monier, Anton, Swedish ambassador xx
Mongolia 5
'Monster of Hell,' military engine devised by the false Dmitry 117-18, 145-7, 212
Mordvinians 179
Morozov, Vasily 74, 209
Mosalsky, Vasily Mikhailovich 78, 83-4, 125, 166-7, 215-16
Moscow xi-xiv, xvii-xx, 3-5, 9, 14-15, 21-3, 26, 32, 35, 37-8, 41, 47, 49-53, 56-9, 62, 66, 68, 80-1, 93-6, 100-5, 109-12, 115, 120-1, 123, 125-36, 139-40, 143, 145, 152, 155, 159-61, 174-5, 179-80, 189, 204, 206, 210, 215; trade with Holland non-existent 5; conflagrations 9, 32; flourishes under Boris 26; unrest 21-2; its refortification 9, 35, 95, 204, 206; Polish embassy 49-50; English embassy 50; famine 51-3; arrival of Danish courier 56; apparitions 57, 134; arrival of Duke Johann 59; embassy leaves for Georgia 66; the wounded from Novgorod Seversky arrive 80; Cossack prisoners arrive 80; packs of wolves appear 81; continual ill tidings 93; disorder after Boris's death 96; the populace is menacing towards the Godunovs 100; the approach of Dmitry's emissaries 102-3; defences prepared against Dmitry 103; the entry of the false Dmitry 109-10; Maryna's entry 127-9; the seclusion of its womenfolk 130; Massa endeavours to procure sketch 130-1; order restored 139-40; Dmitry's spirit causes calamities 145; defence against Bolotnikov 155; alleged corpse of Tsarevich Dmitry brought to 159; lawlessness of people 161; noyades 163, 215; besieged by Poles 174-5; scarcity 175; impending relief 179; relieved by Skopin and Sheremetev 180; besieged yet again 180; Massa's arrival (1619) 191
— ambassadorial chancellery xiii, xix; Chudov monastery 68; church of the Archangel 37, 159-60; church of the Ascension (Dormition) 66, 111; church of Jerusalem 110; church of the Virgin 112, 132; the German Suburb 62; Novodevichy monastery 41; Pokrovka Street 139; Red Square xi; Tver Gate 59
— Kremlin 22, 38, 81, 94, 102-3, 105, 110, 115, 121, 131-3, 136, 140, 143, 210, 215; its reconstruction by Boris 210; plundered by Muscovites 105; Dmitry's new palace 115; tumult in 121; wooden palace built by Shuisky 215
Moskva river 15, 35, 65, 110, 155
Mstislavsky family 45-6
Mstislavsky, Fyodor Ivanovich 45, 74, 76-7, 80, 85-8, 97, 118, 122, 132, 166, 170, 207; appointed Boris's chief commander 74; refuses Xenia's hand 45, 74; forbidden to marry 45, 74; advances on Novgorod Seversky 80; wounded in action 80; slaughters Cossack prisoners 85; orders the evacuation of Kromy 86; receives a letter from the false Dmitry 88; in danger from S.N. Godunov 97; honoured by Dmitry 118
Mstislavsky, Ivan Fyodorovich 10-11

Muscovites 3, 11-12, 14, 23, 42, 54, 61, 63-4, 70-1, 76-7, 82-5, 89, 98-101, 132-4, 139, 170, 173, 180; eager to hear Massa's narrations 3; trade in Astrakhan 11; settle in Kazan region 11, 14; Astrakhan revolts against 12; obtain booty from Crimeans 14; celebrate New Year's Day on 1 September 23, 42; their distrust of foreigners 61; agitated over Boris's attending Duke Johann's funeral procession 63; Dmitry promises to convert them to Roman Catholicism 71; ravage the Komaritsk district 77; their victory at Dobrynichi 82-5; break off in search of plunder 85; their ineffectual siege of Kromy 89; defect to the false Dmitry at Kromy 98-101; vexed at the presence of Poles at Dmitry's wedding 132-4; plunder the Poles 139; their new treason 170; capture Tula 173; their stubbornness 180

Muscovy 49, 54, 65-6, 76, 145-6; brigandage in 54-65; famine in 66; unseasonable frost 145-6

Muscovy Company 187, 192, 196

musketeers 121-3, 128, 131-3, 150

Nagaia, Maria, *see* Maria Fyodorovna Nagaia

Nagoi family 8, 25, 32, 118

Nagoi, Fyodor 132

Narva 25-6, 58, 142

Nashchokin, Fyodor Ilich, rebel governor of Vologda 177-8, 216

Nathan, Andreas, Augsburg merchant 124, 141

Nemiecki, Polish merchant 141

Neverov, Mikhail, secretary xiii

Niemojewski, Polish merchant 124

Nizhny Novgorod 164, 175, 179

Nogai Tatars 12-13, 18, 23, 62, 68, 152, 165, 179, 184

Novgorod xviii-xix, 23, 64, 71, 93-4, 125, 132-4, 137-9, 147, 161, 164, 171, 183-5, 215

Novgorod Seversky 78, 80, 86, 167

Novosil 167

Obdorsk 23, 94

Oblezov, Filipp, head of customs chancellery xviii

Ogarev, Posnik, ambassador 75

Oka river 29, 42, 102, 155, 163, 169-70

Orel 167

Osipov, Timofei 136-7

Otrepiev, Grishka (*see also* False Dmitry) 137, 146-7, 209

papacy 56-7, 120-1, 125, 143, 208

Pashkov, Istoma 162, 169

Pchelna, stream 216'

Pereiaslavl 94, 191

Peremyshl 167

Perm 23, 94

Persia, the Persians xii, xix, 3-4, 11, 36, 46, 56, 65-7, 72; the Dutch seek transit facilities for trade to xii; eager to hear Massa's narrations 3; shah 3; papal legates pass through Muscovy on the way to 56; their embassy to Moscow 65

Peter Fyodorovich, impostor 148, 151-2, 155, 163, 167, 169, 173

Piatigoria 67

Piatigorian Cossacks 13

Pilgrimovsky, Elias, courier 50

Pleshcheev, Naum 104, 211
Pochep 167
Poland xx, 46, 49, 55, 57, 65, 68-72, 93-4, 101, 115, 118, 120-1, 125, 142, 144, 171-3, 180; the Renegade Monk flees to 68-9; the false Dmitry's preparations in 71; embassy to Dmitry 120; Dmitry's plans to attack 142; courier arrives in Moscow from 171; opens hostilities against Muscovy 172-3
Poles 9-10, 25-6, 29, 46, 49-50, 64, 67, 71, 79-85, 115, 120, 122, 124-8, 131-6, 144, 148-51, 154, 165-9, 173-4, 183, 189, 195, 216; attack the Muscovites 9; sue for peace 10; as auxiliaries in the Muscovite army 26, 29; send an embassy to Boris 49-50; discouraged before Novgorod Seversky 79; attempt to desert Dmitry 80; defeated at Dobrynichi 82-5; brought captive to Moscow 85; nobles come to Moscow 120; merchants come to Moscow 124; their disdain for the Muscovites 135; attempt to violate a boyar's wife 135; massacred 136; flee Moscow 144; their insolence 148-9; interned in Muscovy 150-1; complain of the slaughter of their countrymen 154; plot to free internees 165; leave Moscow 168; besiege Moscow 174; their ambassador comes to Moscow with threats 174; their repatriation 195, 216
Pologowski, Bal Jan, Polish lord 141
Polotsk 10, 23
Polucki, Nocholas, Polish merchant 124
Pomecki, Polish lord 141

pope 69-70, 121
Potterloo, Abraham, nephew of Isaac Massa xxi
Pozharsky, Dmitry 184
Prussians 194
Pseudo-Dmitry II 156, 163, 166, 170, 172-7, 180, 184
Pskov 20, 23, 71, 94, 137, 147, 176, 180
Pushkin, Gavrilo 104, 211
Pushkin, Nikita Mikhailovich, governor of Vologda 177-8
Pustozersk 165
Putivl 73, 78, 80-1, 85, 151, 167, 170-2

Radziwill, Christopher 207
Riazan 23, 167
Romanchukov, Savva, conciliar secretary xvi-xviii, 191
Romanov family, charges against 33-4
Romanov, Alexander Nikitich 34, 41, 44-5, 206
Romanov, Fyodor Nikitich (religious name Filaret, later patriarch), father of Tsar Michael xvii-xx, 33, 37, 39-41, 44, 183, 194-5, 206-7; his popularity 33; bequeathed the throne by Fyodor Ivanovich 37, 206-7; hands the crown to Boris 39; quarrels with his wife 41; captured by Poles 183; returns to Moscow 194; his triumphal entry 195; dies xx
Romanov, Ivan Nikitich xvii, 41, 44, 189, 191, 194
Romanov, Mikhail Fyodorovich, *see* Michael Romanov, tsar
Romanov, Mikhail Nikitich 44
Romanov, Nikita 22, 33

Romanovich, Simon 169
Romanovskoe, village near Yaroslavl 176
Roslavl 167
Rostov 23, 94, 165, 191
Russell, William, London agent for Dutch merchants xxiii
Rylsk 78, 101, 151, 167

Saburov family 30, 45, 104-7, 211
Saburova, Evdokia, wife of Ivan IV 204
Safa Girei, ruler of Kazan 10
Saltykov, Lev 14
Saltykov, Mikhail Glebovich 58, 74, 78
Samara 152, 164, 184
Samoyed 23, 147
Sapieha, Jan-Piotr (confused with Lew by Massa) 173-5, 216
Sapieha, Lew, Lithuanian grand chancellor 49-50, 207, 216
Saratov 68, 152, 164, 175
Sardanapalus 15
Schwartzhoff, Wilhelm 48
Scots mercenaries 153, 175, 189
Sebastian the Wallachian, emissary of Ivan IV 13, 204
Selim, Turkish sultan 14-17
Semeon Bekbulatovich 10, 76-7, 204
Semiramis 24, 36
Serebriannye Prudy 167
Serpukhov 42, 102, 155, 163, 170-1
Severia 23, 71, 74, 78, 81, 91, 94, 151, 163, 167, 176; Boris's reprisals in 81; rebels against Shuisky 151; prosperity in 176
Shchelkalov, Andrei 36, 206
Shchelkalov, Vasily 36, 45
Shein, Mikhail Borisovich 210
Shemakha 11, 72
Sherefidinov, Andrei 108-9, 121

Sheremetev, Ivan 14
Sheremetev, Peter Nikitich 152, 164, 171, 175, 179-80
Shigalei, Tatar prince 12
Shuisky family 45-6, 114, 120
Shuisky, Dmitry Ivanovich 35, 74, 152-3
Shuisky, Ivan Ivanovich 35, 152-3, 170
Shuisky, Ivan Petrovich 35
Shuisky, Vasily Ivanovich, *see* Vasily Shuisky, tsar
Siberia xi, xxi-xxii, 23, 91, 94, 147
Sigismund III, king of Poland xii, xvi, 75-6, 93, 98, 119-20, 125, 131, 153-4, 180, 211; accused by Boris of violating truce 75; his excuses 75-6; sends embassy to congratulate the false Dmitry 120; present at Dmitry's proxy marriage to Maryna 125; besieges Smolensk 180; concludes peace with Muscovy 190
Siisky monastery 44
Simon, Swedish follower of Prince Gustav 48
Simonov monastery 174
Sitsky, Ivan Vasilievich 35
Skopin-Shuisky, Mikhail Vasilievich 152-3, 162, 166, 175, 178-9
Skotnicki, mercenary soldier 153
Skuratov, Maliuta (Grigory Lukianovich Belsky), favourite of Ivan IV 24, 205
Slinski, Polish lord 141
Smolensk 10, 23, 71, 95, 125, 147, 180, 184-5, 210; refortified by Boris 95, 210; besieged by King Sigismund 180
Solomon, king of Israel 55
Solovaia, Evdokia, wife of Ivan IV 204

Soloviev, S.M., historian xxiii
Sosnitsa 167
Staritsa 112, 166
Starodub 10
States-General of the United Netherlands xii-xxi, 183-97
Stefan Batory, king of Poland 20
Stockholm xx
Stolbovo, treaty xiv
Sukhona river 196
Suska 196
Sutupov, Bogdan Ivanovich 78, 83, 133
Svyiazhsk 180
Sweden, the Swedes xiv, xix-xx, 16, 75, 93, 106, 116, 154-5, 171, 175, 179-80, 183, 192

Taman 17-19
Tamerlane (Timur-Askak) 19, 23, 67
Tatars 3, 17-19, 25, 35, 66-7, 71, 104, 131, 142, 164, 172, 179, 184
Tatary 106, 116, 123, 167, 180
Tatev, Boris Petrovich 170
Tatishchev, Mikhail Ignatievich, ambassador 59, 66, 161
Teliatevsky, Andrei Andreevich 74, 100, 155, 166, 216
Terek 19
Texel xii-xiii
Thirty Years' War 190
Tiumen 14
Tmutorokan 11, 204
Toropets 10
Torzhok 10
Totma 86, 94, 165, 189, 196
Tournhout, battle 130, 213
Tretiakov, Peter, head of ambassadorial chancellery xiii-xiv, xvii, 188

Trinity monastery 34, 174-5, 190-1
Tsaritsyn 171
Tula 86, 102, 106, 151, 155, 163, 167, 169, 173, 216
Turkey, the Turks 11, 18-20, 29, 66-71, 129-31, 155, 184, 187
Tushino 216
Tver 10, 23
Tyszkiewicz, Samuel 174-6

Udorsk 23
Uglich 30-2, 48, 69, 90, 92, 97, 120, 160-1, 164, 203
Ulrich, Danish prince 55
Upa river 216
Urodliva, Elena, infernal prophetess 78, 126, 171
Ushakov, S.M., ambassador xii
Ustiug 30, 86, 94, 189
Utemish Girei 10
Utrecht university xxi, xxiii

Vaga river 35, 165
Vasilchikova, Anna, wife of Ivan IV 204-5
Vasily III, Grand Prince 6, 16, 203
Vasily Shuisky, tsar xxiii, 32, 35, 74, 90-1, 97, 113-14, 121, 125-8, 133, 139-41, 146, 149, 152-4, 166, 168, 171-4, 178, 183, 212-13, 216; attends Dmitry's funeral 32; swears he has buried Tsarevich Dmitry 90; swears to the Pretender's imposture 97; his conspiracy against the false Dmitry 113; condemned to death 113-14, 212; reprieved 114; exiled but later pardoned 114; his fresh conspiracy against Dmitry 125; helps restore order in Moscow

139-40; repudiates debts incurred by Dmitry 141, 213; becomes tsar 146; his accession is proclaimed through all the towns 149; proposes to become a monk 152; sends an army against the rebels 153, 215; his embassy to Poland 153-4; his new dwelling completed in the Kremlin 166; raises new armies 168; sets off on campaign 171; marries 173-4, 216; sends a letter to the inhabitants of Vologda 178; surrendered into the hands of the Poles 183

Veliaminov family 30, 45, 104-5, 211
Velröes, noble family of Liège province x
Venev 166-7
Viatka 23, 114
Viazma 144
Vienna xii
Vladimir 23
Vlasiev, Afanasy Ivanovich 57-8, 125, 133, 150, 161
Voght, Dutch resident at Hamburg xii
Volga river xix, 10-11, 13, 24, 26, 36, 44, 48, 65-8, 71, 107, 151-2, 164, 167, 169, 171, 175, 180, 184, 190
Volkonsky, Y.K., ambassador 154
Vologda 94, 165, 176-9, 189, 196, 215-16
Volsky, foreign merchant 141
Voronov, Roman Makarovich, chancellor of Vologda 177-8
Vorotynsky, Ivan Mikhailovich 35, 97, 153, 159, 167-70, 216
Vyborg xviii

Vychegda 86
Vyrka river 215

Wassenbergh, Maria van, Isaac Massa's second wife xxi
Wends 62
White Russia 112
White Sea 172, 180
William the Silent, stadholder 3, 203
Wisniowiecki, Adam 68, 112, 140, 142, 151, 174, 212
Witsen, Gerrit, Dutch merchant and politician xii
Wladyslaw, Polish prince 189
Wolski, Polish merchant 124
Wonsowicz, Polish lord 141

Xenia Godunova, daughter of Boris 46-8, 60, 91, 105, 108-9, 119

Yamgurchai, ruler of Astrakhan 13-14
Yaroslavl xvii, 23, 62, 94, 151, 164-5, 168, 175-6, 179, 189-91, 196, 212
Yauza river 162-3
Yazykov, Zakhary, secretary 75
Yugoria 23
Yuriev Polsky 12
Yury Vasilievich, second son of Vasily III 203

Zaborsky, Semeon, secretary to Russian ambassador xii
Zagoria 161
Zaporozhian Cossacks 170
Zarutsky, Ivan Martynovich 183-4
Zernov family 205
Zolotaia Orda 23, 205

www.ingramcontent.com/pod-product-compliance
Lightning Source LLC
Chambersburg PA
CBHW071154070526
44584CB00019B/2779